Guild of PSI

93641
confirmation
code

Guild of PSI

*Psychic Abilities - the Link
Between Paranormal
and Spiritual Realities*

By Eric Pepin

*Higher Balance Publishing
Portland, Oregon*

This book has been transcribed and compiled
from live lectures given by Eric Pepin. Some
elements of the live format have been preserved.

Published by Higher Balance Institute,
515 NW Saltzman Road #726,
Portland, Oregon 97229
www.higherbalance.com

ISBN: 978-1-939410-08-5

Library of Congress Control Number: 2014958642
Guild of PSI: Psychic Abilities - the Link Between
Paranormal and Spiritual Realities / Eric Pepin

Published 2015.

Other Books by Eric Pepin

The Handbook of the Navigator:
What is God, the Psychic Connection to Spiritual
Awakening, and the Conscious Universe

Meditation within Eternity:
The Modern Mystics Guide to Gaining Unlimited
Spiritual Energy, Accessing Higher Consciousness
and Meditation Techniques for Spiritual Growth

Igniting the Sixth Sense:
The Lost Human Sensory that Holds the Key to Spiritual
Awakening and Unlocking the Power of the Universe

Silent Awakening:
True Telepathy, Effective Energy Healing
and the Journey to Infinite Awareness

Waking the Immortal Within:
Develop your spiritual Presence,
Awaken the Inner Master and Explore Hidden Realities

Books by Higher Balance

Bending God: *A Memoir*

To discover more techniques and knowledge from Eric Pepin, and to experience awakening yourself beyond what is discussed in this book, visit:

www.higherbalance.com/experience

ADD TO YOUR EXPERIENCE
READERS ONLY FREE MATERIAL

As a reader you receive special reader-only bonus material you can download for free. You will get new tools and knowledge to enhance all the practices found in the book.

Receive:

Guided Mind Projection: Eric Pepin guides you on an audio Mind Projection session. You'll go step-by-step through the entire process you can use for practice and to better experience your initial projections.

Feels-Like Video: While you learn the language of Feels-Like in the book, the *emotional* element is difficult to capture in print. Watch this video of Eric showing you how to use Feels-Like and what it is.

Shadow People: Advanced Knowledge: An entire advanced course on the energy beings commonly called Shadow People. The discussion begins in the book in the chapter on Energy Beings. However, there is so much information and dis-information on the internet Eric sat for a video explaining in greater detail what Shadow People really are. Then he followed up with a 90 minute lecture giving the most in-depth knowledge to-date on the topic.

Go to ***www.guildofpsi.com/readers-only***

"What I see in Nature is a grand design that we can comprehend only imperfectly, and that must fill a thinking person with a feeling of humility ..."

—Albert Einstein

ACKNOWLEDGEMENTS

This book is dedicated to all of the Navigators, past, present, and future who recognize their quest ... to awaken for the Force.

From my heart to yours.

My sincere appreciation,
To the editing team:

Loretta Huinker, lead editor
Viny D'Errico, assistant lead editor
Ray Ross, editor
Diane Pfaff, editor
Justin Schramm, editor
Deborah DeWet, technical assistance

The proofreaders,

Steve Pfaff and Katherine Malone

A special thank you to *Katherine Malone* for her contribution to the Introduction.

And, last but not least,

To the Higher Balance staff for all of their contributions.

TABLE OF CONTENTS

INTRODUCTION

In my previous books, you have learned the inner workings of your consciousness from understanding energy to accessing your sixth sense.

You have stripped away layers from your consciousness to come face to face with your true self, your navigator, your soul. You understand the interconnectedness of all things and recognize the effects of the energies around you.

Mastering these skills allows you to enter a new realm and I am proud to welcome you to the next stage of this journey. Now you must delve deeper into the phenomena of the Universe and the realities outside of your physical body.

Beyond your brain's ability to comprehend, you will discover a new world filled with experiences and beings that will expand your understanding of the Universe.

Like the planet is filled with many different people, the Universe is filled with beings. From entities to dimensional beings to shadow people, I will teach you how and when to find and contact these beings. Whether these encounters take place in the dream world or in your waking consciousness, you will walk away from each new encounter with a deeper knowledge of the inner workings of your reality.

This knowledge serves to carry you forward on the path to enlightenment. But what is enlightenment, really? And how do you know when you reach it?

In most spiritual circles, enlightenment is an abstract concept without a clear definition. But as you progress on this journey with me, I will reveal what enlightenment truly is. Because without this knowledge, how can you ever hope to achieve it?

Throughout this book, I will guide you through the door that separates the physical and dimensional worlds. I will teach you the advanced techniques you need to explore this new reality and deepen your understanding of everything you have learned and experienced so far.

From dreams to energy beings to a deeper and more complex understanding of what enlightenment truly means, your journey into dimensional worlds is only just beginning. I invite you to walk through this door with me and explore the mysteries on the other side.

Good Journeys
Eric Pepin

Chapter 1

MIND PROJECTION

Astral or mind projection is the ability to energetically leave your physical body. It is possible to do this because you have an energy body that is the exact duplicate of your physical body. The energy body is able to go into places without the encumbrance of the physical body; meaning it can move through objects, ceilings, walls, and travel great distances in a matter of seconds while perceiving whatever you are experiencing.

Astral projection is another way to explore reality. Some people believe there is a silver cord attached to the energy body, much like an umbilical cord. But the truth is that when you project, you use part of your energy, your frequency, to create a probe that you consciously connect to your organic brain. The probe moves out, like a satellite, sending information back to your brain where it is then decoded. Like psychic ability, astral projection is an organic sensory. You 'see' information that originates from the place you are observing.

The frequency of your probe is the same frequency as your consciousness. So this frequency is specifically tuned with the intent of collecting information. As you meditate and you build a level of discipline, you start to get more energy, higher levels of consciousness, and then you reach dimensional consciousness. The deeper your meditations and the more you can stay cognitively aware without mental or structural chatter, the greater will be the effectiveness of astral projection. So when you choose to astral project, your success level is absolutely superior.

Is there a difference between astral projection and out of body experience?

No, there isn't a difference. Astral projection is often called an OBE, or an out of body experience. When you leave your body, that's when the experience becomes an OBE.

What is the difference between astral projection and remote viewing?

Both remote viewing and astral projection use the same sensory. During astral projection, you choose how to perceive and what you believe will happen. That affects how the information will be communicated to you.

What about the difference between astral projection and lucid dreaming?

Lucid dreaming is more of an application to achieve an OBE. If you're in an altered state of mind, it is understood that the physical body will be off balance, or the brain will be off balance so you can sneak off without your governor saying, "Hey, you know that's not possible, so get back here!" It is another method of achieving an out of body experience.

How can you tell the difference between a lucid dream and astral projection?

An out-of-body experience can clearly be defined as a conscious event rather than just being consciously aware in the dream state. When you are in the dream state, it's your internal perception rather than something happening externally. Now, I'm not saying it isn't possible to achieve astral projection through lucid dreaming, but I do believe that your results will not be as good.

For instance, scientific studies have shown that people who suffer from sleep deprivation will have dream-like side effects. It's as if the brain projects a different kind of reality that overlaps into this physical reality. It's similar to a piece of clear plastic that is layered over a picture. With lucid dreaming, I suspect that there isn't much of a difference. You're fooling the brain to project something visually when, in fact, you're not going anywhere. Whether or not you're actually achieving the intended goal is questionable. I do believe some people do achieve it, but I think there are better ways to have the same experience.

How is astral projection possible?

Before I can answer this question, I need to explain my particular point of view on astral projection. Most people think their physical body leaves and travels by floating or flying to their astral destination, but I completely disagree with that concept. Most people also feel that it is their soul leaving their body. It's not your soul in any way, shape, or form. There are energies in your body that you have developed spiritually; astral projection is about taking a part of that energy and moving it outside of your physical body.

The astral body can best be described as a probe. When I say probe, I mean a part of your energy, your frequency, your vibration that is manifested and released from your physical body. Much like a satellite is launched from the Earth to collect data from our solar system as it travels; the probe's frequency is the same frequency as your consciousness. This frequency is specifically programmed with the intent to collect information. So, like a remote pilot you're directing this energy to wherever it's going.

During astral projection, some people are in such a deep state of trance that they feel they are this probe; they've completely forgotten their physical body. Other people are conscious of their physical body and, at the same time, they are aware of their consciousness moving through time and space. So when people say, "I can see my body," I believe they impose that concept through their mind as a way of coping with what they're doing. In other words, why do they only see things within a 90° spectrum of sight that is similar to normal vision? You don't have eyes as energy; therefore, you really should be able to see in all directions. You choose to believe, without rationalizing; you have a governor that determines how you will perceive everything. In other words, all the data this energy is able to collect is being filtered through your belief system.

I don't necessarily believe there is a cord attached to your energy body. I've heard people say, "If you go too far, the cord will snap and you won't be able to find your way back. It's your connection to the body." Again, this is about your *perception* and also about *fear*. The biggest reason why it's difficult to achieve astral projection is because, in your mind, you believe the astral body is your soul; therefore, you are afraid that if it leaves, you will die. This is a survival issue, the most powerful, and it will prevent you from achieving astral projection. It doesn't matter how much you *want* to achieve it. You need to fool the brain in order to let it happen, or retrain your thinking process to convince your brain that it is okay to do that. Once you achieve astral projection several times, it will become easier to achieve it more often. The first five to ten times are always the most difficult.

As you collect your energy, you create a frequency as well as your intent of an expectation. In other words, you perceive that energy in the form of a body. You perceive it in a certain direction, *if you do not set limitations*. Your particular viewpoint or cultural belief can impose certain limitations on your experience. It is like you are programming your experience. You are manipulating your energy to split in half. You are creating a probe which is consciously connected to your brain, *not necessarily your mind*, but your brain. It's moving out and, like a satellite, it is sending you information. That information goes through your brain and is decoded. You're seeing information that you believe to be from a particular place.

Imagine sitting in front of a large movie screen that projects a picture so real, you literally feel as if you're there, but you're at home in front of a movie screen. It makes it even more intense because you feel like you're there.

So are you there or not?

Technically you are your 'I,' your middle pillar, so you're really not there. But it's like you are because of the level of detail that you receive through this probe. For instance, your hand really isn't you. If you reach out to touch something, your experience is where your hand is but it is only an extension of you; your consciousness is there. If something were to cut off your hand it would affect you, but it doesn't affect your middle pillar - your consciousness. So when you astral project, you're really not there. However, the information is so detailed and constant that it makes you feel as if you're there.

What prevents people from projecting?

I would say fear is the number one reason why people cannot achieve astral projection. You have to give yourself permission, and that is an internal thing. Most people who have had experiences with astral projection say they were spacing out. For instance, I once knew of a person who was in the back seat of a car. He said he was physically exhausted but still able to have a conversation. He then shot out over the car and was able to see the car moving while he kept up his speed. He knew he was in the car but he wasn't really thinking about it. He looked around and he could see the highway and the town, and then he thought, "Well, what about my body?" The instant he thought about it, he went slamming right back into his body.

Fear creates a polarity shift, like a magnetic field. If your mind can go to this region, it'll allow the probe to move out from you. The second your consciousness reflects on *the self* it reverses and creates a magnetic pull because it confuses the probe with the idea that the soul has to remain in the body. The soul is hotwired into your physical body as if it were melded together. Only when the heart stops beating at the moment of death and your entire electrical field drops can your soul, or absolute true-consciousness, begin to move or separate from the body.

In astral projection, because you assume that you are leaving your body, you connect right away with your fear of death. If you slip out by accident, the second that you reflect on your physical body, you instantly activate that subconscious fear of death. Before you can even consciously think about it, you're thinking about it subconsciously. That is what instantaneously slams you back into the body. You have to overcome your fear of the soul leaving your body. If you're not having success with projection, there could be psychological issues that act as clamps to prevent you from achieving it.

This is why you must take a closer look at your perspective of astral projection. There's a much higher level of success with remote viewing, or other methods of using your psychic ability to perceive things distantly.

Another reason astral projection is less successful than remote viewing is because it has been visually depicted as the physical body leaving itself, or this dimensional body leaving the physical body. If you can change your perception, you will have a greater understanding of what's really happening and it will make sense to you. Your level of success will leap dramatically forward.

What are some techniques
for a successful projection?

Over the years, I've been exposed to many different techniques for astral projection, but there are just a few that stand out from the rest. One of them is similar to what I teach. Visualize what I'm going to describe so that you will be familiar with this information. Use your imagination to perceive it as a *probe* rather than a body.

Use your imagination to perceive your mind as a probe, rather than an astral copy of your body.

Accept the fact that detaching from this probe is like pulling the plug from a camera that's being remotely operated. It's not going to harm you. There's no way for something to track it back to you, so it's very safe. It's only your fear of "what if something bad happens" that prevents projection from happening.

Some of the other techniques involve working with the body. Physical relaxation is very important. If your body is tense, it means your brain is preoccupied with the tension. If your brain is tense, it's going to manifest in your physical body. Work with your physical body. Relax it; drink some warm tea; do some stretches.

Wear very comfortable clothing; wear things that aren't going to irritate you by rubbing on you or pinching you. If your mind and your brain are not in a relaxed state, you can't relax the body, so meditate. Find a way to use your skills to initiate this process.

Once you are in a nice relaxed state, there are other techniques that you can use. For instance, focus on the area between your kneecaps and your groin area. This area creates a natural impulse known as the erogenous zone, due to the location of the nerves. But in either case, if you simply rub this area for a few minutes or so, there is a sensation that you will get from your energy field that affects the nerves in the spinal area. The brain senses this and tells the babbler to ease off so that you can achieve astral projection. You may feel tingles, you may feel a very distinct sensation that you usually don't pay much attention to.

Could someone use a Dreamscape to achieve astral projection?

I would not recommend using a Dreamscape to achieve astral projection simply because it's not designed for it.

Does the Higher Balance Meditation enhance one's ability to project?

Absolutely. It can be applied to all that I teach because it teaches you to calm the brain and to think from a different state of consciousness, which is the guiding force you will need in order to travel. The second you start to think in words you'll be pushed back into your body. It happens so quickly you won't even feel it happening.

Now, there have been some documented cases of people who have experienced jolts of astral projection For instance, they were lying down feeling relaxed when suddenly their whole body jumped for a second. That is what I call a *semi-launch*. It can happen when your brain is very relaxed and you're really not thinking about anything; you're almost in a meditative state, like in a meditation. Your energy begins to lift off and then your brain jumps in and says, "Whoa, what's going on? Get back down here right now!" This is when you feel the jolt, and the brain says, "Wait a minute, we're falling," because it feels so real. It happens so fast that the brain is not able to process what's going on and thinks you're falling. Your body jolts to catch itself as it falls.

The *Higher Balance Meditation* trains you to not overreact. It teaches you to have self control in between the states of brain and mind. It takes a lot of discipline to direct this consciousness and *the Higher Balance Meditation* is what you need to build that discipline; it's absolutely critical.

What benefits can be gained from astral projection?

The purpose of life is to experience. You're in a physical body and you reincarnate for a reason. The reason is you are trying to learn as much as possible about the physical dimension and, in turn, convert the knowledge into electricity. It becomes part of your energy consciousness. So, astral projection is a way of exploring reality.

In primitive times, this ability was used as a survival mechanism to find water, food, and to alert you of inherent danger. There had to be a sensory to help with survival. The human race was nearly wiped out six or seven times, according to alternative archaeological history. Survival must have been critical, so this human sensory enabled the species to survive.

As our species became more skilled in using other senses, astral projection became a teaching tool to overcome the fear of death. Had we integrated this into our lives, there would be a higher degree of acceptance for moving into dimensional space, or beyond our physical body. Mankind would already be familiar with the process.

When you actually die, you go into a similar state of energy. So, what you are really doing is borrowing from that sense to go out beyond where you are physically.

What is the astral body made of?

All things of structure are made from various forms of molecules that have collected to create different frequencies or structures. At our level of understanding, they become a different form of matter. The physical body is a transformation of these energies that have collected and structuralized. In the end, everything is made from Prana. Prana is the essence of God.

When I say to you, "You have to collect Prana or energy to build your dimensional bodies," it's the same thing. You can program it with your consciousness; it desires to be shaped by you. You are a co-creator with God, but on a very minor level. Your astral body is pliable to whatever you choose for it to become. In this particular case you're saying, "I'm taking some of this energy that I've collected through ... let's say, the *Higher Balance Meditation*." You have built up enough of that energy to create an energy satellite, or probe, to leave your physical body. It's a part of your consciousness that has been designed to communicate with you.

Your intent is to achieve astral projection. To the average person, astral projection means to leave your body and travel to other places. They assume that the projection is a part of them and they are going to see things. That's exactly what happens. It collects information and broadcasts it back to them. Everything is made of Prana that has been given multitudes of frequencies and intentions to create its purpose, its master design. And that's all because of your expectation. Your belief is what creates those complexities.

Is the aura connected to the astral probe?

The astral body will reflect the state of your aura; it's part of that same energy. So you will not have a separate aura around your astral body, you're going to have only one aura.

Is the physical body subject to harm while you're projecting?

It's the same as when you are sleeping. Do you protect yourself when you are resting? Can you wake up if something harmful happens? While you're sleeping, you go into a dream state. Are you physically here or are you somewhere else? Your body will function as if it's in a dream state while you're projecting. The difference is that you're consciously controlling the direction of your mind. Your physical body is just resting and taking it easy.

If something disturbing happens, your mind simply breaks the connection to your probe and you react to whatever's happening. It's not like someone has to shake you to get you out of it unless, of course, you're a deep sleeper. It's no different than when you are meditating. You go into a deep state of consciousness, yet you are still able to react. You are setting your body to autopilot.

There are times when people become so focused on a game, what they are reading, or whatever they're doing, that they lose awareness of their body. It's really no different than that. If you think it is, you will develop fear which will prevent you from achieving astral projection.

Does projection interfere with your sleep?

No, because the brain perceives the projection as another source of information that is very similar to dreaming. It does not distinguish the difference between the two. The difference begins when you start to consciously think about your body.

What happens to your physical body if your astral probe is harmed?

You may wake up and check your body but it will be fine. Since your probe is energy, nothing is going to happen to your physical body. The brain might perceive the injury as being real, but if you're at an advanced level and something attacks your energy field, you only react to it if you still think you're a physical body.

Most people presume that if something shocking happens to them while astral projecting, it's physical. It's seems real to the brain, but there comes a point when you progress to a level where you understand the difference.

When is the best time to try projection?

You want to be sure you're relaxed and you're not going to be disturbed. You also want to be sure you have plenty of free time. In other words, don't do it an hour before you have to get ready to go to work. You want to remove all the excuses that your brain may find to keep you from achieving it.

Naturally you don't want to do it if it's getting too close to your bed time because you will fall asleep then. There's an internal clock that keeps you in a certain rhythm. Your brain follows natural programs and cycles. Choose a weekend when you know you're not going to be disturbed. Do it at noontime because you're not too groggy from just waking up and you've had time to get your brain back in balance. The brain will demand sleep; it's mandatory for all creatures, so you don't want to mess with your sleep cycle.

Find the best time that will work for you. It could be sometime in the early part of the day, or six hours after waking up. If you wake up at 9:00am, I'd say a good time to consider doing this would be between 12:00 pm or 5:00 pm. It's also good to be in a semi-active state of consciousness, so stack as much as you can in your favor.

There is not one perfect time that works for everybody. You have to decide what the best time is for you. Never three hours before your bed time though because first you're going to do a 30-minute preparation and just as you start getting out there, your body is going to start shutting down in preparation for sleep. Timing is everything.

Is projection possible during sleep?

Astral projection often happens when people are sleeping and, in fact, it often does. The problem is that during the sleep state, you are in a very difficult state of brain activity. It somehow buries the information gathered during the projection and, similar to a dream, you might remember it only for a few minutes before it dissipates.

It is difficult to ascertain if you were really astral projectioning and not just dreaming. This is why I tend to steer away from the lucid dreaming technique. There's just too much room to question it. Why go that route when there are better methods that you can use to consciously achieve those experiences? You'll never be quite sure if it is really a dream or if it is real.

Does diet or health factor in?

Do you drink a lot of coffee before you sit down to study? Does drinking too much coffee affect your thinking? If you eat too much food before you work, does that affect *how* you work? You instinctively know the answers to these questions. You should steer away from caffeine and eating heavy, greasy foods. Instead, eat something light and refreshing so that you are alert and conscious. It will be to your advantage if you do that.

If you eat a big, fat hamburger and French fries, washing it down with a large coke, you're going to be distracted while your body's working at digesting this whole meal of grease and fat. You're not stacking things in your favor. You have to ask yourself whether you want to be successful or do you want to just roll the dice.

Are there any foods that will contribute to a successful projection?

There are certain foods that enhance your sixth sense ability. There are amino acids that affect the regions of the brain and contribute to the sixth sense. I know that rye, like rye bread, is good because of the B-vitamins. I'm a big advocate of B complex and, vitamin B12. I also recommend the occasional use of fresh lemons. It's not necessarily for vitamin C, but another element in lemons that enhances your psychic ability. Put one in your drink, or squeeze it on your food.

A large quantity of something does not make it work better, so don't swallow five handfuls of B12 capsules. Gradually introduce any vitamin to your body.

Does it matter which direction you face?

Some teachings from various metaphysical groups recommend facing north. I'm a believer of this theory because there are benefits to sleeping with your head facing north. It's feasible to say that certain minerals will be affected and your entire body will benefit from them.

I don't know if this can be scientifically substantiated or not because I haven't seen anything written about it, but I would probably say there is a connection. I often tell people who have a hard time sleeping to point their bed north. However, it is not always practical to do that, depending on the space in your bedroom. Your brain utilizes the minerals and electrolytes that make your biochemistry and electrical fields function better. So there is likely a strong connection there.

Does visualization aid in creating a probe?

Absolutely. I recommend that you use your imagination, but in a realistic way. Don't use your imagination to create butterflies that have cattails and a cat face. A good example would be to visualize your bathroom. Visualize it to the best of your ability with your eyes shut. See the shower curtain or shower door, the color of the floor and its structure, the sink and other details that might be there. See your reflection in the mirror, the metal as it's curving around on the faucet; evoke all of this from your memory. Do the same thing with any room in your house.

Now, I'm not saying the whole house because that would be too much to visualize. What you want to do is focus on a specific area so that you can sharpen your memory with all of its details. You're helping your brain tune in. It's almost like the picture on a computer monitor that's not quite coming in clear enough. You're tuning the color, the brightness and the wavelength.

You're training your brain to develop a clearer level of perception or memory recall.

One thing that you may find interesting is when you close your eyes to visualize your bathroom or bedroom, the picture will not be as clear as what you see with your eyes open. It is very subtle. You want to work on intensifying colors in your memory. So you might want to think of oranges and blues, or greens and reds and just try to see how intense you can make those colors. Do this for a little while, going through the whole color spectrum and see if you can get them to appear brighter.

There's a difference between just thinking of the color orange versus thinking of orange brilliance from a melted Crayola crayon. The intensity jumps out at you with the second description. So the possibility is there, but your mind isn't trained yet to really work that way. The only time it does that is in your dream state when your brain isn't filtering everything.

By exercising your visual memory without fantasy or fiction involved, just pure memory, you're training your brain to receive data through your probe with a higher level of clarity. The more you do that, the better your visualizations will become. If you're serious about achieving excellent results, you may want to do this for at least ten to fifteen minutes a day for about a week or two. Your results will be pretty amazing. It may take you several months to get the kind of clarity that you want, but you can definitely improve with practice.

Most people will receive the data differently than others. Some people see, but they say it seems like something is covering their eyes. That is how your brain filters what you get. Train the brain to think differently. Once you've exercised it so that it is working with you, you're going to find that it is more efficient when it gets other data that isn't based on memory.

Can you project during meditation?

Absolutely, although I prefer to steer away from that question because it can cause a conflict or misunderstanding of the process. I can give you information that will free you, but just because it makes sense to you and you achieve some amazing breakthroughs, there can also be disadvantages.

Projection during meditation can be profound. Many years ago when I was meditating, I suddenly zoomed into a place that looked something like a research environment. It was a large island in a mountainous area with water lapping against the side of a wall. I've seen posters of a place like this that had white buildings all around. I was instantly aware of all that I could see; which is the first level of astral projection. I could also feel the temperature of the environment. I could feel the movement of the wind, and then I drew in my consciousness because I wasn't thinking with words.

In the *Higher Balance Meditation* technique, you are training yourself to achieve and maintain non-thought. This is so you can reach the higher levels of multidimensional consciousness. Astral projection is part of the genre of psychic abilities, so it's definitely an organic sensory. When we teach to you meditate, we're trying to move you into hyper-dimensional consciousness. It is profoundly more intense than using your psychic abilities, but for all intents and purposes, there are levels where you tap into those abilities and they are profound because you've removed the babbler.

If you decide to focus on a particular image during your meditation, ten to one you will project to that place. That experience will be vivid and clear. It will be far more intense than other methods of astral projection, especially now that you have this knowledge.

You never know exactly where you're going to project to until you learn to guide the direction with intention. Instead of *thinking* about where you want to go, you just *visualize* it. Focus on the place, look at a picture, tune into it, and you will go there.

In my previous example of astral projection, I "popped" in over the ocean. In the distance I saw a mountainous area with white buildings in the foreground. I took a moment to absorb the experience, not quite sure what to make of it, however, I was trained to not babble in my head. I observed the buildings and, out of curiousity, moved closer. I found it so incredibly interesting. At this point, I realized that I was projecting; I just didn't know I could do it through meditation. Early in my youth, I had projected in other ways. What really threw me off guard was the *clarity* of what I was experiencing. Until that moment, I only understood astral projection as it was described from a text book, which was why my experiences were limited.

When I projected through the *Higher Balance Meditation* technique, I had no previous concept on which to base my experience. As I looked at the scene before me, I wanted to move closer, so I zoomed in and saw people. There was one particular house that had a second floor with open windows and fluttering white curtains. They moved softly like thin curtains would, but seemed a bit different. I was attracted to them, so I zipped right to them. At one point, I thought to look back and instantly I was looking back. It wasn't like I rotated. I understood the 360 degree sensory phenomena of being aware in all directions, and accepted that I could see this way.

Your senses can flip because it's not necessary for your physical body to move. You'll find that any time you think of moving somewhere, you will immediately move there. If you think about being closer to something, you automatically appear there. You need to remember that it is energy of a higher frequency, so it is a completely different type of movement. Don't allow your perceptions to slow you down. Just try to go with the flow. Because I experienced this through the *Higher Balance Meditation* technique, I was not as inhibited as I was when I first learned to project.

During my experience, I looked back into the room and saw a huge table with lots of food. The doors in the room opened and people came in, as if they were from a wedding party. I felt a sense of surprise and immediately snapped out of the scene back into my body. It was a very intense projection with absolute clarity. Students come to me with stories of their many experiences. I recall one student who did a meditation, then jumped up and said, "Oh my God, I think I was in Kansas and there was a trailer park and this huge tornado went over a building." In a matter of hours, it was on the news. So he had projected to that particular location, experienced it, and came back.

Having said that; try not to focus on that type of experience because it's not a typical meditation. You want to develop your psychic abilities but you don't really want to focus on the visual effects. What you want to do is discipline your mind so you can get more energy. You want to access higher levels of conscious-ness to reach dimensional consciousness. Then, when you do a projection, your success rate will be superior. When you use psychometry, telepathy, or other techniques, you will have greater success. When you integrate all of this into your meditations, it will take you down one particular path, and you will become more focused. You will find that the old way is a distraction to you; it is very difficult to move back to the process of what you were previously doing.

If you want to experience meditating with the knowledge that you now have gained go ahead and explore, but don't let yourself get too caught up in that process. Try to use a different process whenever possible. Use the method that's designed specifically for astral projection. It may be a little bit more work, but it definitely has its rewards, and you will have profound breakthroughs with this method.

What are the Astral Planes?

The astral planes are really dimensions. There were times when different cultures didn't know how to explain what the other realities were. Sometimes they were so surreal that they deemed it the *astral plane* or the *ethereal plane*. Energy is not as limited as physical organic matter.

You can move in this physical reality and also in the other dimensions. The other dimensions have textures, colors, and perhaps life. Those things may be very different and may seem like fantasy or surreal to you. Plants may glow, objects may be neon colored. When you observe the art work, paintings, and imagery of

India, you see how they have used vibrant colors in many of their spiritual deities and images. Even clothing for their spiritual rituals is alive with color and very bright.

There are places you may pop into that have a fantasy-like appearance. The problem is that until you are relatively well-trained in astral projection, your brain could interpret your experience as *just your imagination*. When you see something surreal, your brain thinks it is a dream so it can't be real. This is when another problem occurs in astral projection with your brain, or *the body probe*. The internal governor is designed to keep you at the 'normal' level. It wants you to be a red cell, an organism for the planet. You are pushing the barriers of practicality as a creature on this planet. Your brain still has its instinctual barriers to control that kind of evolution.

For instance, you could be in Egypt looking at the pyramids where everything looks so real and amazing. As you look at the scene, you suddenly realize how much whiter it is instead of how you had imagined it would be. You see the heat coming off the ground and then, a car or school bus floats through the air. In your head you say, "Oh, now I see that this is just my imagination." Your brain is lying to you. Your brain is introducing the school bus or whatever metaphor it chooses because it's trying to compute this. So it's overlaying your imagination upon the canvas of what's actually happening. It plugs things in to mix up your perception.

So the challenge now is to train yourself so that doesn't happen, or if it does, don't over-think what you see. If you can stick with what you see, the bus will actually fade away. But the rest won't, it will remain vivid and clear. This happens often, but most people don't have the ability to hold the image of their energy probe while it's collecting the information. The connection is lost because, in the back of your mind, you say, "Oh, it's only my imagination." Your internal knowing directs you, but you utilize your brain to deflate the process.

Are there astral beings?

Actually, there are astral beings. When I was much younger, around twelve years old, I knew these two other kids that were about sixteen or seventeen. They knew I could do all these spiritual things and they knew about the cases I'd been involved with. They were family friends. I recall them asking me about some of my astral projections and I told them about some of them. One of my experiences was with an Afro-American man in a wheelchair who would often visit with me. This, of course, caught their attention, so they asked if there was a way for them to learn how to do it too.

At that time, I really didn't know how I did it. I don't remember if I made the suggestion or if they did, but I recall we lay down on the floor together and held hands. I talked to them and said to just repeat what I was doing. All three of us were able to astral project together, and I was able to move them to different places. We started off talking out loud, and then switched to mental communication without realizing it until much later. We saw each other in a physically transparent form.

As time progressed and we got better and better at this, the textures of how we perceived each other became more and more transparent, like a luminescent energy. These are things I recalled later as I grew older, although we didn't pay much attention to it at the time. It just seemed to make sense to us. We went on several journeys and had experiences that were rather amazing.

On several occasions, we met up with other beings that were very curious about us. I remember one particular being that was golden-yellow and felt like a feminine energy. There really isn't a masculine or feminine gender in that reality, but since you're projecting, you carry your unrefined masculinity or femininity with you. If you are spiritual, you can let go of that mindset and become an indifferent kind of energy or hold a state of balance.

This particular being seemed to be a very feminine, loving energy. She was curious about us, and I remember her wanting to know where we were from and why we were there, but not in a negative way. She took us to different places to show us things. It was as if she was another person projecting with us. She brought us down through a canyon pass that was similar to a mountainous landscape in Israel.

I've never physically been to Israel, but I remember a large building that was similar to a scene from one of the *Indiana Jones* movies. It was built into the side of the canyon wall. It looked massive inside in the movie, but when we went in, it was a lot smaller than I thought it would be. We quickly came to a dead end and I remember being very surprised by that. I had a conversation with my older friends after the projection, and they commented on how amazing it all was. This feminine energy, or what I believed was another girl astral projecting, went on her way. It was the first and only time we had ever met.

I brought both of my friends to the Afro-American

man in the wheelchair. To this day, I have a very strong affinity towards him. He was one of the best advisors I had at that time in my life. But it was a very short-lived relationship for some reason, though we did have some time with him. I suppose that, eventually, I forgot about visiting him, or we moved during that time in my life. I want to say he transcended to a higher dimension and that was his departure.

My point is that you can meet other beings during astral projection. You can have companions there, but you don't hear about it happening very often. Maybe it happened to me because I was young and more open to the possibility. If you have these experiences, it's easy to become so fixated on what you're going to see that you don't even think of communicating with other beings or even the possibility that it will arise.

Earlier in my life, I was very interested in the Bermuda Triangle phenomena. It was a big thing back then and I was young and wanted to explore. One time I brought the guys with me, and we believed that we were caught in the Bermuda Triangle. It was like a magnetic pull, like two loops downward and then one loop up and back out again. That's the only way I can explain this.

It was like a magnetic pull. Two loops downward
and then one loop up and back out again.

We went through the loops and ended up in a place that looked like another world where there were no trees and it was very barren. It looked like a pond just before it completely dries out. It was like gray clay, reminiscent of a school yard in the desert. There were no hills or mountains or anything to use as a reference of size. The sky had a hint of green or a dark slate gray color.

There were a few older airplanes and a few old boats, but they did not have any paint on them. In fact, they had no sign of wood, leather, or even any springs left in the seats. I remember looking at the seat of a plane, or whatever it was, and it no longer had any springs. It was just a metal structure. What remained looked like acid had eaten it away in places. It was pitted in certain areas. I interpreted it as the ocean water had constantly washed over the ground, and maybe these were objects that had manifested through the Bermuda Triangle.

I don't claim to know what it was and it happened such a long time ago. Maybe I need to reinvestigate that as an adult with fresh eyes and a mature intellectual capacity.

Later on, I tried to describe our experience to a friend who was a physicist. He worked with energy patterns and was intrigued that, at such a young age, I was able to sketch such a complicated energy pattern. I was describing the same things he believed happened at the Bermuda Triangle, so he was totally fascinated when I described the scene to him. I said that I felt like the material objects were being deconstructed in a molecular sort of way. It felt like it had happened instantaneously and when it reached a certain point, *poof*, it was all over. It was more like it had broken down as it came through the triangle, redeveloped, but all that was left was the metal structure, not the organic matter.

I brought the guys through this experience and we discussed it in a state of awe. We did this on three or four different occasions and it was absolutely fantastic. I don't know why we ever stopped. I could probably share a multitude of stories like this, but I don't think it's fair to just provide stories and get people excited about them. It's more important for people to experience these things for themselves.

The interesting thing is that I have not physically astral projected with another person since my childhood. But the fact is that I certainly believe it is possible. I recall that we open mindedly lay down on the ground to go on an adventure like it was any other day. We had the attitude that this was what we're going to do, and we just did it. We never thought twice about it.

It reminds me of a game called "light as a feather" where someone lies down in the middle of a group of kids. Then everyone puts two fingers underneath the person in the middle of their back, and that person goes through a death scenario. They are supposed to believe they died. Sometimes the story gets embellished until they all begin to chant, "Light as a feather, light as a feather." Everyone says "lift" and the person is lifted as if they were weightless. They are held there for a second or two before being brought down ever so gently. When you try to do that normally, you can't move them. We were kids and we lifted an adult-sized kid over our heads.

The reality you experience has much to do with your perceptions, your social and cultural beliefs, and how you reflect those back into your reality. All of this is held within the Matrix or the Gaia Mind. It's what holds us all to our limitations.

It's the same thing with bringing the guys on astral projection adventures. I didn't think anything of it at the time and neither did they. We just did it. They believed, were willing, and allowed me to control the experience because they trusted me and my abilities. We simply lay down and I walked them through the process by telling them what was going to happen. They asked early on what it would be like and what they would see, so they had an expectation. I think my energy field acted as a conduit for their energy to create the possibility for it to happen. I was the wind; they offered the boat and the sail. I filled the sail and moved all of us in the same direction. It made perfect sense to me then, and it makes perfect sense to me now.

How do you communicate on the Astral Plane?

Telepathically. You internalize what you want to communicate; you just simply know. When we spoke, I'm sure it was an emotional relay that moved from one probe to the other and bounced back to the main central, which was me. My brain translated that information into words. But really, you just know. You *know* the emotions for everything; you just fit the knowledge to it. So we were able to have these lengthy conversations about what we were experiencing.

What do you look like when you are projecting?

You imprint your image from whatever your consciousness believes you're going to look like. When people think of *astral projection*, they think it's their physical body they are projecting, so right away, they imagine a transparent physical body that wears clothing. As you begin to let go of that thought, you begin to change; there's no longer a shape or structure to your energy. The image disassembles, but you don't feel any pain; you feel safe, you feel normal. It's like a child who doesn't think anything different about running around naked in the winter. I would look at the being next to me and know who it was. At death, a being will hold on to their shape for a certain amount of time and still be recognizable. Their presence will be familiar to you. In fact, we would recognize anyone's presence.

Even though we both might see an energy form, because I'm a little more experienced, I would see it as energy rather than a body shape. I would know it as a being, but you may interpret it differently and form an image from the feelings that you recall. As your memory or involvement wanes, that image no longer holds its texture for you. This is classic for things beyond life. This is a tool we can use to progress.

Can animals or people see your probe?

I believe that animals or people can pick up on your probe, but it depends on the strength of your probe, how much energy has been put into it, and how much its frequency will drop to be able to maintain itself in this dimension. In many cases, animals see at a higher frequency than people do. This is why they sometimes chase or react to things that don't appear to be there.

You might see something out of the corner of your eye. When you look directly at the probe, there's nothing there because you see at a higher frequency out of the corner of your eye. You're going to see dimensional beings or objects with your peripheral vision.

You have to remember that, as energy, your frequency vibrates at such a high rate that it can become so unique that people don't always relate to seeing others during astral projection. More often, you hear about places they journey to, but you don't really hear about live creatures or the people they see.

I suspect the reason is that time is very different. You're moving at such a rate that stationery objects appear to you, but life forms don't. I think if you slow down your energy field, then you might see the manifestations of human beings and animals.

Do you need to consciously program your probe to project it?

That's a yes and no question; I think each person will approach this a little bit differently. When I've projected in the past, I didn't think about programming it, I just did it. Astral projection is almost obsolete for me at this stage of my development. I now have a process of sending my mind to wherever I need it to go, but it's still that same probe. I no longer have to go through the steps to do it.

To me, astral projection is the same as remote viewing or psychometry. They are different methods of moving the mind to achieve the same results. So, it really comes down to how much clarity you want to achieve. If you visualize your bathroom, you may not see it as clearly as I do. Nevertheless, it still works perfectly for you. I don't really feel a necessity for the same detail and clarity that I had earlier in my life when I went to the places I've described.

I still suggest that everyone should experience the detail at least once in their life. It will add to the structure of the development of your sixth sense abilities, yet it is so much more than that. The experiences will yield a vast amount of information like it has for me. I'm only describing about two percent of the information I gleaned from that experience and how it emotionally affected me.

If you are energy, you have to ask yourself how you would know if a spirit is a spirit. How does it see you without any eyes? How does it hear you if it doesn't have ear drums? So here I am in energy form and yet I'm having those experiences. I experienced these things because my brain perceived it as such. I didn't hear sound, but if I did, my brain would have created or mimicked the sound for that particular experience. My brain could no longer relate to what was real and what was not so it would overlap to fill in the gaps. It doesn't mean that the experience wasn't real or that it was a dream, but my brain assisted with what was happening. Keep in mind I didn't hear any people speaking. When they all came into the room during the one experience that I described, it startled me, but I don't remember them coming up the hall or hearing any sound. I saw the door swing open and that's what startled me.

There are many things I learned from that astral projection. It is why I'd rather teach people to have these experiences rather than just read about them in books. I could spend hours breaking it all down and describing that one projection on audio and video if I wanted to put that kind of time into it. I'm just glossing over it like you would gloss over any personal experience in your life. I encourage you to have an experience like this because it really gave me a lot of insight into what was actually happening. There were many of levels of information there that helped me to look at things differently as I progressed.

How do you see if you don't have eyes?

What you can gain from this is an understanding of how entities see us by utilizing a different form of sensory. This information you're getting right now is going through your pupils, your eyes cones, but it's reflected light. Everything you see is reflected light and your brain assembles it to create structure.

I suspect the energy field sends it the same way your eye cones take it in, but instead of having eye cones to send this data, your energy field sends it to your brain to assimilate. We use eye cones because they are a biological necessity, but there are other methods of communication.

How does an image go to a television if it's not using eye cones? There are other scientific processes at work, and so it is for energy. An entity no longer has an organic brain like you do. It's like trying to watch television on a radio. Since the entities can't use organic processes to communicate, there must be a different mechanism at work. The idea piques my curiosity.

Why is it easy to see but not smell or hear?

Sight is the most frequently used sense. Sightseeing is the first thing most people think about when going somewhere. Think of the term *sightseeing – seeing sight*, or sightseeing. What we perceive in our reality is not just what we smell, hear, taste, and feel, it's our whole perception of things. It's not to say you can't have all those other experiences, but we mostly use sight and it's the easiest because it comes naturally to us.

Let's put it this way, your eyes see frequency in a different format. Your other senses are designed to absorb information on a structural level. When you touch, it's a different process of integrating information. We don't really have an equivalent mechanism to utilize in an energy form. We don't have a physical body that translates structure into energy. Sight is the best level between the two and it seems to be the main area in which this information is relayed.

Can your consciousness become trapped outside of your body?

Let me be very clear about something. Not once in all of my life have I ever heard of a single person who went into a coma or their body stopped working or they left and never returned. In fact, there are some people I know that would be thrilled if they could just get up and leave like that. It is so hard to project outside of the physical body that you have to go through a lot of effort just to get glimpses and pieces of information. Rest assured, you're consciousness is fixated into your physical body. The second you think about your body, even if you're on the other side of the universe, you will be slammed so quickly back into your body, you won't even have a moment to think about why you thought about coming back.

The biggest challenge is to learn to focus long enough to achieve this experience. Everything you are learning is meant to prevent you from thinking about being in your physical body. Just thinking about it is like a homing frequency; you're going to slam right back into the body. I could tell you not to do that, but I guarantee you're going to do it anyway. You're going to think about it unconsciously.

The fear of projecting out and not coming back is absurd. Your body will call you back for many different biological reasons. You are not physically leaving the body. It is a probe and this probe is a mirror of your energy. Anything you feel on an unconscious level will respond to your thoughts. You're telling the probe to go up, down, left, right, but the second your body feels hunger, it will manipulate you to come back to take care of it. The second you have a sexual interest, you feel the need to come back to take care of your procreation needs. The second your body feels a twinge because the cat is walking on your leg, it will respond. It's going to want you to respond to your survival senses if it's getting too cold in the room.

You have everything stacked against you when it comes to achieving this goal. It has to be this way, otherwise life would not exist the way it does. There has to be a powerful mechanism that wants to keep you in this organism. The planet wouldn't have Red Cells and White Cells if there were other options. You depend on the living organisms within you to do their jobs, the same as the Earth depends on the Red and White Cells to do theirs. You are designed to serve your existence, your "X" number of years minus disease or accidents. You are hot wired for a purpose at this moment.

Those of us who are Navigators, those of us who feel that we have a higher purpose, a higher need to serve the Force on another level; are the ones who push the realm of all possibilities. We aim to reach past the limitations of our physical bodies, much farther than we have evolved even though we are not fully developed within the areas that are needed to assist us. We're trying to kick start this engine, and when we get it turning, we do not always have it in park. We have all sorts of different circumstances going on. So, don't worry about shooting off and not coming back. You'd be happy to stay out there for as long as ten minutes, trust me.

I remember watching a Shirley MacClaine film once called "Out on a Limb." There was a terrific scene on astral projection and it's probably the best part of the entire movie. She's outside in the hot tub at night, relaxes her body, and starts going through her spiritual training. At one point, she finally let's go and leaves her body. The next scene shows her moving up above the hot tub and, from that vantage point, looks down and sees herself below. She continues to move upward and observes the land mass, the evening night lights, and the surrounding village below. As she continues to climb, she sees the cloud mist and moves higher still. But the second she thinks about her body and starts to worry, she immediately comes back in again.

Do floatation or deprivation tanks make projection easier?

Deprivation tanks certainly do have their purpose; however, I do not see much of a difference between them and a good hypnosis session. A Deprivation tank can be very expensive whereas a hypnosis session is reasonably priced. Let me expound on this: A sensory deprivation tank is a temperature regulated; salt-water filled, soundproof, lightproof tank that isolates you from various forms of sensory input all at once. Its design and purpose is to find out what your brain will do when it is placed into a tank all by itself and left alone for a while.

Inside the tank, because there is no light, there is no sense of vision. You experience the kind of quiet that allows you to hear your muscles tense, your heart beat, and your eyelids close. The extreme buoyancy of the water provides an almost zero-gravity effect. The lack of a temperature differential plays with your ability to perceive where your body ends and where the water and air begins. This provides a means for your mind to escape, or to astral project. The problem is that you can manifest some deep-set fears you were not previously aware of before. You are alone in the tank without the assistance of a therapist if that happens.

A good hypnosis session can give you excellent results. During hypnotherapy when in the deep theta state of mind, you do not feel any physical symptoms. You relax the conscious mind, quiet the babbler, let go, and allow the subconscious mind to surface in order to get the results you are looking for. Science simplifies things, but I personally believe that deprivation tanks are overrated. I have not had a lot of experience with them, but with the experiences that I have had, I do not really see an advantage that outweighs hypnosis.

Can you improve your probe?

Absolutely. It is just like anything else. The more you practice doing this, the better it gets. We learn from our trials and errors. I have certainly improved my probe and my ability to tap into things, and it has also helped me develop a lot of other alternative methods of gathering information. Much like my experience with the island event that I mentioned earlier, I learned a great of deal of information through self study, which led to improved methods and other techniques. My goal is to provide good, sound and applicable information that will give you better results.

Now, the kind of experience you have will be based on your frequency, which can be controlled through your chakras. For instance, if you want most of your experiences to be on the physical level, you would focus awhile on your lower chakra before you go into an altered or hypnotic state; more than likely you are going to have more physical experiences in this physical dimension.

If you focus on your heart chakra and you develop a very happy, positive feeling, you are going to move into the astral planes or the level that I was talking about earlier consisting of very unique dimensional places.

If you focus on your mind chakra, it is as if your mind now shoots into space. It moves you into the Universe in a kind of galactic experience. You can also combine different chakra frequencies and experiment with this. For instance, if you work on the lower chakra and the mind chakra, you may go to other worlds, see other life forms and different circumstances of life in the world.

Are there baby steps to projecting a probe?

At first, you are going to have visual effects – probably little blips and pieces of information. Maybe three second runs to ten second runs then twenty second runs and then into full minute runs. Usually the brain will interfere to cut off the information. So, to get a few seconds in the beginning or *blips*, as I call them, is usually a good sign. Then they will turn into longer runs. Your brain is going to jump in and stop it. Sometimes you can have longer runs and, for some reason, your brain will not interfere. It really depends on where your focus has been that day, how well you have adjusted, or how many sessions you have done.

Another good sign is when you feel that jolting effect and then catch yourself. I would call those baby steps. Feelings of elongation in your meditation and the sensation of leaning to one side or the other are also good signs. In that particular case, you are stretching in and out.

Another method that is utilized is expansion-retraction. You want to see yourself blowing up, swelling up, and then decreasing in size during the hypnotic state. It prepares you to build a second body.

It is not natural to think you are going to get information visually. When I say "you get blips of information," that information may not be very vivid or clear. It may not be rich in color; you take it as you get it. Just like in meditation, do not discourage yourself.

Be careful of setting any expectations. An expectation is a marker for the brain. You are capping yourself by doing that.

The brain automatically assumes you cannot reach them. You are really preventing yourself from getting the little pieces that build up to the bigger experiences. You just sit down and let whatever happens, happen. If you do not have a breakthrough the first time, wait for the second, or the third. I assure you, with that attitude you will have a profound breakthrough. A lot of times when you think you're not going to set a standard, you have already set an expectation; it is very hard to fight that. That is why it's important to practice your *Higher Balance Meditations*. You will always have more success when you apply those skills to astral projection.

Do you determine where your probe is going to travel?

It is not always as easy as it sounds, but for the most part, yes. The more skill you have, the easier this will be. It is just like remote viewing. You pick a particular target or area and you hone in on it.

With astral projection, most people just randomly end up somewhere. They are so excited about having any experience at all that they have not given much thought to where they want to go. It is like winning the lottery and taking a vacation to a random destination because you're excited about all the possible places you can go. Subconsciously, it is difficult to focus your mind on one thing; therefore, you are not really strong enough to choose your destination.

As you practice and improve your ability to astral project, begin selecting a place to go to. Get a magazine, look at a picture, put it down, and expect to go there. What I mean by "expect to go there" is that you just assume that is where you are going to go but do not dwell on it. It's a way of getting around the Babbler. Sit down and go through the relaxation process and do not think about where you are going to go, just know. Nine times out of ten, that is where you are going to end up. Then you can broaden the horizons of whatever was not in that picture.

How is it possible for a picture to be the place that you end up going to? It is possible because somebody took that picture and, through their energy, the information of the location moved into the Gaia mind. It is data that is accessible. It is the same way that remote viewing, psychometry, and other techniques work. It is all interconnected. It is as limited as you choose it to be. So when I say, "Do not think about it," I mean that as a technique. *Do not rationalize with your brain* because you are setting the possibility of what you can achieve. Just for a moment, allow yourself to believe it is possible and done on a regular basis. Not everyone can think that way, so just do the best you can.

This is why hypnosis is very helpful for accepting that idea. If you can accept that idea, you will have profound experiences. It is what a therapist is trained to do. Their successes have built a level of confidence that enables them to do the things they do. Their reality is not perceived as most people understand it. They understand a higher level of possibilities. Therefore, a therapist has access to things most people shut themselves off from.

How do you know where to go? Does the time of day make a difference in where you project to?

When projecting, choose a place that you want to go and you will simply go there. It comes down to intent: If I am in altered or hypnotic state and I want to go to Egypt, then I go to Egypt. You also have to think about time sequences – you know daylight versus night time. Think about what it would be like to be there at the particular time you project so your brain is not confused with the information you get.

I recall one person saying they went someplace - I do not remember where - on the other side of the globe, and another person rationalized right away, "How could you have seen all that if it is night time there? It was 2 am when you did that and it is (such and such) time here." And the other person replied, "Well, I do not know. But, I could see everything and I am confident and sure of everything that I saw."

If you are energy and you can take this data back with you, who is to say that you are unable to see things while you are in a higher spectrum? If there are night vision cameras, who is to say your energy body, your probe, is not more advanced than that? Who is to say the image that is broadcasted is not reflected light?

Do not perceive your experiences as a human being. You set limitations by locking yourself into the perception that everything you see and experience will be the same as how you do it in the physical body. It is a huge problem. Even I fall into that habit occasionally because I do not think about it; it just happens automatically.

I recommend not choosing a location for the first three months because it can be difficult to choose a location in the earlier stages. Therefore, if you try to do that and you fail, you will be disappointed. You are setting an expectation and creating a barrier in your brain that will affect your mind and prevent you from achieving your goal. So I recommend convincing yourself first that you have had these profound experiences. Go through all the rationalizations of your different experiences and see where it moves you. See where the Universe wants you to go. After you have done this for awhile, then apply what I have said about choosing a location.

Is distance a factor?

No, distance is not a factor. It is only a factor if you think in terms of moving from point A to point B as if you're walking. You are controlled by this factor as long as you allow yourself to think in physical terms. I think you can move anywhere in the Universe instantaneously. You are connected to everything. You just have to choose to become aware of it.

Some people say that when they project, it all goes blank.

That happens because they subconsciously perceive distance as an impossibility. They base their experience on the assumption that they should already know what is there. The fact is, they do not know what is going to be there and a part of their rational brain is saying, "Then you cannot know." Have an open mind and simply assume you are going to go there to experience whatever you are going to experience. That is when you will start to see things that are just mind blowing.

I remember once projecting to Triton, a moon orbiting Neptune, and I was recorded. I do not remember the name of the person recording it, but he was a parapsychologist. I remember there was a space probe, the Voyager 2 that was taking pictures of the outer solar system. I saw what looked like volcanoes spewing ice, and I remember hesitating and wanting to tell the parapsychologist that I saw a volcano, but there was no lava coming out of it. It did not make logical sense to me and I felt like I was fighting with myself not to say it.

Much of a person's accuracy is based on fear. Most psychics are afraid of making a mistake or being called a fraud. So they hesitate or limit the amount of information they are willing to give on a particular subject, especially in a test situation. I think many psychics cannot perform under stress because of that same fear – it is an internal, psychological fear of failing.

I had enough training and experience so I said, "Well, I am seeing volcanoes with something that looks like liquid ice coming out of it." I think it was a matter of eight months later when one of them brought me a copy of Omni magazine. There were pictures of an orbiter that was taking pictures of Triton, and they were amazed that there were volcanoes that were spewing liquid nitrogen. It was documentation that basically confirmed what I had described to. So you cannot go in with a certain expectation.

When I was projecting and looking at the volcano, I remember the image was fading, and I was trying to get it back. I was internalizing and trying to accept what I was seeing; understanding that my brain was cutting off the information because it could not logically accept what was coming out of the volcano. So, in essence, when some people astral project, everything goes blank because they have set their governor to shut it off; they do not accept what they see. Just by saying they cannot imagine what is there stops them from having the experience.

I remember projecting once to a world that reminded me of a scene in *The Wizard of Oz* when Dorothy and her friends were running through the field of flowers that put them to sleep. I remember projecting and coming across this giant field of flowers. They were like glass that was refracting the light and making rainbows; it was beautiful.

There were fields of rose-shaped plants that felt like liquid. The shimmer of color was like fog, or a morning mist, yet it was different. It was like the Northern Lights but on a micro level and intensely more complex. My brain was trying to understand what it was that I was seeing. Even though I am describing it to you, you are only getting ten percent of the reality. I am at a loss for words to explain what I saw because it was so vast, and I remember there was something in the distance. I do not know what it was, yet something very large. The only way I can describe it is, the Emerald city in the distance and a beautiful path of amazing-ness. I knew it was alive, that it was a living thing. It was not like glass. It was not like crystal. It was like liquid glass, alive!

Do you need to be spiritually evolved to project, or can you just be psychic?

You can be psychic. I think Red Cells who have not yet ventured on their spiritual path are absolutely capable of it. If they begin to astral project, they will develop a dimensional body. Just the fact that they have become interested is another part of the process of building it. You start off biologically, and then you develop it into energy before you develop a dimensional body; just like a soul is first created. By reflecting, you cause this energy to begin building itself within you. There are now more spiritual advantages because you are now open to new possibilities instead of being limited by what your brain allows, filtering the information. That is the only difference that I see.

Is it possible to create a probe while you are conscious?

Yes, but it takes a lot of skill to do that.

How can you be consciously here and aware of your probe simultaneously?

The same way that you remember what your mother's house looks like. Think about it right now; it is the same as thinking about astral projection. You are doing both at the same time. It is just a matter of which one you direct more of your attention to. In fact, you can probably think about five different things at the same time. It is about the quality of information that you are visually getting.

Can you create multiple probes?

Absolutely. I do it all the time.

What about with multiple destinations?

Why not? I do it all the time. As I just said, you do multiple things at the same time. Imagine that you are driving a car. You are watching the speed, listening to the radio, looking at the mirror on your left, looking at the mirror on your right, and having a conversation with the person next to you all at the same time. There are many things going on; it is just a matter of perception. But you could not have done all those things if you just jumped in the car for the first time and had never driven before; give yourself a realistic amount of time to get to that level of skill.

Will entities be aware of your probe?

Yes, there are entities out there that may feel intruded upon by you and may want to find out where you are or where you live. I've had experiences like that. One or two were a bit unpleasant. The chances of that happening to you are about the same as you swimming in the ocean and getting bit by a shark. If you constantly live in fear of that happening, you will never explore the Universe or learn to do anything. I am not going to paint a false picture that everything is rosy. I am always going to be truthful.

There is always the chance that you will come across a negative entity. It is possible they will feel your energy and zero in on where it originated from. It works in the same way as someone who finds a missing person – they hone in on the person's energy or use remote viewing to find their exact location. The entity usually cannot get your location fast enough, but if they can they might want to. If you use your High Guard (explained in *Igniting The Sixth Sense*), you will not have a problem.

Could you unconsciously send out a probe? Could one just pop out unexpectedly?

Yes, if you start projecting regularly, your brain will learn to use it as a form of sensory. In the same way that you reach out and grab a glass of water, you will not even think about doing it. It won't bother you. You will dismiss it. You will only give it your attention when you want to direct your attention to it. It is not bad, it is a good thing, and if you want it to stop, just stop projecting. After a week or two, it will slow down on it is own.

How much of astral projection is brain work and how much of it is mind work?

I would say about fifty percent will be brain work. You need your foundation; you need the platform to operate from. The other fifty percent will be all energy and frequency.

Is the mind chakra the central point of projection?

No, you cannot just look at one chakra as being the entire focal point for astral projection. A projection is really a part of your completeness. That is why it works so well for gathering information. Remote viewing is actually the same thing; they are separated by perception. Think of it as a harmonic balance of all of your chakra points; your 'is-ness,' and do not be concerned about what chakra point you are projecting from unless you are putting intention into it.

I have heard of a technique where you place items with a certain scent around your home and then you attempt to recall the scent to project there. Is that a productive technique?

Well, that is another interesting way to use your sense of smell for projecting. When you are walking outside, you may smell a certain scent that could trigger an instantaneous flashback to a certain place, or a sensation that you may have experienced before. You are utilizing that mechanism to *jump*. I recommend that you do not use the sense of smell because it is secondary to sight because of pheromones, or scent molecules that are put through a different level of receptors. It is more difficult to use that method than the previous methods we have already talked about.

Does your probe retain your physical size? Does size matter?

Size does not make a difference with energy; at least in our perception. You will more than likely perceive yourself as a larger embodiment of energy that is appropriated to your physical size because, in your mind, it is how you perceive yourself. You give it a size based on your perception.

When I projected during my youth, at first I saw a transparent version of myself that eventually became more energy. It got to the point where I saw myself as three or four feet in size but just energy, kind of like a cloud with ribbons of energy going through it. Unconsciously, you feel most comfortable at that point after you have done it for a while. Everybody's experience is a little bit different. When people do not think they are doing it correctly, or are having an experience, they immediately think they have failed when in fact, they are actually achieving projection.

If you were to stand up and look out, you really cannot see your body. You just see what's in front of you. So a lot of people think they are just getting images in their mind because they don't see their body or probe. It is really just a matter of how your brain interprets it. It will change as you get better and better. You learn that your brain has set comfort levels for certain things.

Could you project your probe into a micro verse?

Absolutely, again, it's about perception. If you can look through a microscope and see the minuscule life on the slide, then you can exist in micro life. If I can go to the beginning of time and see the fabric of creation, I am within the level of protons and even smaller than protons. It is unbelievable for us to fathom when you think about it. If you close your eyes, you already know what it looks like under a microscope. Can you not see it? Can you not move these little globular things around you? They look like eggs when you crack them open. You just make them bigger and you move them around. There is no limit!

Can your probe continue to collect data when you return to a conscious state?

It depends on your intent. Most people have the probe return because they assume when they open their eyes they must be in their body. When you evolve to a certain point you can actually let it out and it will collect information.You are in more than one place at the same time. You are doing something that you are not paying attention to and then later, when you focus your mind, you realize all the things you have done.

Why is it hard to move when you project?

It's based on your perception and belief. You are projecting what you think is your main reality onto something else. It is just a matter of learning to do two things at the same time. It is similar to the way an athlete learns to walk a balance beam, or a juggler tossing several items at once. You can walk and talk at the same time, but in the beginning you could not. You had to give your full attention to either walking or talking. When I projected to the Greek Isles, it was only because of my curiosity. As soon as I became curious, I moved toward it. I did not think about how I was going to do it. I just did it and that is the secret. Do not complicate matters with what you are doing or how you are doing it because you will solidify yourself and limit the possibilities of your normal everyday functions in life.

Could you affect a physical object with your probe?

It is certainly possible, but it would take an intense amount of energy to affect the energy fields in our current reality from that place. There are other methods of manipulating a kind of psychokinesis or "PK" energy for that purpose. Psychokinesis is the ability to energetically move an object. As for achieving this during projection, you would have to be extremely advanced in order to be able to do that on a regular basis. You might get lucky with certain things once in a while, but I highly doubt it.

Is it possible for your brain to take over and slip you into a dream state?

Yes, it is possible. That power comes from what you give it. As I said from the very beginning, do not do it around the time you normally sleep. You want to stack the odds in your favor. You are starting to move over into its territory if you are pushing into your rest period.

Are there universal laws governing projections, or where your probe can go?

Well, yes. There are only certain dimensions that you are going to be able to get into. The type of energy that you will be projecting is not going to resonate with certain dimensions; you would have to die in order to do that. You would have to leave your physical body permanently in order to go there. Death is the only universal energy frequency that has the potential to reach those places, and even then it is based upon your frequency. The level of your knowledge will determine the kind of place you can move into.

Is that why sometimes when you are projecting, you feel you should not be in certain places?

If you do not feel you should be there, one of two things is happening. Your instinct is telling you that you really should not be there and you should listen to it. Go find something else to do. There are plenty of interesting places to visit. Or, you have fear because it looks a little foreboding and that is how you perceive it.

Here's an analogy. Let's say there is a biker bar and it looks pretty rowdy in there. You are imagining stabbings, drunkards, and breaking bottles over people's heads. Your buddy rides a bike and he says, "Oh no, I go in there all the time, it is wonderful! You know John, the bartender, and Bill is a lawyer and he has a big Harley." Once again, it is just your perception.

So, while projecting, you may see something that seems intimidating and you register it in a fearful way; this is what creates that barrier. It could be one or the other; it is very difficult to judge those two things. If you do not feel that you should go there, then do not go there. Build up your strength and as you mature, your perception will change. Then, re-approach that scene and see if you get the same vibe.

If your body is safe, why not push your probe?

Well, there are really nasty entities that just do not want to be bothered, and if you are encroaching on their environment, their energy field is projecting a feeling of "Stay away! Leave me alone!" and you will feel it on a psychic level. You can decide how you want to handle the situation. If you are going to provoke it, then you get what you deserve, and that is your own fault. If you see and hear a rattle snake and you say, "Oh! Look at that tail rattle. I want to see what's in it. Let's go pet the snake." Then you get what you deserve. If you interpret the rattle as being what it is meant to be, a warning, then you probably got the right message.

Internally you know right from wrong. So you can be stupid if you want to or you can act intelligently; it is up to you. It's like swimming out in the ocean. Do you have a sense of how far out you want to swim? How do you know? I would say, use the same common sense. If you feel a resistance or danger or that this may not be wise, then you have to wait until you feel you have the stamina or the ability to swim that far.

I am not saying not to do this, nor am I saying only wade up to your ankles or your kneecaps. There is a reasonable level of confidence and you decide what that level is. But do not be foolish. If there is an energy out there that says it does not want you there, then you need to respect that. Just because you can project there does not give you a license to intrude on other beings.

Other being's presence, or field of energy, is like their home. Would you drive by someone's house and intrude on their privacy just because you want to see what the place looks like? You know there is a door there and if it is locked, you should presume that they don't want you in there. Just because you have a car and a hand to open the door, does that give you the right to walk in? Every place has its levels of respectability; certain things want to be approached, and certain things do not want to be approached. They have a right to decide when you should approach them, not you. It is ignorant to think it's your right to do whatever you want.

How can you tell the difference from that inner knowing and your Governor?

The same way that I explained before; human beings are explorers. Most living things are explorers of some type. There is going to be a time for you to push your boundaries and experience will tell you how to decide when that time has come. You will understand after awhile through other experiences how to reassess that same experience when you go back to it. Then maybe you will realize it was your own fear that was preventing you from exploring it. Or you will realize that was really a rattler warning you to stay away.

Treat the Universe as you want to be treated. You will feel what you need to know to survive in the same way you have survival senses for your physical body. You can see danger, you can hear danger, and in some cases, you can smell danger. You will naturally have the senses you need to inform you, you just have to pay attention to them. Don't be concerned with running out of places to explore.

Let me put this another way; do you feel there are plenty of places in this world that you can freely explore to satisfy your curiosities? Or do you think the whole world is one big house and there is only a tiny back yard that you get to play in? It is a big multi-dimensional universe out there. Don't be concerned with where you may not be able to go and think that you are missing something. There are plenty of other fantastic things out there to explore.

How can you send your probe
to a place where there are no pictures?

It's potluck. Your assumption is that there will be something out there and, hopefully, you will discover what that is. When Christopher Columbus discovered America, his assumption was that he would find new land, but he did not know for sure. Eventually he came across it. There are a whole lot of `something's` out there. It s just a matter of projecting out in any direction, discovering what is there, and making the best of it. If the universe is the body of God, then there is a collective consciousness for everything. So there is a map that you can tune into that will help you get there. It is already there, it is already part of you. You must reach a level of accepting the information.

Can you send a probe into the past or future?

Absolutely, but you cannot interact with it. In other words, if you were to project here, in this time, someone might see your probe and think they are seeing a ghost. You can only project into the past if it has been recorded in the Gaia mind. It's as if you go through its memories; like a holographic journey that you can move through. In a lot of ways, it's the same for the Universe. So there's really an infinite level of possibilities.

You can only project to a certain point in the future because it isn't written yet. It is like the analogy I've given before about the super computer knowing where the bouncing ball will stop in a large room since it can calculate the probabilities of this happening. If I threw something to you, you would already be positioned to catch it because your brain is guesstimating what I am going to do. You can predict what will occur in the future if you work through the Gaia mind or the universal collective consciousness.

Does time pass differently while projecting?

It certainly can. You might project for thirty minutes and you will swear that you were out there for five hours. Or you might project for two hours but it feels like it's only been five minutes. Time can condense, and the condensed moment is so detailed that the brain perceives this as a normal occurrence.

When you dream at night, it seems like a very long time; but when you wake up, you realize it's only been a short period of time. It depends on how the brain processes the data from the higher dimensions. While projecting, you are experiencing a higher level of consciousness that is similar to multidimensional consciousness, so you are not limited to the organic brain to process that data. The brain filters a lot of information because it just will not accept it.

The same filtering was occurring when I saw those glass-like plants. I was stuck trying to organically process the data my probe was receiving. I might have looked at that for five minutes, but in my organic brain it was looping and I felt like I was looking at it for two hours. It is absorbed differently, and my brain was trying to thread different concepts: plants, glass, liquid and build a foundation to understand what I was seeing.

If the image starts becoming fragmented and processed by your organic brain, wouldn't you notice that time is looping in a strange way?

No, you will realize it later as you become more experienced and gain the ability to analyze that.

Can your other energy bodies create probes?

All of your energy bodies become a piece of the probe. It's all one harmonization of the sum total. The only difference is that those bodies are able to transcend this physical life. They in turn will also shed as you metaphor into something that becomes a much higher energy being.

What about evoking a certain emotion to project?

It would be just the opposite of creating a probe to send out. It works the same as when you choose an image and then choose to go there. The more emotion you can evoke, the better. On the same token, it can also be a downfall. What you see in the picture and what you think is going to be there might not match the real frequency, but you have now added information that you did not need to put in the mix. If the frequencies do not match up, you are not going to be able to enter that place.

In most instances of remote viewing, you will only receive an alpha-numeric code. That is all you have to work with, nothing else. You do not know if it is a person, a place, or an object. You use your sensory to give you the data that you are getting from the Gaia mind. You are getting it from the super subconscious that is connected like a grid, a matrix.

You have to rely on your feelings and thoughts to give you a free flow of data, rather than rationalization. You go with that free flowing data and you start to etch it in your mind, or you can let it flow visually. But now that visualization is another form of astral projection or remote viewing. These are really all the same thing, in my opinion. They are from the same family of sensory.

I've included a relaxation technique at the end of this chapter for both remote viewing and astral projection. It will get you started, and you will learn to enhance your skills as you continue to practice them.

Remote Viewing

You are going to need two other people to work with. The reason for this is to avoid any suspicion that, somehow, you were tipped off or you telepathically read the information from the other person.

The first person will be secluded from you; it could be someone you don't even know. The second person will be your assistant and is going to relay the information between you and the first person. The first person will randomly choose a picture from a magazine, a photograph of something, or even a painting. Then, they'll take that picture and assign it an eight digit code that is made up of numbers and letters.

For instance, let's say that I saw a picture in a magazine of the Taj Mahal. I would assign it the code *84D63928* and write that down on paper. It's very important that the first person is looking at the picture, feeling it, and burning a very clear mental image of it into their memory, and then feeling what random number comes up. They will then fold the piece of paper so that it can't be witnessed; preferably, put it in an envelope before handing that piece of paper to the second person, your assistant.

So, your assistant has no idea what's in this envelope. They will sit down with you at a table during the session. You are going to need a notepad and a pencil instead of a pen. When you're ready, you will have that paper, or envelope handed to you. When you open it, you are going to focus on the code and *feel* what it means to you. Interpret it, and see what images and impressions flow through your mind. Your target can be anyplace in the world, even beyond the world; other planets, universes, whatever you like. The selection of the location is not very important.

Instead of choosing a picture, the third person can physically go somewhere. They can pick a place in a town, call the second person, look around where they are located, and then give them a code. For instance, if I were standing in the middle of a park, I might say on the cell phone to the second person, "849FG632". The second person needs to write that code down, and no other information would be exchanged. Then, they give the written code to the remote viewer to digest and interpret what it is. What comes from that code? The room that you work in should be quiet with no interruptions, no children, pets, barking dogs, etc. You definitely need to have your paper and pencil ready. You also need to have an honest discussion with yourself and remind yourself that it will take time to develop a level of good, clear accuracy.

This takes time and practice, and it's okay to be incorrect. Remember, practice makes perfect. It's important to understand that the information is not going to be crystal clear like an image or a moving picture. It's important to understand that it usually appears like a faded or dim image. In some cases, you may see a close-up of a chair leg, or you might see a beach. You might see bird feathers close to its wing and not be able to see the rest of the bird. You should not spend time trying to understand what kind of bird it is.

Jot down the information that you get and don't try to decide if it's a Blue Jay or a Robin: Just 'bird, feathers'. If you see a color, write down the color. If you see a pattern of red, blue, and black write down the pattern that you see and move on. *The secret is not to allow the mind to try to interpret the information.*

Information can come in a variety of ways: a feeling, a hunch, a smell, an idea, the feeling of texture, or an overall sense of knowing without really knowing the source of how that is possible. It's as if you are guessing, but without applying the effort. It's your intent to gain information that allows the ideas and images to come through.

You don't have to think about what you're doing, you already have the intent to see what this information is. So, try not to think about the information, or wonder what it means, or place a meaning on it to make better sense of it. The bottom line is that your brain will instinctually try to place concepts on the information you receive, so ignore it and allow it to flow unconditionally.

Your training from the *Higher Balance Meditation* will make a big difference in the results you get.

Sitting in a chair, place your hands on your lap. Breathe through your nose. Breathe in, and exhale through your mouth. Do this two or three times. Become aware of your physical body. Think about it. Notice the feeling of the clothing you are wearing and the chair that you are sitting on.

Now, change the direction of your awareness of your body to the room. Observe the room around you and apply special attention to details, such as the kitchen counter, its design, its texture, the curves, the color and the style of the refrigerator. See the handle, the objects that may or not be on it, the coolness of the metal door.

Observe the floor. Notice its pattern, its textures, and flaws. Now, smell the air; discern any noticeable scents and then search for different ones in between those scents. Listen to the sounds of the room. Become aware of a clock ticking, the hum of the refrigerator, the sound of silence.

Close your eyes, and breathe in through your nose and exhale through your mouth. Then visualize your bathroom with as much detail as possible. Then, imagine your bedroom, the colors and texture of the covers on your bed. Recall the feeling of climbing in bed and pulling the pillow up close to your face. Recall the smell, its feeling. Pulling the pillow close to your face and smelling it. Look at the closet door. See the color, texture and the details. Look down at the carpet. Acknowledge the color and texture of its fibers. Recall the feeling of it when you touch it. .

Then, open your eyes and breathe in deeply through your nose and exhale through your mouth. Notice how you just recalled the sensations of those memories and how clear or refined they were. Notice how your memory recalled the feelings and textures. The information you receive will be very similar. Set your expectations for that in the beginning.

Now, breathe in deeply through your nose, and exhale through your mouth. With your eyes closed, think about the space in between your ears. Then inhale through your nose, and exhale through your mouth. Now open your eyes feeling clear. Accept the folded paper from your assistant and with a clear mind, look at the code and inhale through your nose with the desire to know what this code represents. You may leave your eyes open or closed now. It's a matter of preference. Allow yourself to feel, imagine, sense, recall, or simply know pieces of data. Pick up the pencil in front of you and begin to release your thoughts and feelings onto the paper.

No matter what, do not second guess yourself. Just jot it down and move on. Begin by internalizing a desire to know if it is a land mass, water mass, or structure. Internalize the feel of the environment. Does it feel like a library, a home, an office, a church, a factory, a school, the beach? What are the basic colors involved? What comes to mind? What are the vague images coming though? What are the textures? Does it feel warm, or cold, metallic, fibrous, or smooth? Allow yourself to flow with this information. Do not allow the information to be interpreted by your expectations. It is as if you are recalling information rather than experiencing it firsthand. It's like thinking about your bathroom or your kitchen and recalling those memories. Recall what this number is saying to you. Does it have an emotion like happiness, distress, calmness, excitement, hopelessness? Is it active or still? Sketch your images. Write your thoughts down. Trust your instincts. It's that simple.

You may want to switch things up with a slightly altered version of the same technique, only using a picture, an object such as personal jewelry, or a wallet. The second person, maybe the person these items belong to, will ask you generic questions at first and eventually, as you build your confidence, they'll ask you more complex questions about the item or picture. Most importantly, you must always have feedback. You need encouragement when you are learning remote viewing. Encouragement always increases your accuracy as you learn to trust your information flow, rather than filter and screen it. And remember, the more you practice this technique, the more accurate you will become.

Astral Projection

Do this technique no more than two to three times a week for the first two weeks. Your experiences with the *Assimilation Technique* (Chapter 3 of *Igniting the Sixth Sense*) will come in handy when learning how to project. It is helpful for you to be in a relaxed state, but not too relaxed. If you use it right before bed, you will likely fall asleep, but you may have many interesting dreams. However, I highly recommend that you do this technique during a time when you are not overly exhausted.

Be careful of what expectations you set. An expectation is a marker for the brain that sets a level. In essence, you are capping yourself. As you practice and get better, begin selecting a place to go. Don't do this for the first three months as it is difficult for most people.

The frequency of your probe is the same frequency as your consciousness. So this frequency is specifically tuned with the intent of collecting information. As you meditate and build your level of discipline, you start to get more energy, higher levels of consciousness and then you reach dimensional consciousness. The deeper your meditations and the more you're able to stay aware and cognitive without mental chatter, the better will be your projections. So when you decide to project, you will be more successful.

Visualize the details so that you train yourself on different levels to incorporate this information. Use your imagination to perceive this as a probe rather than a body and accept the fact that it's a probe. Physical relaxation is very important. Work with the physical body; relax it; drink some warm tea or find something that relaxes you; do some stretches. Wear very comfortable clothing.

Prepare through emotion to determine the kind of frequency you are going to pop into. For instance, if you want your experiences to be more in this physical level, focus awhile on your lower chakra. If you focus on your heart chakra and you develop this very happy, positive feeling, you are going to move into the astral planes. If you focus on your mind chakra, your mind will move into the Universe and you will have a galactic type of experience. Sometimes you can combine these frequencies. You can work on your lower chakra and your mind chakra. Then you tend to go to other worlds and see other life forms.

Secure a quiet and safe location where you will not be disturbed for the next 90 minutes. Turn off all phones and place a note on your door with the time that you will be available. Also, be sure to let immediate family members and friends know what you are doing in case they accidentally disturb you and react with a level of concern.

Place pets in a secure area where they will not disturb you. Lighting should be natural. If it's daytime, the blinds should be open. If it's nighttime, have a light on with at least a 60-watt light bulb, but not directly above you. Sounds, such as T.V. and radio should be limited and heard only in the distance. There should not be any strong odors, such as incense or room deodorizers. Have a light blanket or covering to place over you, especially if it is the winter months. Your temperature will drop, just as it does when you are sleeping.

If, for some reason, you fall asleep during or after the session, there is no reason to be alarmed. You will awaken naturally, as if from a short nap. When you have set up your environment, you should take a moment for some basic stretching. Once you have completed your exercise, lay in a comfortable position with your head slightly elevated. You may use a comfortable pillow, but be sure it is not lower than the rest of your body. Your feet should not be crossed, rather side by side and not elevated. Place your hands down by your sides; do not place your hands on top of your body. As you begin, this will become very comfortable for you. Each session will yield more results as you progress and gain more experience.

Once you have yourself in a nice relaxed state, there are other techniques. In the area between your knee-caps and your upper hip, almost up to the groin on the inner thigh, simply rub in this area for about five minutes. There is a certain feeling that you will sense about your energy field. It affects something in the spinal area that gets the Babbler to ease off so that you can achieve astral projection. Feel the finger texture, the moving and the rubbing. Do it for a few minutes. There is a very distinct feeling that comes from it. You may feel tingles or you may feel a very unique feeling that you don't pay attention to very often. Combine that as part of the process of preparing to astral project.

Begin by choosing a spot on the ceiling to stare at. It's okay to blink, but try to keep your attention only on the spot. Slowly inhale through your nose, and release through your mouth. Focus your attention on the spot, and become aware of the feeling of your clothing. Feel the weight of your body pressing downwards, sinking into the bed, the weight of the flesh on your face.

Then, imagine the distance between you and the spot on the ceiling. Feel it. Now, close your eyes and become aware of your chest. As you inhale slowly and deeply through your nose, become aware of how your chest feels as it's expanding, and imagine the space within it. Then, exhale through your mouth, and become aware of your body; your feet, your calves, your thighs. Think about them; your torso, your intestines, and stomach.

Next, you're going to focus on your inner chest. Experience your inward and outward breath. Feel your chest expanding and contracting. Now, become aware of your shoulders. Imagine the distance between them. Feel the space. Become conscious of the space. Your arms, elbows, wrists, hands, and each finger tip. Become aware of them. Feel your neck, your throat, your cheeks, and your jaw. Become aware of them. Feel your eyes resting in your skull, your forehead, your ears, and imagine the space in between them. Become aware of the feel, and the weight of your body. Imagine the space within it. Feel your breath pulling inward through your nose, and flowing out through your mouth. Breathing in, feel yourself expanding, and retracting as you exhale.

Next, inhale, and imagine your inner space expanding larger than your physical space. Exhale, and come back within your physical space. Again, feel your breath move in and imagine your inner space expanding larger than your physical space. Feel it and become aware of it. When you exhale, come back within your physical space.

If you're just learning to project, you may see deep, intense, hard-to-explain colors in your 'mind's eye' during a session. Instead of stopping and marveling at the color for too long, look or 'feel' beyond the 'colors' you experience. When you become familiar with the Assimilation Technique, in Chapter 3 of *Igniting the Sixth Sense*, you can use it to discover more about these colors. Usually the intensity of the colors will be an easy anchor point for you to focus on.

During Mind Projection, you may encounter a brilliant range of colors; some are so intense they cannot even be measured by our eyes. Don't get wrapped up in the fascination of the colors themselves so much as what is behind the visual phenomena. This can also happen with people who discover auras and train their eyes to see them better. These colors are actually just the surfaces of dimensional phenomena outside of your brain's current ability to process or digest. By reflecting on the frequencies of those colors, and using non thought, further information or insight can occur.

The secret is to not allow the mind to try to interpret the data it is receiving. Information can come in as a feeling, hunch, smell, idea, or what texture it would feel like, an overall sense of knowing without really knowing the source of how you know.

You don't have eyes as energy, so therefore you really should be able to see in every direction – 360 degrees. If you accept that you can see this way, it's as if your senses can just flip because it's not a necessity for your physical body to move.

Sometimes, while you're experiencing astral projection, you'll find that anytime you move, it's like zoom... you're there. You can move forward, but if you think about being closer, sometimes you just appear there. You have to remember that it's just energy movement but it's completely different. Don't slow it down by your perception of it. Just try to go with the flow. You can move anywhere in the Universe virtually instantaneously. You are connected to everything. You just have to choose to become aware of it.

When your projections progress, you will have visual effects such as little blips and pieces. When you get a few seconds of blips in the beginning, it is usually a good sign. If you feel a jolting effect when you go to catch yourself, you are progressing. You may feel elongated in your projection, just as you sometimes do in meditation. It's as if you are leaning to one side or the other. Look forward to it rather than trying to ignore it.

The second you begin thinking about your body, it's like a homing frequency. You're going to go right back into it. When you finish, lift your right arm up, and then place it down. Lift your left arm up, and place it back down. Open your eyes to the here and now.

Chapter 2

JOURNEY INTO THE COSMOS

I want to give you an idea that will provide you with a better understanding of the vastness of the universe, your role in the universe, and the potential of what you can become. It is pivotal that you understand how meaningful your life is; yet, in another aspect, how meaningless it can seem. I've always believed that when you understand something better, it frees you from this low level of consciousness to a higher level of awareness.

Most people just deal with their everyday life, their problems, and the ritual of going to work to make some money so they have a place to crash at the end of the day. Those of us who quest for a higher state of consciousness, a higher state of being, a higher state of existence, are reminded every day of our typical, mundane life. Most humans live their lives like push-button machines. They simply go through the motions as if they are sleepwalking. I visualize that type of existence as living in a maze. In this maze they just move forward, and when they hit a wall they either go to the left or right. They walk through their life with minimal thinking on their part; this is true for most people.

If you allow it, life will push you through the years and you will grow old before you even think to question where those years went. Eventually, without aware-ness, life grinds you up, you're spit out, and it's all done. After your death, all of your experiences are weighed to determine what you've become. Most people's collec-tive experiences ultimately weigh nothing at all. Their energy dissipates back into the universe because there was no soul, so there is no afterlife. That concept is one thing I want to discuss. I'll also give you some new exercises and review exercises to help you feel the energy inside your body.

To become enlightened, you have to have an awareness of the environment in which you exist. I'm not speaking of just the world, or your home, or country, but also the universe. You must comprehend how the universe functions in comparison to your body. You need to grasp how your energy works and how your mind works in comparison to the total universe. You're not supposed to know these things, but if you can reflect on what I'm saying from time to time and start to understand and grasp the "un-knowable knowledge," that act alone will harmonize your energy. That reflection raises your conscious-ness, it allows you to become more psychic, more gifted, more spiritual, and more in tune with the universe.

It seems like such a daunting task, but you already know the entire universe because you're made of the same fabric. You just have to choose to ignite it within yourself so that you can experience it. I understand that you may not realize yet what you need to ponder, what your mind needs to understand, what to feel, or even how to even begin to comprehend what it is you're trying to look for. That's what I'm here for; I'm going to try to show you.

To not ponder on who you really are is no different than an animal roaming around eating, mating, raising cubs, and starting the process all over again. You would be just letting your life trickle through your fingertips like sand or water; you've got to try to remember your purpose, to awaken.

I reflect on the rituals of life; the customs, rules, regulations, laws, adulthood, and the conventions of marriage within our society. Every country argues and fights over which customs and beliefs are correct. It's just so senseless in the end. Our lives on earth are so menial, so infantile. It is nothing in comparison to the big picture of our existence. Becoming fixated on these earthly things is the beginning of being consumed by everyday life. When this happens, one forgets about the universe. If you can think about that, it makes all the problems in your life seem very small. It forces you to realize how little you are.

Only two things are promised to you in this life; you're going to live in this world, and you're going to die. That's it. You start and you finish. Unless you do this one thing, it will all have been for nothing: you must build the energy in your body. You must learn to control the electrons in your body. This is the same energy that, when you touch something with your finger, moves to your brain to tell you what you feel. That experience was a translation of energy which moved through your body. You must learn to control that energy. You must learn to become aware of that energy and you must use it. You must exercise it in the same way that you lift weights for the health of your body. You must physically, actively, work the energy in your body so that when you die, you don't just evapo-rate. Otherwise, your very existence, all that you have learned, and all the things you have become from all of your life experiences will just dissipate like throwing a sugar cube into the ocean.

You must build this energy inside your body. You must learn to become aware of it. Forget about being enlightened. Forget about becoming a conscious being on the planet. The first thing you must realize is that you are more than just a physical body. Just like a frame of a car, your bones are the frame of your body; the engine is your heart, the wiring and everything else is your intestines and your machinery. Your body is just like a machine and you are this living force of energy that is lucky enough to exist within it. But will you exist when it's done, when it has expired? Will you move on? Will you exist when you die; will you exist beyond this life? Do you even want to? I certainly do.

The only reason that people embrace death at all is because they get old and their body gets tired, so they begin to think they are their body. When the body gets tired; they believe they're ready to die. They're ready to give up their life. That is why most people don't live after death. They associate their physical body with their energy body, and when the physical body dies the energy just dissipates because that's their last thought. You must have the will to live beyond this life. You must will forth every single day, every single moment, and try to think about your other self; the energy being that's coexisting in this physical mass, this machine. The universe is a mirror to you and you are a micro-verse, a miniature version. To really see, feel, and ponder the universe is what raises your energy. Describe this universe; describe the vastness of what Earth is in comparison to this universe.

It's like a cell in our body, but even greater than that, a cell in our body in comparison to the earth.

The Earth, the entire planet that we exist on is like the tip of a pin. That pin tip fits into one of these little bumps. (See the example of a pincushion). And where each pin tip fits is a galaxy. When you look at the rest of the universe, each of the bumps represents just one galaxy, one galaxy that holds everything, and each galaxy is another "little bump." In fact our entire solar system fits inside of one of these little bumps. We are nothing, we're *absolutely nothing.*

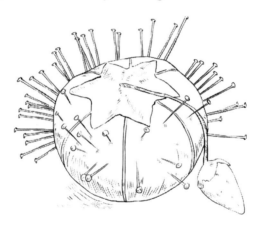

Each pin tip is a galaxy, like bumps on a pincushion.

The movie *Contact* depicted one of the best visual portrayals I've ever seen as to what is really out there in the universe. This aspect of your learning is so important to your development because it gives you the drive to press forward when times get tough and you feel that life isn't worth it. I've always thought; if I didn't know these things, I would have given up long ago. Life in the machine lacks meaning.

In the opening scene of the movie *Contact,* one of the interesting points the directors made is about the speed of sound. The speed of sound is fast, right? The sound closest to earth is the newest sound. So, if you can move at the speed of light, and you were to follow the sound audibly from the 1990's (when the movie was made), you can conceivably travel through time and space. The sound moves from the 1980's, the 1970's; all the way back to the 1920's when the sound waves were first broadcast as a signal. At the same time, the sound is still moving through space. We can actually move through space and catch up with a signal that was broadcast in 1921 and hear it as if it is happening right at this very moment.

Your body communicates via electromagnetic impulses. Your internal organs are told how to function by these impulses as they listen to the signals that move through your body. The stars throw off radiation and the radiation bombards the planets, and the planets tell us, as living organisms, how to function. You send the same intention throughout your body to all your cells and organs. So your kidney and liver are like giant galaxies in comparison to the molecular living organisms within your body.

You are a giant universe to these organisms, so vast it seems incomprehensible for the signal to travel through to them. However, it's no different than you trying to conceive the vastness of the entire universe. Physically, you could never move to the end of the universe; you wouldn't live long enough. But you could as an energy being.

You would be the same energy that moves through your entire body when your finger touches something; the energy visiting and experiencing millions of galaxies as it travels to your collective consciousness. When you die and you can hold your energy together, you can leave this world and travel the multi-universes and choose to live lives in other worlds, other galaxies, other beings; lives beyond your comprehension.

If you ponder the universe, visualize it, and try to comprehend it, you become that tonal, that vibration. Your mind begins to merge on a level of that energy and you become like the Universe, like God. It's not just what you can do; it's what you can understand. The more you understand, the more liberated you are. It frees you and the massive amount of energy inside you. There is more energy in one human being than is comprehensible to you; it's a different kind of energy that no human being can understand. It's like a molecule that we haven't yet figured out how to spin in a certain way, but when we do, the possibility of it is beyond our understanding.

Watch the opening scene of the movie *Contact* and really understand what you are seeing. It's so important for you to feel the moment, to try to conceive the unimaginable vastness and ask yourself what you really are. You're nothing but a little tiny microscopic cell. And in comparison to the universe, the planet looks like a lowly cell. The entire galaxy, when you move far enough away, looks like a tiny dot.

If you would zoom into the galaxy, zoom into the solar system, and zoom into Earth, you'd realize that you're nothing but a spot in the middle of a barren desert — absolutely nothing. What are you then in comparison to the galaxy, the universe, the multi-universe, the cosmos? You are insignificant. The only way you can become something more is to become aware, to become this frequency of energy that says you must experience rather than simply exist.

If you expect to experience God someday, since God is everywhere, you must become the frequency; you must become a little tiny prick of pain or the little feeling of joy that runs up your arm as a tingle for the moment that you reflect on it. You must insist that the Universe looks at you and that is only by awakening, it's only by becoming.

When you first watch that scene from *Contact*, you'll realize how insignificant you are. But so is an atom and an atom can become an atomic bomb. You are made of billions, and billions, and billions of atoms. What if they were all to ignite at once? You would become known to the entire universe. That is what enlightenment is. By doing so, your will can be imposed on levels that are incomprehensible, but it all depends on your energy, your awareness.

It starts now. It's a journey and everything in life tries to keep you down, spiritually. Everything in life tries to stop you. The Darkside doesn't want you to awaken, The earth tonal doesn't want you to become more than an organic species for the planet serving it, just like you would not want the cells in your body to become independent; you need them to do your will. So does the Earth want you to do its will? You are a cell to the Earth as your cells are to you. As the Earth is to the solar system, as the solar system is to the galaxy, as the galaxy is to the total universe.

You must go beyond what you think is free will because when they say you have free will, you really don't; you're just a push-button, biochemical creature that responds in pre-determined ways to thousands of variables. You use your will by becoming and realizing the things I'm saying.

I'll walk you through some exercises in this chapter that will help you to become more proficient in energy movements. If you consistently do these exercises and you pay attention to the energy movements in your body, you will become alert, and your energy will build. Just because you haven't noticed a huge difference does not mean you're not on the verge of attaining a profound awakening.

You may wonder how it is possible to become a part of this huge vast thing - the universe. A microscopic part of your body could, for a moment, have a tingling sensation, but still get the attention of the entire multi-universe of you. You get the attention of the absolute cosmos in the same way; it is a living thing. It's just a matter of what you do with your life, your personal evolution, and whether or not you achieve that level of awareness. Will you reach that level of energy consciousness, or will you fail and become like millions of other beings that just exist for a moment and then that's it, they're gone?

If you just choose to live life without any care, then you shouldn't even exist now. You have to ask yourself if you want to be something more than all of this. If the Earth is so vast, and there is so much to explore from Tibet to India to China to Europe to Africa and everywhere else, can you imagine what it would be like to explore our galaxy? Think about it; that would take hundreds of millions of years to accomplish.

What are those conservative religious people thinking when they say you go to heaven after you die and that's it? Do you check into heaven and play shuffleboard? If they believe in God, then they have to know that God created a vast universe. God wants us to experience and explore, and the only way to really truly experience something is to live as an organic being in a physical dimension. You experience a 100-year life span, or however long it turns out to be, for that species. You have that time to learn what it's like to exist in this world. Think about it.

One of the reasons you are here is to gain knowledge. I am offering knowledge to you; whether you accept it depends on you. I tell you about these things so that you can become aware of them and that is what moves and pushes electrons in your head. It takes a stagnant mind and fuels it. Just pondering and feeling the excitement of what we're talking about moves the molecules in your mind. It moves something inside of you that science has not fully understood yet. It awakens the sleeper in you, but if you don't think about it, you stay asleep and then you die.

If you do think about it, if you ponder, if you talk about it, if you share it with others, it breathes life into you; the knowledge itself is exercising your consciousness. It's like doing push-ups, running, or jogging. By thinking about it, you accelerate this energy. Your consciousness is like a car going from 0 mph, to 5, 10, 50, 100, to the point where you move so fast you becomes energy - pure light.

The more you ponder these things, the more you go out into nature to look at the trees, the ground, and see the faces of all of your friends, you realize how menial, how predictable, life is. You turn to the sky and look at the universe and breathe in, and you feel the pulse of the country, the world, the galaxy, the universe, and you think how microscopic you are, but how truly connected you are. It awakens something in you.

The tonal of the Earth is a constant tide. It slowly washes away what you attempt to build. Like a sandcastle.

By ignoring these things and letting them go into a slumber, which is the low tonal of the earth that evades your mind, they slip away. The earth tonal, the Doe, is like the tide; as you built a sand castle and it starts to become something beautiful, the tide sweeps in before you complete it and slowly washes the castle away until there's no trace of it whatsoever. The Earth says you're an organic being; your purpose is to serve it, mate, and raise more of your species - to create more cells to serve the earth. It just washes you down until you become a smooth surface that never existed. So you must fight to think of these things.

Drugs make you forget the fact that you are a dimensional energy, a universal consciousness. They convince you that you are part of the organic earth, just an organic response for the planet, similar to the cells in your body. Likewise, people are organic; they are just cells doing their job like the cells in your body. They work, eat, sleep, reproduce, work, eat, sleep, and reproduce. Repeat – repeat– repeat!

You must raise your consciousness and think of the universe, think of your vibration, think of your energy, so that you can awaken and become something more than what you are now in order to experience things that are incredible, vast, and miraculous. It's just an incredible journey.

So you must be aware of the energy in your body; it's the first and simplest thing you can do. You must exercise these teachings, you must reflect on what I've taught you numerous times in previous books. You must create a perpetual motion of thought in your mind that will affect you in everyday life. You must be a human being. So you're going to have to work, you're going to sleep, use the bathroom, have sex, and do all these things. Hopefully, everything that I've taught you about raising your consciousness will be enough to sustain you when you mingle in life. If I don't stress this enough, it will simply be washed away like that sand castle until there's nothing left.

That happens to a lot of people, I see it happen often. People come to me to learn and then they leave, excited, and they think about everything I taught them. Then life hits them like one big wave and they forget everything they learned. It becomes washed away and they forget about this quest, this journey that they're on.

The Fourth Way students believe that conscious knowledge is limited, like the supply of fuel. There is only so much of it around and only the chosen people of a certain intellect will get it. They get it because they work on their consciousness, they work on their mind, and this energy is attracted to them. They are like a beacon, summoning this knowledge. All of a sudden, everything starts making sense in their mind and they become aware.

Others who are working harder at it start to drain your pool of information. You start to forget what you know, and it fuels somebody else because they're working harder at it than you. So it's like a Law of Attraction, whichever of them is the strongest, succeeds. There's some truth to this. So, you must exercise your mind, exercise these teachings, share them with other people, and express them.

Studying what you have learned is like moving an entire river of logs. Contemplation is what moves these thoughts instead of allowing them to congregate and create a dam. Your mind is flowing when you talk about it. You make new discoveries and have new realizations. Your tonal rises; It's adding to your inspiration, it's adding to the meaning of your existence; it's completing you.

If you don't talk about it, if you don't think about it, if you don't inspire yourself by reading something, by watching something, by doing anything to inspire yourself, then you're depleting yourself. It comes full circle; the act of teaching propels this knowledge back to me.

The first exercise is one that we do often, but not often enough and I stress that point. You know it but you don't use it, and if you don't use something you lose it, so that's the first problem. If you're not using it, you're losing it and that's why you lose your consciousness, your understanding, your desire, your purpose of moving.

Keep in mind that you have to reflect on the feminine energy within your body; you must look at the feeling and the emotion inside of you. It takes time and it takes practice to do this. If you can feel the muscles in your body, then you can move electrons in your body.

It's just that you've never thought about moving the electrons in your body. You have never thought about the energy that makes your muscle expand and retract. And you have never thought about that energy doing other things. Well, light is energy. It's the same kind of energy in your body, moving and manipulating electrons.

Energy is energy, it's just a matter of how much or how little is being manipulated. When you consider the energy in Karate, Tae Kwan Do, and other forms of martial arts, you're not pushing somebody through magic; you're vaulting them with your electricity. It's like sticking your finger in a socket. All the muscles tighten up and that's why the person seems to fly through the air, you just shocked them. You can generate this energy and get it to do what you want it to do, even to exist after your physical body dies. Your thoughts – your mind is electrons. Your body is energy. You are really not flesh at all; you are electricity moving in different degrees on its own.

Keep something in mind; you may have a physical body but the energy that's within it stays by choice. Energy can move through matter. In other words, the energy in your mind stays there and works with your brain because it chooses to. It can pass right through your brain as it exists within you, so it doesn't need a physical body. It can depart from the physical body and exist as if it's inside of you. It can use you like an ATV: to touch, smell, and experience. Everything is converted into electricity in your brain. It's like the radio and TV signals that are moving through us right now, but we're unaware of them. We need the TV in order to translate and capture them for us so we can see and understand.

Energy is not capable of experiencing this earth: the chairs, the flowers, the sun, or anything sensual. It needs the body to capture the sound in your ears, the taste on your tongue, and the smell through your nose to convert it all into electricity through your nerves. You don't need the body; you only need it to experience this dimension. When you learn to control this energy, you will become more aware of it. It has the capability of doing things you've never imagined, but if you don't exercise it, if you don't move it, you will lose it.

One of the easiest exercises to learn is to place one hand down on by your side and place the other hand straight out. It is just the fingertips that you are paying attention to. Most of the nervous system travels up the spine to the brain. Through the center of the body, parallel to the spine, there are a lot of nerves. These are your chakra points. The breath is used because it synchronizes you. If you breathe fast, you think fast. When you slow your breathing down, your mind slows down. So breathing is connected to your thoughts.

Take your fingers and point them down where your chi center is, just below the navel, and move your hand up to the top of your head like you're scooping an elongated hand of energy into your lower intestines. When you move your hand up, concentrate on the feeling and you will detect a subtle tingling, like the sensation of energy moving upward. Just imagine scooping it up and slowly moving it up with a slow *whoosh*, and then bring it from the top of your head back down again.

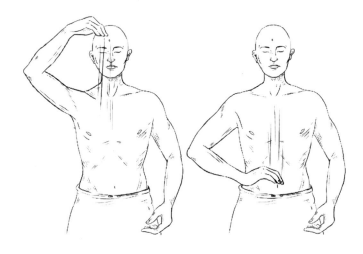

Move your hand up, concentrate on the feeling of energy moving up. Push it back down, feeling the flow of energy that follows.

Visualize it in the interior of your body. Your hand is just a representation of where the energy is moving. Now a slow *whoosh* back down again. If you feel nothing, put your hand there and just imagine it. You really have to focus on the inside of your stomach, and this takes practice. Nothing is done instantaneously; it's through practice that you realize that you feel something.

If you feel a tingle, ask yourself what inspired that tingle? What is a tingle? A tingle is electricity that is going through your nerves to tell you it's there. You caused it to happen. It didn't happen by hitting something, or because you got hurt, or because you ate something bad, but because you just mentally said I want to feel something. You just felt, for the first time in your life, the interior of your body. You have to think about that, that's pretty amazing!

So let's do it again. Sometimes it takes up to five tries before you feel something. You want to focus on the inside of your body and use your hands as a form of lever, almost like a light bulb getting brighter, and brighter; you're going to pull this energy up. Take a deep breath in, and then out with a slow *whoosh*.

Now, cup your hands and place them on your lap. I want you to notice how you feel. You should be experiencing a relaxed, comfortable, peaceful feeling. Now, just allow yourself to stare straight out and notice what that feels like. It's comfortable right now and I want you to just open your hands and rest them on your lap. Ask yourself if you feel different now. It feels almost as if its cooler, like energy is just flowing out of you now. Bring your hands back together and lay them back in your lap. You'll begin to feel this energy start to rebuild again into your inner area.

These are very subtle feelings. You may not even feel them right away or wonder whether or not you are feeling something. But the point is, if you feel something or you work at feeling something, it is part of training your energy. The little steps become huge steps once you become aware of them. If you notice a difference, then what is that difference? If you can feel that little bit of energy what else can that energy do? It can do amazing things. You just need to teach it.

Your hand is the most sensitive body part because it has the most nerves. What I want you to do is take one hand and feel your other hand. Pay attention to how it feels when you touch it. It will probably confuse your body a little bit. Think about this; your hands are made with a frame, like a car; it has an inner structure. If you remove the inner structure your hand would be like Silly Putty.

Feel your hand and explore this now. It's got all sorts of flesh which are muscles, cells all bunched together. Little tiny circles actually, with nuclei of energy, billions of them. And then you have nerves moving through each finger to tell you what you're feeling. Every time you touch something, it's like a spark, an explosion, a microscopic explosion for every single millimeter that you touch. And those explosions move through your arm all the way up to your brain to tell you exactly what you're feeling. There are blood cells that are being pumped through your hand. They're like laborers or workers; if you damage your hand, those "workers" start to rebuild, repair, and replace everything with the design it was before it became damaged. It is, in itself, an entire living cosmos right in your hand.

Now, leave your hand straight out for a moment. It almost tingles, doesn't it? That's because there's billions of electronic signals firing. If you could see energy it would look like your hand was a glowing flame. Now, what I want you to do is imagine the sensation getting stronger and brighter in your hand. Do you feel something? Like a warmth in your hand, almost like a fuzziness? Where is that sensation coming from? Nothing's touching it now. You did stimulate it but you could switch hands and you could do the same thing with the other one. That's energy, and that energy can move through things, it's you. *Your mind is in the palm of your hand right now.* Your consciousness doesn't reside just in your brain, it simply communicates there. Your mind is all over your body.

If you reach out with intention and you touch something, you can will your mind into something else. If you touch another person and you connect with them, you become one being. You use your brain to feel what that other person is feeling. There are no limits. It's only limited by your perceptions. You limit yourself by what you believe to be true.

Put your hand back down; take a deep breath in through your nose and exhale through your mouth. Now, take your thumb and touch each fingertip for a second, almost like you're playing musical chords. Feel the feeling. Each time you touch, electrons move through your fingertips to your brain.

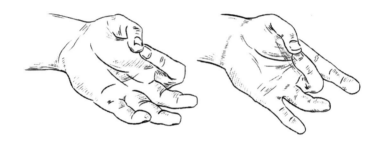

Each time you touch, electrons move
through your fingertips to your brain.

This is called a *mudra* and is a form of meditation. It helps your mind to be quiet. The more you focus your mind on energy, the more you become aware of it. The more you become aware of it, the more you can do with it. Wax on, wax off.

Now, stop on your pinky finger, place it out and have a little attitude. Imagine you're a spiritual master and you're doing your thing. Take a deep breath through your nose as you think about that spot. Did you feel any tingles through your body, did you feel anything? Switch it to your next finger - with attitude. Think about being superior; think about the energy in your body. Just like you were going to will forth a giant storm to take out a giant forest fire in nature, you have the ability. Now imagine as if you're just willing it forth. Take a deep breath in, then out.

When you truly believe, when you truly touch your finger and shift your consciousness, it will happen. You can control wind. You can control health. You can control rain. You can control animals. You can do all sorts of things, but you must remove every ounce of doubt, every ounce of negative thought. Don't *will* it to happen but *allow* it to happen. Allow your mind to work, allow it to flow. You can't will something to happen. If you look at a tree and you say to the tree, "I want the flower to fall off," or you want the leaves to fall off of one particular branch and you will it to happen, it's not going to happen. You have to allow it to happen. You have to caress it with your energy and simply intend it.

Intention. You know that you want the flower to fall so why visualize it falling at all? Why want it to fall, simply *allow* it to fall as if you *expect* it to happen. As if you *know* it's going to fall. It's no different than knowing if you hit a light switch; it's going to come on. *When you can truly allow something to happen, you can change this dimension.* You can make something happen. But if you want it to happen or you try too hard to make it happen, it won't happen.

When your consciousness is shifted, you allow things to be shown to you, you allow yourself to fold time, you allow yourself to fold dimension, and you allow yourself to experience all these things. But if you force your will on it, you will get nowhere.

Touching your body or even just thinking about it makes you aware of it. Nobody thinks about their body. The only time you think about your body is during sex. But for the most part, you don't think about the contour of your body. You don't *feel* it; you don't become aware of what it *feels* like. This is the most astonishing thing to me.

Feel your cheeks with your fingertips, the flesh hanging on a skeletal structure that supports it. It would completely collapse and fall off if you didn't have a strong structure of cells. If you removed your bottom jaw, there'd be a big hole there. That is your esophagus. This contraption that we call a body is really nothing like what you really are; it's simply a structure that is containing you. If you can reflect on that and realize that, then it frees up your energy because your energy recognizes, "Oh, I'm not *this*? I don't have to be limited by the design and structure of *this*? I can expand out of it?"

When you realize that, you become more aware, more spiritual, and you allow yourself to expand. You allow yourself to feel the universe. You allow yourself to *feel*. If you sit on a mountain peak or go into nature, don't think about nature; allow nature to happen to you. Allow whatever is inside of you to unfold and envelope you; trust it. It's only because you don't trust yourself that your energy won't move outside you. Humans are naturally afraid of everything they don't understand.

When you think about energy, when you think about touching your fingers, whenever you think inward, you become silent. You become relaxed. You start to feel what it *feels like* to be a physical body experiencing this dimension. You will become what you think about. That's the secret. *You have to let the universe work with you, the energy, not your body in this physical dimension.* You have to let the universe shape you.

The only way the universe is going to shape you is if you're receptive to it, if you're trying to listen to it, if you're trying to experience it. If you're trying to unfold yourself to the universe so that you are pliable and formable, it will make something of you. But you must keep your mind clear. The more your mind is clouded, the worse it becomes, because the universe can't shape it.

If you know how certain things in the universe worked, would they stop working?

That's partially true, but there is more. Everything is interconnected. There are some things you can understand now and other things that make more sense later when you can add to them. The universe is still being created. It's not been created, it's in crea*tion*. There are fringes of the universe that are only starting to unfold. There are certain things that exist right now and there's no reason why they should exist. They exist because they are the imagination of God. They are holograms, this is all a hologram. But it's hologram where all of us are real.

There was once a TV show called *The Outer Limits* and they depicted something very interesting. In this series, the world kind of blew up, and there was this one guy who had a computer that created a giant hologram that he could exist within.

In this hologram, he could touch, smell, and feel everything, but it wasn't real. He was real, but the rest of it wasn't. For instance, he couldn't drink the water; he could touch and feel it, but if he drank it there would be nothing there. So, the computer had different characters that looked as real as you and me, and in the process of it all, the computer fell in love with him.

So he said, "You can't fall in love with me, you're not real." And she said, "Well, what is real?" And he turned around and swung; he passed through her and said, "See, see, you're not real." And she turned around and swung; she passed through him and said, "Well you're not real to me!"

They're all holograms but they all correspond to each other. So what's real; him, or the hologram? They recently made a movie about this same theme.

They believe they're real. They recognize themselves, and by recognizing themselves they think, "I think therefore I am." He's saying they're not real, he's real. They're saying, "All of this is real to us. I can drink. I can taste. I can smell. I can dance. I can party. I sweat. I feel the sweat. But I'm just a hologram for you to program. But to feel all these things, whether I'm programmed or not, they are real to me."

So the point is, the way reality works is like a hologram. It can change if your mind wills it enough to change, if you understand how it works, or it begins to make sense to you and starts to work a certain way. In some ways it would cease to work because it wouldn't work with everything else.

If one shoe is made a certain way and you compare it to a similar shoe, it does not make sense to you why one shoe can do something and the other one can't. The differences are so minute. There shouldn't be any reason why one can float thru the air and a similar one can't. Therefore, the hologram resets to whatever the strongest program is and the floating of the shoe ceases to exist. You won't even remember it existed because it's evaporated from your consciousness.

So in some ways, some things cease to exist by recognition of them and it limits the mind. But the universe is still in creation, nothing is permanent and nothing ever will become permanent. It will evaporate someday in some age far into the future beyond what you can conceive. All of this will cease to exist someday.

I was wondering about being at different levels of consciousness, of awareness, and letting myself "unfold". When I'm out in nature and I begin to feel it, does it go beyond just intensifying or being enveloped by the feeling?

Oh yes, the levels beyond are limitless. It all depends on which perspective your consciousness takes. I can go there sometimes and I'll just zone out and go to whatever level I end up on, which someday you'll be able to do, hopefully. But all of a sudden, I'll hear the sounds of the forest all start to hum together and it gets really loud, and I will just snap out of it.

There are other times when I can let myself go and everything takes on an illumination; it's almost as if everything has a neon glow to it. Not that you can see where the light's coming from, but it's a glow; a fiery energy glow that everything seems to have. The more I go into it, the more intense it becomes until solid objects disappear and everything becomes like a giant neon forest where I can see the energy lines, like the electrons moving through it. I start to see pulses in trees and billions of sparkling lights moving through living things.

It all depends on which level you can let your mind go or what your mind is ready to accept. This is why I tell you to *allow* it to happen to you, or allow yourself to think about it from a spiritual perspective.

The more spiritual things you think about, the more spiritual you become, the more these things happen to you. Some students have been at these peaks and then they have a decline, which everybody goes through because you're constantly being bombarded by life. Then there are times you work really hard at being spiritual. If you ask these students about the things they experience, they would tell you that many spiritual things happen at the high point, but nothing happens at the lows. When they focus on their spirituality again and start to move up, then the things start to happen more.

They tell me what they've experienced and then they say, "I don't experience it anymore." That is because, at this particular time in their self-growth, their life is so challenging that they have strayed from their course. You can be very spiritual and maintain a personal relationship with someone without losing all your energy, but then one day when you're making significant progress, something bad happens. Now you have to deal with that. All of a sudden, you are snapped back down to a lower tone and you're having a hard time getting back up there. You're literally stuck here. You want to get out of that because you know what exists up there, but you feel like it's now out of reach. It's just too much work.

And then you have an issue at work. Perhaps you just got fired or you have a big time-consuming project assigned to you. That can snap you out of the higher dimension and bring you down into a lower tonal, and that's where you'll reside until you climb back up again. Those higher regions also get more and more intense. Eventually you get to a point where it no longer matters if you get pulled back down; you just rebound because this becomes your true existence.

Your tonal is set by how far you move through the dimensions of energy, which become your vibration. The more you talk about it, the more you reflect on it, the more you learn. It's like a tuning fork; you resonate at a higher pitch and as you move through the higher pitches, the higher you'll go until you get to the point where you start to experience more.

These things I'm talking about really do exist. You could take shortcuts to try to get up there. You can do certain things, but either way, it's really about getting the frequency of your consciousness to move with momentum to reach that plateau.

It's also very easy, when you do reach a high level to fall back. The simple fact that you *did* reach that level is what makes you lose your path and you go back down again because you're so in awe of making It that you stop doing what you did to get you there and you lose that vibration.

You have to reflect on how you feel. Most people don't pay attention to how they feel when they're moving up. They simply look at all the reactions, the stimulation of how things look or how they see or sense things differently. They don't really reflect on what it feels like to be there. You must train yourself to be at that vibration. You might get more interested in all the quirks and all the amazing things you're seeing, experiencing, and doing, that you rebound because you didn't spend enough time familiarizing yourself with what it *feels like* to be on that level. When you rebound, all you want to do is get back to that level, but you won't remember it enough to get back there.

In either case, you are exercising your spirituality by living and being in a spiritual state and it will propel you. Don't worry about life. Life will make you interact with it. Don't worry about getting lost in your spirituality because life will force you to work, pay bills, and exist in this reality. You don't have a choice in that matter. So you have to live as spiritually as you can because it will propel and hold you in these higher levels. Hopefully you'll keep working your way up until you either make it or you collapse back down again. Then you'll just have to climb back up the ladder, and it's a long ladder but it's one that you always desire.

In a similar way, visualize the energy in your hand, don't just stare at your hand; *feel* it. Feel what it feels like. That's something you don't do normally. You don't think about what it is to feel your hand, to feel the energy, to become aware of that energy. Right now, can you feel the heat on your face if you think about it? Think about the unusual things. That's all related to energy. You're making your brain think differently. The more your brain thinks differently, the more skilled it becomes.

I always say to my students "wax on, wax off". This saying comes from the movie *The Karate Kid*. In the movie, the teacher tells his student to wax all his cars a certain way, but the student wants to know what that'll do for him. When the teacher goes to swing at him, he blocks it instinctively. The point is that you've got to fool your brain to do things for you because you've been told your whole life you can't do these things.

You are a product of society. You're mental thinking is limited by what you believe you can do, and it's very firm; it's very rooted. It has been rooted since childhood. I'm not saying to, "Pull the roots out," like they do in Hinduism, and be a Yogi for 30 years before you can do anything. What I'm saying is, "Fool your brain." The mind is very, *very* capable of doing amazing things. All you have to do is learn to use your brain in different ways. If you can learn to think in different ways, it'll get used to it and be able to do all these things as if it were always capable of doing them.

For many years, people believed that anyone who suffers from brain damage would never again remember certain memories, walk, or do certain things because the damaged parts of their brain is like the worn out (chemical) gears of a motor. Now, *what I'm saying is very, very important* because it stresses the point that you are more like a machine than you are spirit because spirit is energy; *it shouldn't matter which area of your brain is damaged.* That energy does need tools and your brain is one of those tools.

The important thing here is the memories. If the memories are stored somewhere in your brain, it means that you are mainly biochemical - a machine. However, tests have shown that it's the machine that helps you to bring forth the memories that are damaged. The memories are still there, no matter what part of the brain is damaged, which means thought is *energy floating.*

You are an energy being; a consciousness that does not need a body. With certain therapy, different parts of the brain can be used to take on memories. Once that mechanism is rebuilt into the brain, the memories can be restored. So you never lost them. It's only the steering column of the car that you've lost, or a tire. But you, the driver, have not been damaged. *It's the vehicle that you are using* that is not conveying the message, and by putting a new tire on the vehicle, it will function just fine. That's simply amazing!

So that means you are your memories, your thoughts, and your recollections. How you rationalize with your thinking process is by comparing experiences. So if you are hit in the head and you lost a part of your brain that holds all the memories, it was previously assumed that your memories would be gone. Now it's well-known that there's really not just one place to store them; somehow, the information is stored everywhere.

So the more you think about these things, the more you think about your energy, the more you think of your awareness, the more you will become. If you don't think about it and reflect on it, you will not move the log jam in your brain. You will become a biochemical responding machine. Most human beings are like robots. Somebody hits your car, you get out, and you think about how you want to deal with it. It's almost as if your brain processes which way it wants to deal with the situation.

When you get into an argument, there's a part of you that doesn't feel angry but there's also a part of you that says you should feel angry. You decide how and what you want to portray to the person you're dealing with. Which part of these are really you? If you are sitting there witnessing the moment, is that really who you are? Or is it simply you acting out what you are supposed to do? Are you no different than the robot hitting a wall and backing up because that's the response it's supposed to give when it hits something?

So, biochemically, every time somebody argues with you, you decide how you want to deal with it. That's not true consciousness. True consciousness is simply reacting. You're making decisions based on what you have been programmed to do. *You're using*

your brain to think rather than your mind, your soul.
That's the secret. You must remember this. You'll really
have to work so you don't forget what I just said
because it's unknowable knowledge.

So how do your emotions tie into that?

Emotions are only ten percent yours while the other
ninety percent is a chemical release in your brain and
your body has to act it out. By acting it out, your body
releases the opposed chemicals to neutralize the
original chemical, thus, calming you, or making you
more excited, or whatever your response is. Different
chemicals respond based upon how you believe you're
supposed to react. For instance, if you're supposed to
react to anger, your brain will start flooding your body
with chemicals that make you more frustrated or
physically stronger so you can fight. But you are aware
of this; you can actually feel yourself deciding what
you're going to do.

You're on autopilot ninety percent of the time. Almost every decision you make is actually made by your
brain. You're not supposed to realize that you're
thinking about your reaction. If you catch yourself
thinking about it for a second, you begin to wonder
who's actually making the decision. It happens so
quickly you don't even realize it, you simply react, but
there was a moment when you made choices very
quickly. The sheer fact that you made choices point out
that this is not really you. These are chemical decisions
because chemicals are a slower release than pure
energy, which is the soul.

So, if thoughts are largely biochemical, do emotions really exist? Does love really exist?

Yes, absolutely. Ten percent is real, but you have to let that ten percent rule instead of the other ninety percent- the chemicals. Emotion is really a fast process of thought. If you can reflect on what you're thinking and feeling then remove all of the biochemical responses and your true feelings will come through. That's your higher consciousness.

If you are able to remove all the chemical responses and just mellow out to a more abstract feeling and will your mind to do what you want, you heighten your psychic abilities. It's like using pure sensory to sense things psychically; you allow things to happen. It's the complication of all these chemicals that keeps your mind from unfolding to higher levels.

Whenever I do something psychically, I clear all the biochemical responses in my brain until there's nothing left but a feeling of pure existence. That's what the spiritual part of me is; it's what the spiritual part of everyone is. But it becomes congested with biochemical responses in your brain and images of how you're supposed to act, which are now highly reinforced by television, so that is the product you become. You are a machine.

The trick is to remove the thought processes of the machine so you're left only with the true self, which is similar to what the Fourth Way teaches. It is also taught in Buddhism and in Hinduism. If you can remove all of these unnecessary things, you will be left with your true self, so that's what you have to think about.

Most of your thoughts and reactions are biochemical; they're really not you. By removing these things first, you will discover who you are, your spirituality, and your higher states of consciousness. Everything else will make itself known to you; do not try to understand things, rather *allow* them to be understood and it will come to you.

Another problem is all the other biological machines – all the other biochemical thinking people. Their drama is what keeps them grounded. It's what keeps them - and you - in the doe. This is part of the system of the earth. In the same way that your red cells are kept as laborers and not allowed to become anything more for your body; the other cells keep the other similar cells intact.

I've tried to teach this repetitively in many different ways. Think about what I just said about keeping yourself in a higher state and how other people's drama brings you right back down to the drama of the world so you are not able to evolve. Let go of your old friends. Let go of the people who are in this lower tonal because they will keep you there also or they will bring you down to their level when you desire to rise up higher. Sometimes we have to let go of friends and we have to let go of family, to a certain point, so that we can evolve.

Let's look at it from a different point of view, let's climb up on the other hill and look at the same valley from a different angle. By biochemically bringing you into my drama, I'm really trying to get you to respond on the same biochemical level as me; this is part of social functionality. People try to keep each other functioning on the same level as they are. And this is what everybody else does to you, as you are supposed to do to them. It is self-stimulation. It is security. It is a feeling that you're doing the right thing. This is how the planet assures that you're not going to wander off too far because everybody else keeps you at a lower tonal. It's about attacking you so that you're forced to release these chemicals and choose a reaction.

This is human functioning. We're supposed to watch this and be observers and not become part of it, but to watch it is to say "I see it for what it really is." Now that I'm on the outside I can observe it and make a note in my mind that this is not what I want to become a part of.

It's all frequencies. It's all channels. There are a billion channels of what *not* to be and there are ten channels of what *to* be. The only way you'll know what to be is by pinpointing each channel and locking them all up until you're left with the result that feels right to you. If you go into reverse it doesn't work so easily, it takes three times longer.

The problem then is battling the tonal of all the other people. You've got other people with their typical lives trying to make you see the world from their point of view. They're trying to bring you down, like they did to Christ and other spiritual masters. If you don't get it, which most of us never will, they stone you. So one way or another, they'll get your attention to come down to their level.

What they don't understand is truth. They can't see what we're talking about, because their minds can't perceive that level. So, when I tell you to keep one foot in this reality and one foot out, I also mean dealing and interacting with the red cell world without letting them know that you are.

Yes, you can go to a higher level. Yes, you can convey this knowledge. By conveying this knowledge, you're raising your tonal because you're forced to think about it. You have now flipped a switch in your brain that doesn't go along with any of the other biochemical functions that society has taught you. Think about that.

It's against your whole programming because it's making you question who or what you really are. It now has put you into a flux in which your brain will either realize it, or retaliate and say, "I don't buy any of this," and its going to shut you down. Or it'll say "Hey lets go home and just get high," because it doesn't want you to go to this level. This is the level of spiritual beings. People often think that level of spiritual beings is serene and it's not; it just starts that way.

Think of the opening scene in the movie *Contact*. You start off in the noise and confusion, which is life. As you peel away all this jibber jabber in your mind, all the biochemical thoughts and emotions of who you think you are, it's like you're traveling through all the noise. The further away you get the less and less noise you hear until you eventually reach a point of silence. That point of silence is a placid, peaceful state of mind. But what you don't realize is, you're really traveling; you're moving without moving. You just think it's this peaceful quiet mind but you're moving through dimensions.

This is why I can see the dimensions illuminate in front of me; I'm becoming aware of them. They just appear to me when they *were* invisible before; like a shadow world rising, but much more complex. As I'm going through the peacefulness, instead of all the gibberish, there's a different kind of noise. It's not words; it's not biochemical's, its pure energy con-sciousness; which is true awareness. It's like thought, but a billion times sharper than what it should be.

So that peaceful, placid state is a temporary state that indicates you're going in the right direction. It just means that now you've hit cruising speed and now you're going to move through these dimensions. When you've gone though enough of these lower frequency dimensions, you start to get to the higher dimensions of energy and light; then you reside from there. You operate in this dimension but you really exist there. You are physically here, but you're in a million places all at the same time.

So the peacefulness is just a temporary state. It's peaceful because you feel whole. Peacefulness means you feel more whole than you ever have before in your life.

Is that the true self?

It's the rinsing. It's the washing. Then, as you approach the light, you become who you are because it's an energy state of consciousness; you become part of that. That's what's represented in some movies, but they can't take it any further so they bring you back into this world, this moment. I could interpret that as being a part of the truth because, if you're an old soul, you've gone through this journey and you've chosen to come into this life to live as a mortal; to feel, to taste, to touch, to do all these things. The problem is, you've gotten so caught up in it that you've forgotten who you are.

I want you to think about whom you are now, all the noise and confusion – all of it. Then, think about moving through space, which is almost dimensional if you want to look at it that way. You move away and then you hit a light and the light is who you truly are. You see the world and you realize for this moment that your life right now isn't truly who you are. You came into this world and lost all your memories because you wanted to see how you would react without them. Just for a minute, you've realized that you're really not who you think you are; you're really a super being.

You move, you hit the placidity, you see this bright light, and you realize *who* you are. You've awoken out of a coma. Then you look into your eye; now you're looking out of it. You see your body, your face, and then you're looking out of it. You realize, in your instant of realization, you're not who you think you are. I am not Eric Pepin. You are not "you." You realize you're this other being, but you forgot who you were.

If you don't move on when you die, is it because you didn't remember who you were? You didn't awaken in this life?

If the remembering doesn't quite happen, then it ends. All your other lives don't matter; it doesn't matter whether reincarnation exists. What matters right now is right now. Right now you're in this world; you're part of this world.

Visualize the planet, think about it, and hear all the music and noise, which is really the biochemicals in your brain reacting to life, to work, to everything. Now, imagine you're moving away from the planet and realizing there's more to everything. As you realize, you start to awaken. You hit the calm of the universe until everything becomes light, and you awaken. The light is in your head; you really aren't who you are.

That's what you're trying to achieve. You're trying to let go of everything here. All the stuff that keeps your mind here, everything that says you are a biochemical machine and you will function with the rest of the machine. The rest of the machine will make you think on this level and be a part of this level. You'll react as a machine and, before you know it, you're going to forget about everything that we've discussed, everything you've just learned, and you are just going to become part of the machine.

Creation. From nothing comes the expansion; multi worlds, multi levels, universes, cooling, forming, solidifying, clearing. It becomes just an entire dark universe with brilliant gleams of shining stars and universes within its depths and surroundings. It forms universes and in seconds you are seeing billions, and billions, and billions of light years happening instantly in super-fast motion in front of you.

Stars are exploding in supernovas at this very minute, taking out entire universes around them. Recooling, re-solidifying, and growing into new universes; each bubble is an entire galaxy in itself. The universe is expanding, growing, and getting bigger and bigger, foaming and frothing at the edges.

This is all part of 'God's' imagination. Its thoughts directly influence reality, just like ours do. We are the consciousness of God. We are the inspiration of new thought. Somewhere in your brain, in a tiny little molecular spot, is a new inspiration of thought. These thoughts from different people collectively work together and get bigger and bigger until they become a global consciousness.

Not only that, but you reflect it out to the rest of the universe and the rest of the universe takes it on; it then unfolds and becomes bigger and bigger. If I touch something, I can feel millions of electrons. We are just one tiny electron moving through consciousness, just on a more complex level. For example, think of Helen Keller; how she created an entire universe in her mind, a reality.

Is that reality actually a place where another consciousness can go?

It's not another consciousness; it's just another process of realization; another point of view. Is something really black, or is it tan to everybody else, or is it a shade darker or a shade lighter? There are a million different perceptions. So is that a million different views? God perceives through all of us. We are the micro consciousness of God, or at least the earth, and the earth to the universe. We are the *experiencers* for God. We *are* the imagination. We are the frontier of consciousness.

Now keep in mind, I don't think God is a thinking entity. I think it's more of a very complex organism. But in either case, we are part of that electrical imagination. And we are free thinking just as much as the cells in your body think within you, but they are still part of you.

Are the cells in the body you, or are they all individual and separate from you? But they all think. But who do they serve? They serve you; they are you. You exist everywhere but yet, you don't exist anywhere. They all may imagine, they all think. What they experience or what they do affects you, doesn't it? Doesn't it become part of your reality, or make you think? It inspires new thought, it's a database. We're all part of a giant database. We can draw in information, and we collectively give information, we're all in this together.

We call it 'collective consciousness', but for a computer it's like a database. You can have a listing of names in one program while another program has pictures, and another program has license plates. You say "Mary Sue" and get a picture from one database and her driver's license from another, even though they're separate functions. So we're all separate but we're all collectively working together.

There's a million ways of explaining the same thing and I'm always trying to find different ways of explaining it because you never quite know when somebody understands what you're trying to say to them. So you have to present it from a million different angles.

Like I said, we are on one side of a valley; let's go up to the other side. We'll be looking at the same valley, but we can see better from that angle. Most people will not reflect on any of this because it'll be gone by tomorrow morning. It'll evaporate just like Gurdjieff believed that knowledge is limited. You won't really have the photograph, you'll have the negatives.

Think about these things, think about your consciousness, think about your feelings, and think about energy. And *reflect*. Nobody ever reflects on these things. Thinking about them is one thing. If you reflect on what you know, if you reflect on your classes, you reflect on what you're feeling, you're going inward.

Chapter 3

ENERGY BEINGS

In this chapter, I will cover ghosts, spirits, entities, and other dimensional beings. Many people have asked me, "What is the relevance of entities such as ghosts and spirits to someone who is spiritual, meditates, or seeks to find higher consciousness?" Although entities fall into the paranormal category, they also deal with life after death; who or what you will be when you leave your body.

One of the most difficult things for a person to do is to let go of the ego or 'self' in order to have the best meditation possible. Once you have gone through a variety of different experiences, there is always something else needed to trigger the greatest release which enables your access of the highest levels - to experience God fully and to reach true, full enlightenment.

That brings us back to the topic of life and death. The fact is, you are afraid to die. You are afraid to let go of your physical body. Somewhere in the deeper subconscious of the mind, no matter how much you want to tell yourself you are capable of doing it, you just can't let go.

Your fear could be caused by several different things. If your probe leaves your body, your fear might be that you'll never get back; it is what you may be thinking subconsciously. So you can experience a large variety of experiences, but in the deeper psyche of your mind there's that fear of death. That's the most prevailing belief that all human beings have, no matter what culture you're from.

When I write about spirits, entities, and ghosts, you gain knowledge. Through learning comes understanding. Through understanding comes liberation. If you have a greater understanding of hauntings and why spirits, entities, and ghosts do what they do, will not be so afraid anymore. By having a greater understanding of these things, you will remove your fear. By removing fear, you remove the vices in the deeper parts of your subconscious that keep you from having greater experiences. You have less fear of death because you understand death now, and you look at it differently.

When you think of the word *death*, you think of *life and death*. "That's the end." When the subject is *ghost or spirits*, immediately you accept a different paradigm where there are living beings without physical bodies. You don't equate the fact that there's a bridge between the two. You fear death because you fear there is nothing after life, but you do believe in ghosts, so there has to be something afterwards. You should not be afraid of the unknown. You just need to understand what it is.

Let's start off by talking about ghosts. Are ghosts real? When I was very young, probably eight or nine years old, my father's family was having a séance. They were doing *automatic writing*. It's like using a Ouija board, but instead you use a pen and paper. You put the alphabet and numbers on the paper and you draw a cross on there. Then you ask, "Are there any spirits here?"

I remember that I was not allowed to be part of it, yet my father was very open-minded, so he let me sit in the background to observe. I recall them saying out loud, "If there are any spirits here, make yourself known." It was a spooky, candlelit vibe. It must have been dusk because I remember having the light on. I recall looking across the room and seeing this purple or blue illumination hovering over the stove in the kitchen. It seemed to me that nobody else was very aware of what was going on; they were very focused on the writing.

I remember pointing this out to either my father or my aunt. They all jumped up when they realized that and everybody moved very quickly to a different part of the kitchen. I recall moving by the staircase and being fascinated by this illumination. Either my father or an aunt said something to the effect of, "Give us a sign." And I thought to myself, "Well, how is it seeing my father? How is it seeing the people in this room? It doesn't have eyes. And it doesn't have ears or ear drums to hear. It doesn't have lungs. So it can't say anything."

It always perplexed me how people interpret ghosts as being these table rapping, talking entities who tell people, "Get out of my house," and things like that. Over the years, I've often reflected on that memory. As I became older, studied, and investigated experiences like this one, I've come to realize certain things. What you think of as hauntings aren't really hauntings at all. Most of the time, you are not even aware that an entity is around you, so that opened up a lot of questions for me.

Does an entity have the ability to see or hear you?

An entity cannot see you because it doesn't have eyes or eye cones. It doesn't see light the way you do. It's very different. I'm not saying it doesn't see, but it certainly does not see in the same frequency, the same vibrations; you interpret your physical dimension by the reflection of light on your eyes.

It doesn't have the ability to hear sound or talk the way you do. Imagine how sound changes underwater. It sounds very distorted. An entity is made of energy; it's not physical matter as you are. When you assume that it's hearing you, it's just an assumption on your part. It doesn't have eardrums for the sound to reverberate off, so it can't possibly hear you talking to it, at least not in a format that you can understand.

An entity is not going to say "Boo" or "Hey Bob" because it doesn't have lungs; it doesn't have vocal chords; it doesn't have the ability to project sound in the same manner as a physical being. Now, I'm not saying ghosts cannot communicate. Maybe it can speak. I've had some very interesting experiences. The real question is, if it is doing something like that, is it a ghost?

I believe that a lot of other things are misinterpreted as ghosts. For instance, why couldn't it be an alien from another dimension? Why does it have to be physical? Why does everything have to look and function like us? Just because you can't interpret it, you immediately think it is a ghost, spirit, or something deceased. That's not usually the case. It can also be an intelligent creature or a being that's in our dimension. All of these are beyond your understanding; therefore, you automatically bunch them all into one group -

ghosts, spirits, or entities. There are also multidimensional beings. About seventy percent of the cases are not hauntings at all, nor are they entities, ghosts, spirits, or aliens.

What typically causes a haunting if not a ghost, alien, or dimensional being?

From all of my personal explorations and experiences, I do believe there is a certain amount of truth to the stories told about old houses having spirits or ghosts. But I believe these are actually recorded sounds in the walls. Hauntings generally occur in old houses on the East Coast or in England with the majority occurring in cold, damp environments; however, there is always the odd case.

This recorded sound effect is a very specific grouping. When you look at those old houses, you'll find that the walls are often made of slate. The walls are made with a mortar paste containing a heavy mineral base with crystallizations in it. Chicken wire is used to keep it all together, and then it is rubbed back-and-forth to smooth it out. This is a very crude, but effective type of material.

So when there is pressurization from weather, the house creaks and the boards bend; this is energy. We don't usually think of it in these terms, but it's energy. If we go back in time a bit, people in those older houses didn't have television or radio. They played cards, games, had conversations with each other, and laughed a lot. In the right place, at the right moment, somebody was laughing, or talking, or screaming because someone's tickling them. They're having a good time, maybe having a few drinks, and the sound is somehow recorded in the hallway or in some other part of the house as the walls are arching from the weather: the cold, the damp, the heat, whatever is inducing itself on this environment. The house records those projected sounds. It's a million to one chance, but it does happen.

As time progresses, the weather changes and this pressurizes the house again, releasing energy, and in some crude format, it makes the sound play. It's going to sound very distorted. For example, somebody might say, "Hello Bob. Can you hand me that picture?" It will sound like, "Bob...hand...me...the...picture." It's going to sound very creepy to us, but it's actually distorted. If you can walk in certain angles, you might hear it. But a person standing next you, who might be in a different position, may not hear it at all. This again gives the effect of fear and a heightened sense of, "We don't know what's going on." So fear creates panic.

So, sound is captured in that way in many old homes. In unusual cases, it's captured even in modern homes. In a program I watched years ago, there was a potter's wheel and what looked like a needle for a vinyl record player but different; the needle was a little wider. They were actually using it on an old pot to pick up pieces of a conversation that were recorded in the pottery. They suspected that the potter was having a conversation with someone standing in the doorway, and it was actually recorded onto this pot in broken pieces of sound.

We know sound moves through the air. If you put your hand up, you can feel reverberations from a speaker. If you have the right elements, it can record itself. The majority of hauntings in most houses aren't truly entities; they are recordings that are playing themselves. In most of these cases, people will say they hear things but they don't really see things. So that validates this theory.

I often think of the paranormal investigators who go to old places, like the Queen Mary. There was a person who went on that ship and used tape recordings to document their findings. They put in blank cassette tapes and let them run for two hours or so. The investigator played them back and heard what sounded like conversations. Now, maybe there's a chance of picking it up on radio waves, but I think they are also picking up a frequency emitting the same reverberation. It's faint and there's a million to one chance that the circumstances needed to capture it are present. The majority of the cases follow that one particular format.

Some people will tell you that they saw things just like that. When you hear something spooky and you know that no one else is home, your adrenaline is running, your senses are pumped up, and your imagination's moving a mile a minute. There is a fair chance you could create something out of your own imagination. So I'm not saying this is not a possibility.

It is possible and it probably contributes to some of these stories of hauntings. When you understand this is a very real possibility, it calms you and you can look at it more rationally. If you ever come across a haunting or you purposely seek them out, you will have a better grasp of what's happening in that environment and you'll get more information out of it.

I was wondering if holograms are part of hauntings.

Many hauntings with visual sightings are actually holograms. By watching television and movies, society has progressed enough intellectually now to understand the concept of holograms. To somebody fifty years ago, or even thirty years ago, holograms were not understood, but the times have changed.

We are still discovering new levels of science. If the condition of the weather is right, pressurization, or what pilots call *the ceiling*, lowers or rises. It determines the altitude that airplanes can fly or if they can fly at all. It is the same pressure that amasses on a household's environment. It is one of the key elements to creating an energy in a house. A person can walk through a hallway, go to a bedroom, move around in the bedroom, pick up some clothing, and walk back. And for a few moments, it is actually recorded. It's like the lottery – a million to one shot, but with billions of houses, it happens over time.

There is the possibility of distortion of the quality as it's replayed, or it may be a very good quality. The house pressurization from the weather or electricity in the walls; copper piping, circuitry of various televisions, or almost anything, can contribute to an energy field that triggers the right possibilities to recreate these events. All of a sudden, you see a silhouette, hologram, or what looks like a ghost, walking through a hallway, going into the room, or doing something. Often people will see a ghost move down a hallway, turn left or right, and then just walk through the wall. And the question you ask yourself is, "Well, my God, did I just see a ghost?"

The real question is, "Did the ghost respond to you at all?" In most cases, it does not. It's as if you didn't even exist. They were calm, cool, and collected. They walked down the hallway and hung a right. If you did some research, you'd find that the house had been renovated. If you can find the old blueprints, ten to one you'll find that there was a door where you saw this entity move through the wall.

So it's literally following a recording of what used to be there.You're just not seeing the door anymore. There are a number of other possibilities, but it's not a conscious, thinking entity. It is a hologram or projection of light. Again, there have been situations where one person can see it and somebody two inches away can't see it. Or you see it, turn your head, and it's gone. You look back again and you can see it. It's as if you're catching a spectrum of light that's bending a certain way so you can see it. That's why people say they didn't see anything, but the other person wonders how you missed it. There could be numerous possibilities of what is going on, however, this is a hologram and that is how they function.

In some cases, just by moving objects in the environment of a real haunting or perceived haunting, you collapse the energy field that allows the entities to exist within that environment. That, in itself, resolves a whole haunting problem. There are situations where you can see entities but they are just holograms. If someone was to ask me, "Well, how do you know the difference?" I usually say to them, "If you can see it clearly with clothing, hair, and a face, it is usually a hologram and not a ghost."

A lot of times people will see what appears to be a female spirit looking through a window. From my explorations, every town has a white witch, the lady in white, or something similar. These are actually projections of people's expectation. People project their ideas of what they expect to see; thereby, creating the supposed ghost.

The human brain is a major contributor to hauntings. You have to accept that most hauntings aren't really hauntings, but there is also the possibility of real hauntings. At a distance of one hundred feet, in just the right lighting, if you see a stump of a tree and it has a short branch to the left and a short branch to the right that's been cut off, it looks like a body. The brain will automatically add arms and a head to it. It's constantly trying to create an image for you. The eyes do a lot of the work to create what you're seeing, but the brain will actually add things that are not really there because that is its job.

So, when people go to graveyards and they see things, in this particular case, it's not a hologram and it's not audio. It is really their heightened sensory, their fear, and looking with an intention of seeing something. The intent in a graveyard isn't to find a frisbee or a balloon, it is to look for ghosts.

If you're going to look for ghosts, you're expecting to find something, so your eyes are already searching for some kind of visual sign. So again, you can't really trust those particular scenarios. That doesn't mean you can't find an entity in a graveyard, but you need a clear mind when you're approaching it.

If you want to find the real thing, you must have a level of scrutiny, a level of doubt, or a level of filtering your own thoughts in order to find the gems in the ash. Personally, I think it's fantastic if you see a hologram that looks like a ghost in this particular place, but it's not at all what I'm interested in finding. I want the truth. I want to find the real deal.

How do you know the difference?

When you're deceased, there is really no reason for you to have arms, legs, and a head. You're energy. So why would you keep that physical form at all? I find that most aware entities and consciously awake spirits or ghosts tend to be balls of light. They look like foggy forms of energy moving through a room. There's no need for physical shape, so why would they have one? The entities that maintain a physical shape, that are real hauntings, are not even aware that they're dead.

In the case of a ghost that doesn't know it's dead, what is its purpose for haunting a house and scaring the occupants?

In this case the ghost is stuck in a dream loop, and cannot fully rationalize intelligently. They are in our reality, haunting, but to them it's a dream. They haunt the house because they feel that this is their home. People move in; they move out. New people move in; those people move out. They can't understand why people that they don't know are in *their* home. So, they rationalize that they have to get rid of you or that you shouldn't be there. It's not necessarily because they think you're evil and they have to haunt you.

On your end, you see a ghost coming at you and you're thinking, "This is bad; this is freaking me out. What is this?" But in the ghost's mind, it's trying to figure out why you're in its home. It doesn't remember that it's been haunting that place for about a hundred years. To a ghost, it is only seconds, minutes, or hours. It doesn't have a sense of time. It's in a constant loop.

So, when the entity does have a moment of consciousness it steps out of its dream and sees all these strange people. The entity is trying to communicate with you because it senses something is wrong. It knows that it is stuck, so it is trying to communicate without vocal cords to talk with, so you can't hear it. It tries to touch you, but you can't feel it. For a moment it sees our reality instead of some stasis consciousness.

How does it even see you? If an entity sees you, it tries to contact you because it senses that out of everyone else in the house, you just stopped and felt something move across the room. Or you saw something out of the corner of your eye and you looked back. It notices that you sensed it. So now that it senses you are aware of it, it's excited. It's trying to talk to you but you still can't really hear it. This is why it does strange things.

Sometimes it might muster up enough energy to pinch you, push you, or move an object. In our reality we freak out. We're like, "Oh my! Something evil is in the house; something horrible is going on." Again, there's this instant fear, but the entity is thinking, "How do I get their attention to let them know that I'm here?" So this creates a rift between your reality and their reality. You are trying to talk to them. You are trying to touch them. You are trying to see them with your eyes, but you are using all the wrong tools.

How do psychics and mediums who don't have this understanding communicate with spirits of deceased relatives?

I don't believe these mediums or psychics are actually talking to the spirits of deceased people at all. I'm not saying it's not possible, but not at the level that they claim. It would be like having a multitude of entities just hanging around with nothing better to do than to watch us cross a street, or evaluate people in our lives. As a human you tend to hang onto the people that you lose in your life. You want to keep them with you, so in your mind, in your spirit, in your energy, you hold them here.

When someone dies in your life, the reality is that you have to let them go at some point. It's selfish to want them to just linger behind and be around you. They need to move on to the next level of wherever it is they need to go. The majority of entities are people.

When you die, if you have a certain level of consciousness and a greater understanding of things, you remember all of your lives. You become much wiser, but that doesn't mean you lose your identity. It's like reading a bunch of books and gaining a lot of wisdom all of a sudden. You know that you need to move on and that the people in your life will be fine; you have nothing to fear. If you understand there's life after death, why do you need to linger around? You will figure things out on your own.

If the mediums aren't communicating with real entities then where and how do they obtain so much personal information?

All the information known by mediums and psychics either comes from the collective consciousness or it's telepathically broadcast to the psychic without your conscious awareness.

The collective consciousness of the planet is also called Gaia. Some people call it the Matrix. Call it whatever you want. Gaia is a collective of all the consciousnesses of the planet; that makes one consciousness for the whole planet. On a psychic level, you are capable of plugging into that. Every human being has a specific frequency. When you isolate that frequency, you tune into their life, their information, and what's going on around them.

There's also a level of telepathy. You so desperately want to hear from a certain individual that you project this to the psychic. They telepathically feel this or see this. In many cases, they misinterpret it as being a spirit or entity in the room.

You meet people all the time and there's a natural psychic instinct inside of you. When you don't trust someone that is a survival instinct from primitive times; it is purely psychic and from a different part of your brain. You have senses and feelings about this person, but you ignore them because the person seems to just be telling a story. They win you over in time, so you have certain senses that help you to discern the truth. Sometimes they're right and sometimes they're not.

I'm always amused when I hear of these things because there's a level of accuracy and there's a level of non-accuracy. There is always the occasional, "Well, I didn't know that, so it must be a spirit that told them that. Otherwise, how could the psychic know?" A lot of people forget certain things that they knew before. Or, some of it is telepathically connected while other parts are pulled out of the Gaia consciousness, which has a greater source of information than the person giving you this information.

As you know, I don't believe that everybody has a soul. When many people die, they give their consciousness to the Gaia consciousness – like raindrops into an ocean. For those people who have passed away and have not developed a soul to move on, whatever they knew is given to the Gaia consciousness. So, someone could selectively tune into that person's frequency and acquire the information. The psychic isolates the knowledge that the deceased person has contributed to this higher consciousness.

Similar to a library, they pull that information out and give it to you. Some of these people truly believe they're working through spirits; they don't realize that they're actually pulling the information telepathically.

They've convinced themselves that they're able to communicate with spirits, so they create certain images from their own mind. The brain is powerful enough to create artificial realities to work with you. There are identities that are working in your mind, but it's really you. It's just very complex. It's similar to a popular book that was written in the 1770's called "Sybil," a woman with multiple personality syndrome.

If an entity can't sense things in the same way we can, what's their reality like?

An entity's world is not very easy to describe, although in some ways, not so difficult. As a human being, you perceive the world through your five senses. We've already deduced that an entity is energy. So as energy, what an entity perceives is going to be a little difficult to explain, but it's more energy. It's colors and structures of energy. Think of when Frodo wears the ring in the movie *The Lord of the Rings*: he switches into this other reality where he sees these dead kings in a gray world. The entity sees a silhouette of our world, but it's a totally different world for them.

For instance, trees seem to be more like neon filaments. You can see all of the veins of a plant; they would see a green structure of light. It's absolutely beautiful, but very different. They might see a human being as a faded illumination of very complex light density. They see your energy rather than your organic matter. In some cases, it can be very faded.

The strength of your illumination will be determined by your vibration and how much you're connecting with their reality. Your frequency is like a tune, a vibration that elevates higher. As your vibration gets louder, not audibly, you'll illuminate more in that dimension. That's why you can feel more in that dimension. You can then sense other beings and entities and some of what they feel. You're entering more of their world the same way that they solidified their energy into our dimension.

They're not really designed to be here, but they can exist here to a certain degree. However, it's very difficult to do. That's how they sense and feel us. The number of dimensional beings or entities that come into our world and reside in this frequency is as miniscule as the amount of people that can feel their world. So it's very few or slim to none. It's not every day that you can feel spirits or see entities, but some people have this ability.

How do entities interact with their reality?

A ghost sees energy rather than organic structure. In our dimension there are walls and structures for boundaries.

In their dimension, they don't have a sense of boundaries; they have a sense of integration. We reach out and touch something to feel it *externally*. They move into it to feel it *internally*. We reach out and smell a flower and feel the flower on our face. They move it into their body and the two become a sort of communication; it is unique and different. Where they see structures of energy, they move into it rather than observe it. For them to interpret it, they can see structure but it does not hold the same importance as it does for us. They internalize or become one with it.

In fairy tales we're told that the spirits live in the trees. Everybody visualizes a little village carved inside the tree. How do you envision a spirit living in a tree? What does that mean? It means that an energy being lives within an energy realm; they merge with it. It becomes them and they become the tree. That's how they communicate; that's how they learn; that's how things go on.

Entities or spirits move into each other and communicate rather than talk across the room. It's very alienesque, unique, and different, but it's more beautiful and fascinating. When we think of their reality, we want to think of beautiful colors, but the truth is that they don't really see the beauty in colors. If you were looking through their reality in a pure entity perspective, you wouldn't see the colors; rather you feel them or you become part of them. You would be independent in one way but completely part of something. It's like when I say, "All is one."

We are all part of something bigger. The cells of your body, the living organisms in your body, are all separate and independent of each other, yet they're part of a bigger organism. It's true to say that entities are separate in their frequency or dimensional realm, but they are also part of something bigger, moving inside of it, one with it. Instead of reaching, smelling, touching, and using the five senses like we do in this dimension, their senses are very different. Their senses are more internalized. They become the spirit of things.

When an entity moves through you, you feel a massive tingling sensation move through you. That's their energy mixing with yours. As a living creature, the more intelligent you are the more in-control you are of your frequency. When a spirit tries to move into it, they're pushed away or popped out. Your energy holds to a type of frequency that they cannot merge with. It just doesn't work. If you were purely energy, then you would mix with others and you wouldn't be afraid of losing yourself. It is just a different kind of communication. It's a profound and beautiful experience.

When an entity passes through you, is there an effect on the physical body?

Yes, if they pass through you, the tingling is because your nervous system reacts to their energy. Your muscles open and close because of electricity. Your eyes open and close because of electricity. Your heart, liver, and lungs – everything is electrical. So, when another electrical field hits it, you feel it. You interpret it as a very physical reaction, different than what the entity would sense.

If the entity is conscious enough, this is how it communicates with you. It's not trying to possess or harm you; of course, this is the very first thing you think of. You panic because this is alien to you. The spirit is doing what is natural to it. It's trying to merge with you like it would do with another energy being. In most cases, they're just misunderstood. That is because the entity is so uniquely different than anything you can perceive in this physical dimension.

A paranormal investigator's job is to seek out entities, and just by seeking them out, they're opening themselves up to communication. That's a given fact. Also, if the entity is powerful enough, strong enough, or conscious enough it can project its thoughts to a person. An entity does not have vocal chords. It does not have the means to sit down and write a note to hand to you. This dimension is very difficult for it to operate in. It is not supposed to function in this dimension, but it is intelligent and powerful enough to *want* to function here. On the other hand, the human body is designed to interact with this dimension and relay its experiences to your soul, your spiritual energy, which is very similar to a spirit.

Now, here you are trying to communicate with an entity. And now the entity, who is very powerful, very mentally capable of concentrating on you or the paranormal investigators, is projecting its thoughts, feelings, and emotions telepathically. An entity doesn't say, "Hey, how are you doing?" It projects the feeling of, "Hey, how are you doing?" There's a very complex language in emotions; it's more complex and more defined than the English language or any language in the world. Emotion is a universal language, not just in our world, but the universe. Everybody knows the difference between sadness and joy.

If an alien visited us and it was sad, it would just be a matter of time before you started to understand that it was feeling very sad. Or if it was very happy, you would know it. You may not understand the specifics, but you would know. Emotion is a very complex language when you begin to decipher it. So, the entity moved its vibration, its feeling, in a very telepathic way into you.

Your brain is designed to convert electrical impulses, energy, into biochemical structure to create your feelings and your emotions. So the entity has imposed its emotions on you, and again, it gets back to fear. The fear creates the anxiety, the panicking, the nervousness, and immediately you feel frightened. You feel that this must be a very bad thing. It's something you've never experienced before, and you're terrified.

So those paranormal investigators felt a powerful presence communicating to them. It clearly had something to say and they felt and experienced it, knowing what it meant.

If I say to my students, "Close your eyes, relax, and think about something cool, soft, smooth, white." And then I say the next thing is, "Dark, thick, hot, rolling, and moving over the white, cool." Now, if I was to discern what that meant, I would say it is hot fudge over ice cream. Your imagination already started to figure out what those emotions are or your sensory already started to decipher them. You already interpreted or began the interpretation.

Is this where the concept of possession comes from?

Yes, when one projects massive emotion at you for the specific purpose of communicating something, your brain begins to interpret those feelings and where they came from. It does not mean that the entity was trying to possess you, but it probably felt like that to those investigators, especially if it came from an entity that was very capable of projecting it. In many cases, this is confused with a form of possession.

During your meditations, you may feel things moving around in the room, or you may occasionally hear the sound of voices. So how do you know whether those things are just being created by your mind or if their being caused by real entities or spirits? It's very difficult to say.

When you reach certain levels, particularly using the *Higher Balance Meditation* technique, you are enhancing psychic abilities - the sixth sense. It's a sense that goes beyond the five that you already use to interpret this reality. That sixth sense is what takes you to this higher dimension. It allows you to enter this dimension where there are spirits and entities.

The sixth sense allows you to communicate, hear things, and know things. You're plugging into the matrix, or the Gaia consciousness of the planet. Since you don't have a certain control yet, you're sometimes hearing thoughts, or what sounds like voices, moving through you. Or, you're seeing things while you're moving through the silhouette levels of consciousness.

So it doesn't necessarily mean it's ghosts and spirits; your mind is plugging into a database of consciousness and it's adapting to sort it all out. Each time you get in there, your mind is learning to cope and deal with those things so it can interpret and understand them. Your sensory may be moving in a direction that allows you to pick up on entities and spirits that may be in the room with you. They might be attracted to you because you're reaching a very rich frequency which they're detecting.

When you're in any form of meditation, I've never known entities that would want to interfere with you, unless you're looking for them. If you're just doing your meditation, you're building your consciousness, so it's a different kind of frequency. You literally have to want to attract spirits in order to get that kind of response. It's like a frequency; a TV channel that you switch on.

The parapsychologists were at a specific house to find spirits or entities. That was their intention. If you're meditating, it's not your intention to speak to an entity or spirit. You're not really going to come across them. If you have that idea in the back of your mind, that particular desire, there's a very good chance if there's one nearby it's going to present itself. If it's involuntary and it surfaces, it is not an entity. You're plugging into the Gaia consciousness, the Matrix. You're getting a reverberation of thoughts moving through you.

I've had a great number of experiences with spirits, ghosts, and entities. One time when I was about fifteen years old, I had a few friends at my house. I lived in an old house at the time. We decided to see if we could get some spirits or entities to come into the room. I had this old, three-foot-high candle stand made of heavy, knobby wood; it must have weighed about twenty pounds.

We placed the stand on the middle of a coffee table and we were all standing around it. It was lit and threw off a lot of light. There were also some other candles in the room. It wasn't a séance because we really didn't know what we were doing. We just wanted the spirits in the house to come. After a few minutes, something resembling a hand just reached out in the middle of the air and smacked the candle stand. We watched it fly through the air and go out. Thankfully, there was more candlelight in that room. It was just astonishing because the hand came out of nowhere.

When I was about eleven or twelve years old, my brother and I had bunk beds. I don't remember the exact time, but it was late. I was in bed and felt something in my room. All of a sudden, I felt something grabbing my ankle. I wanted to scream or react, but it was very quick. It jerked me completely out of my bed and threw me on the floor so fiercely and powerfully that the blanket was still on my bed. It pulled me right out from underneath it. My mother entered the room but I was still shocked. I thought, "What just happened?" I was sleepy so I got up and crawled back into bed. I don't remember my brother reacting at all. I assumed that he was sleeping.

I had another experience one time while visiting my father who was teaching me how to see auras. When I went to bed, there were bunk beds for my brother and me; I remember feeling the need to awaken because something was wrong. I opened my eyes. Then I wished that I hadn't. To this day, even with all that I know now, I'm not sure that I can even explain what happened. That's the scariest part.

In my bedroom, the doorway was facing straight ahead from my bed and a little to the left. In the doorway, I saw something that looked like my father, but it wasn't him. Maybe an alien who thought that taking on the form of my father would somehow relax me or make it feel less threatening. It had the same build as my father, looked like my father, but the skin was a brilliant, fluorescent green. It wasn't a dull green. It was darker than lime but illuminated, like neon. The eyes and beard were both blacker than black. It was a very shiny black.

I remember it walking towards the bed. I wanted to scream but I couldn't. I was panicking, but I couldn't move. My mind could not believe what I was seeing. It was just beyond imagination. It was walking towards me and I wanted to run and scream. To top it all off, it got to the end of my bed and was touching my foot. It was running its fingers up and down my leg. At that point, I screamed out loud. It must've been a bloodcurdling scream. I closed my eyes. When I opened them, it was gone. My father and my stepmother came running into the room saying, "What's wrong? What's wrong?" I was crying, saying, "I saw this thing." I described it to him and my father said, "You're just excited. We've been looking at auras all day. You're scared. Your imagination is getting carried away. It's just your mind. Don't worry. It's okay. You're safe." But I didn't sleep at all for the rest of that weekend.

You're probably wondering why in the world I would ever even dabble with more ghosts or spirits. There was a part of me that did it for the same reason that people love roller coasters – for the thrill of it! I wanted adventure. Entities tortured me, or scared me to death because they were very curious about me. But I also have a very strong curiosity about them.

I've had many paranormal and psychic experiences in my life. I've had friends who wanted to see if I could read cards, or do psychic or other really cool things. This really excited my friends that I had when I was young.

When I was about fourteen, there was this boy and girl that I vaguely knew for a short period. I went to their place, an apartment on the bottom floor in the corner of the building. They had a Ouija board. They wanted me to help them conjure up some spirits. Of course, I was always ready to please. We played with the Ouija board and we got a response. I had seen so much really intense stuff already, so I wasn't terribly impressed. I said, "We're not really getting anything."

It was early evening and the sun already began to set. I went out their door and I should have taken a left, but for some reason I took a right instead. I just wanted to look there; I don't know why. As I walked through the building area to a slightly grassy hill, I saw a man walking a little dog. It was strange because no one was supposed to have dogs in this apartment building. I'd never seen anybody with dogs. They just didn't allow them.

That was the first thing that caught my attention. The second thing that caught my attention was that everything about this guy was black - his jacket and his skin. He had something like a wizard's hat on, but without a pointy top. There was a big brim going around his whole head so rain would run off of it. You couldn't see his face as it was shadowed. He had a trench coat on and everything was dark gray and black about him. I realized that the leash was black and the dog was black. I thought, "How strange that this guy is wearing all these dark clothes."

I looked again and I knew this was not a human being. As an adult, being much wiser, I'm now wondering, "If it was a ghost and what was it doing walking that little dog?" How absurd this must seem. He just turned and looked at me. Instantaneously, I knew that he was there to check me out. He was interested in me.

Of course, the fear then kicked in as I knew this was not a good guy. It wasn't that he did anything bad, but I could feel him all over me. He wasn't touching me with his hands, but his mind was feeling me. He was scanning my mind and feeling my energy field. He was very intrigued by me. I didn't like it. I felt like it was something very bad. Could you imagine a stranger just grabbing you physically? That's how I reacted.

I spun around and just ran. Then I started pounding on the kids' door. I said, "Let me in." He wouldn't let me in. He was scared, too, for some reason. He must have heard the fear in my voice. And said, "No, I am not opening up the door." I think he happened to look out the window from his house, and must have seen it also. That must be why he didn't open the door. So I ran home.

If it is a ghost what is it doing walking the little dog?"

Was that entity a spirit of a deceased person or was it a different type of entity?

There is a group of beings called shadow people. Shadow people move in the shadows because photons of light affect their body. This affects ghosts and spirits in much the same way, but a little differently. That's why I always say that there is a little truth to every wives' tale. I believe there are a species of entities that move into our dimension through darker spaces of shadow. Sometimes they seem wispy as they're moving.

Some people say they see the silhouette of their face or their structures because they look human in some ways. There's very few stories about them but I think, in many cases, they're confused with ghosts and spirits.

Are shadow beings malevolent?

No, as frightening as it may sound, I don't really know of anybody being attacked by them. They seem very curious about us. They seem attracted to people who have some psychic ability. They keep their distance and they will just step into the shadows and disappear again.

At other times they appear in the corners of a room, even on the ceilings. I recently read on the Internet about somebody who placed a camcorder on top of their computer. They kept saying, "I know there's something in my room at night," and it actually caught this entity coming out of the ceiling in the room for three or four frames. It was still a little bright – like it came into our dimension and knew it couldn't stay. You could see the silhouette of the body manifesting like black smoke. But it's not smoke. It's fibrous. That is the only way I can describe it, like silky strands of structure. Then it just spun around and disappeared again. If it wasn't artificially produced, it would be consistent and accurate.

I have spoken with some trustworthy people who came to me for counseling. They told me that there was a young entity child, like I just described who seemed about twelve or thirteen years old. The child was in the kitchen and it just stared at the two of them. They all just stood there looking at each other in shock that each one was watching the other. Then the child got the nerve up to move. It spun around into the dark of the wood in the kitchen and it just faded away.

In ancient times, there were cave drawings of what looked like shadow people. There's also some books written by people who interpreted what they thought were ghosts, but really may have been shadow people. They are known for wearing the long trench coats and hats. They are the same thing that I saw when I was very young. They're much more common than most people realize, but they've managed to stay out of the limelight.

An entity is an intelligent being. That doesn't necessarily mean it's a ghost. When I think of ghosts, I think of the projected sound, holograms, or a lost soul. An entity knows exactly what it's doing. It's not in a dream world, it's functional. It's consciously here; it has an intent to be here. It could be an alien, or an intelligent being who is purposely here, not caught in the dream world.

Whenever an entity comes into a room, there is a noticeable drop in temperature. That is a classic sign of their presence. Whenever you go into a building where they claim that there are ghosts or spirits, there is often a 5° to 20° temperature drop. This is because entities must come from somewhere.

In this reality you don't enter a room unless you open the door and come in. When you open that door, if it's cold outside and warm inside, cool air is felt coming in. Well, if an entity is going to come into a room, it's going to create a vortex or gateway. When it does that, molecules are affected. Our energy fields are affected. That's why it creates a dramatic temperature drop.

Somehow, it changes the energy in the room. This is why the temperature drops dramatically when an entity appears or when they enter a room. Whenever you investigate a haunting and you feel the temperature dropping, you know something is going on. There's something moving into that room from another place. Most people are going to be scared but, if you know what's going on, try to stay calm. Be thrilled! You're probably looking for the entity or spirit anyway, so now, at least, you're on guard.

Smells are often associated with spirits and entities. Smell is directly triggers the resurfacing of specific memories. The spirit who is in that dream state is usually so strongly attached to a certain memory that it projects the frequency of that memory which creates the smell associated with it. In many cases, you can smell either sweet odors or perfumes.

One time I went to an old haunted hotel, and when I went into the hotel room, there was an overwhelmingly strong perfume smell. I thought to myself, "I really need to get away from this. I need to open up the doors. There's too much perfume in here." It wasn't in any of the other rooms, just this one room. As soon as I thought that, I felt the static charge of the entity move past me. I felt the emotion that I needed in my chest.

You can't talk verbally to them. But emotion is energy, so you can project it. So, that particular entity felt my need for fresh air and met it in a friendly way. I felt a static charge move past me. It went to the window and the window swung wide open. Of course, we looked at the window to double check.

So, that was the smell from this particular entity. As it turned out, the entity was a girl who was supposedly murdered there. She was a prostitute and did not have a lot of money. Of course, they used heavy perfume to camouflage natural body odor. This was the smell of that person. It was a lilac scent, which would possibly be affordable or accessible at the time.

Often, negative spirits have a sulfur smell. It's like rotting eggs, a smell that's very repulsive to us as human beings. There are times when you smell something that evokes the memory of a place where you've experienced it before, and it's very powerful. It almost jolts your memory; it works the same way for entities. The entity is so stuck in a certain frame, like this particular one with the lilac smell, that they project it outward and we can smell it through our sensory.

This projection is still energy, so it's a form of communication. For them, it's a profound memory. You can walk out to your car and smell something that brings you back subconsciously to the place and time you smelled it, what is that? That's an emotion. It's a pure, powerful emotion which contains very complex information. Emotion is a language; you feel it and your brain translates it using its interpretations of that data. This gives you a profound experience for a few seconds.

That's what the entity is doing. They're reliving a memory; they're stuck in a loop and that smell is the memory they're experiencing. That's why you smell it. It's like they are trying to communicate with you in the sense that if you smell it, you will have that same memory. It's a form of communicating.

There is a place that I used to go called the lost village. It was a town in the middle of the woods. To get there, you had to hike about a mile down a dirt path. I've taken many people there in the past to experience it for themselves. Sometimes you can hear different sounds, like a horse and carriage, cows mooing, people talking, or kids playing. You can hear a number of different sounds there.

So, why could you hear all those sounds?
Were they recorded sounds being projected?

I believe there is a time loop in that place. I found out later that there were a lot of stones in the dirt. Not only were there stones, but there was moving water throughout that area. You could say it involved quantum physics or energy development of some type, or maybe the valley is holding energy frequencies. The sound was recorded during that time period. It wasn't recording new sounds but it kept randomly looping several different sounds.

You would hear a noise, but when you tried to move towards it, it moved away. It's almost as if it were at the end of a twenty-foot stick. As you walked, it moved twenty feet away, no matter how you approached. There were some parapsychologists who said they heard children. They kept trying to find the kids, but they couldn't find them. They knew there was no way those kids would be out in the middle of the woods alone.

I've heard the horses. The mooing of the cows was also very interesting. As a psychic, I would scan the area thinking there must be a cow or something there. I'd look with my normal five senses and see nothing. I'd psychically scan and I wouldn't see anything either. I couldn't feel any presence, but there it was, "Mooo." We'd walk the whole area for miles in each direction. It's in the middle of nowhere and there are no cows out there.

There's an explanation for this: it is either a time loop relapsing over or it's recorded, projected sounds. One of the interesting things I found is that there are cellar holes and walls there. The people who lived there had built some stone structures and framed them with wood, but there's no wood left anymore. You can see that a village of some type used to be there.

On the main pathway, there were three or four trees. I always felt that these trees were significant to the vibration of the place because you can constantly hear these sounds. We always had excellent experiences when I brought people there. A hurricane hit the area and when I went back to that area again, one of the trees had fallen down.

These trees were the same size - very big, tall, straight, and strangely placed in front. They were like tuning forks that for the ground, the stones, and the water underground. I felt they were very much a part of what was going on. When the tree broke, about 80% of the paranormal phenomena just came to a screeching halt.

Science has not evolved enough yet to supply the answers for everything; there are many freak coincidences. The people who planted those trees were probably not expecting to have a mystical experience, and I doubt that they did it on purpose. I think they just planted them because they thought the trees would look great. It was a freak accident that they affected something on the paranormal level, which is what created that effect. A paranormal or metaphysical event is still science because science is metaphysical. It's just a matter of understanding what's happening.

There is a graveyard on top of a hill in the village. I've had several experiences of entities and spirits there. I've also seen moving balls of light, which are entities. I think the metaphysical energies of that place attract entities to it and that is why paranormal things happened there.

One time, I took a group of college students there. One of the professors, who knew and respected me, arranged for the students to go with me to see if I could convince them that there were entities. They were all nonbelievers.

Nothing really happened in the village section of that area; they didn't hear anything. They were nice about it, but you could tell they were indifferent. One of them had an old Polaroid camera that takes a picture and develops it right away. He was a bit of a smart aleck. We walked through the whole village and then I showed them the graveyard.

As we were coming back down, I noticed there was a pile of stones. I felt that it was a marker for a grave site and the people who were buried there were on the run. I felt that it was a baby or someone very young that was buried there. Anyway, I was explaining all of that and I said, "Oh, I see a glowing light, an orb above the pile." So I looked at them and asked, "Do you see it?" Of course, everybody looked at me like I was insane. I do this from time to time. I see it, so sometimes I forget that everybody else probably can't see it; I just assume that they can.

The smart aleck with the polaroid camera said, "Well, where is it?" I said, "It's right over the stones." So he took a picture with his camera, and, when they looked at the picture, the orb was floating above the pile of stones. They now had to rethink their whole philosophy about whether or not spirits and entities really do exist. It made for an interesting ending of the day.

Is it possible for a non-physical entity to move a physical object?

Moving objects is extremely difficult for an entity, but there are cases where they have done it easily. So, if it's so hard to move an object, how can an entity push a window open? Sometimes, unconsciously, we can do miraculous things. There is a law of physics in their reality just like there is for us. I've heard of instances where a panicking woman was able to lift a car up so it didn't crush her child.

Other miraculous stories constantly defy physics. An entity *movng* a paperclip a tenth of an inch would be equivalent to a person moving approximately eight hundred pounds. Would it be easy to do? Could you do it with enough effort? Probably. Would you be able to get it far? You'd only be able to move it a slight distance before you exhausted yourself.

This is what it's like for an entity to move something because our physical dimension is so different than what they're used to. For an entity, moving even the tiniest object would take an exhaustive amount of energy. When it wants to get your attention it may decide to move a small object but by the time you move away from it and return, it has already exhausted itself. So then you think, "I could have sworn that I put my keys in that spot." I can just imagine the entity freaking out because it was trying to get your attention. It's hard to get this sequence into our reality.

For an entity, moving an object is extremely difficult unless it is a very, very powerful being. What makes them powerful is that they are able to draw in our frequency like sucking in smoke and that enables them to adapt to this physical dimension. This is an ability, a conscious act they are able to do; they assimilate the physical body.

I remember watching some recorded footage of an entity having a fit, kicking a Rubbermaid garbage can. It dented the can and slammed the cupboard and cabinet doors, wreaking havoc through the house. It was a modern house but the people had moved out because of this entity. It was able to use its energy to have a very, very potent and powerful effect on the physical room that it was in. This situation is very rare. It's even possible that it was an alien in our dimension.

When anger is focused into our reality, it can create a very strong manifestation. This kind of entity is usually called a demon because it can be very intimidating, very destructive, and it seems to be full of anger. You have a sense of fear within you. You already know that the entity doesn't have good intentions, so you know that you should get out of its way. An entity that is this angry is capable of doing certain things that are very powerful.

There was one particular case when some parapsychologists were investigating a haunting and they went up to the attic to check it out. They were filming what they saw but they didn't get anything on tape. Supposedly, all the noises and sounds were happening in the attic. But when they were leaving, something grabbed the last person and pulled him back into the room, carrying him through the attic to the other side. There was a rope and it actually put a noose around this person's neck, hung him up and left him there. The other parapsychologists ran up to the attic when they heard the commotion and were able to get him down in time.

Now, that is a fascinating story, but whether or not it is true or just an urban legend, I really can't say. I didn't see the real footage of it. From the source I heard it from; I think it's entirely possible. I've heard hundreds of stories like that. From my own personal experiences that happened to me, I certainly believe it's possible.

I do not see ghosts as being that bad, but entities can be. Ghosts who are communicating can affect electrical fields, energies, televisions, and radios in certain ways. Entities can affect them even more. They're not going to sit there and tell you, "Get out," like in the horror movies; it doesn't work that way. That's Hollywood. You can feel an incredible sense of energy when this thing projects fearful energy at you. You're going to know that something doesn't want you there.

It is capable of pushing you, biting you, and doing certain other things. But they have what I call "gusts" of ability, and then they're exhausted. They only have a certain amount of time before they exhaust their energy. In all of my studies, it's very rare that an entity has actually ever attacked a person; so don't feel that you have to be terrified about it happening to you.

How often have you been bitten by a dog? It does happen, but for those who are around dogs all the time, there's a greater chance that it would. If you're going out looking for spirits and spending a lot of time doing that, you're going to come across certain things. You'll probably be excited, just like when you're on a roller coaster. You'll say, "My God, it bit me." I would say this is fantastic!

In some cases, if an entity has a very strong, powerful energy field, it can move through electrical instruments and it sounds a certain way. It sounds scary to you and, of course, you're scared because it's something happening that you don't understand. It's a natural instinct. But you can arc speaker wires a certain way and it makes an electrical sound that also sounds very intimidating.

Just as your brain envisions a tree stump as a body, the same thing happens when you hear a sound. If it sounds semi-human, your brain already starts to create a being. It automatically assumes the sound must be an entity. That's not necessarily the case; you always have to be careful how you interpret things.

My "golden rule" is to always try to come up with three different interpretations. If you're out ghost hunting, your first interpretation will be that it's a ghost. Make certain the other two are something more reasonable. Deduce some level of logic because you don't want to chase and believe those illusions. If you spend your life believing everything you see, you miss the real thing. And if you find the real thing, you might really find something incredible and fantastic behind it that yields even greater experiences.

Be very selective of what you accept as legitimate. My rule of thumb is to go ahead and deduce the experiences as paranormal if you want, but look for some logical answers. Many hauntings where people claimed to speak with spirits or saw ghosts moving objects were all fraudulent. In my opinion, about ninety-nine percent of séances were fraudulent.

There were two sisters who had fooled a lot of people into believing that they were dealing with entities. There was table tapping and other sounds; and they would say, "If there's an entity here, let us know." Then you'd hear a snapping sound. Later on, as they got older, they confessed to moving their knees in certain ways to make that sound. I think that sometimes people are a bit lonely or want attention. If you want to be foolish and believe everything you see or hear, that's up to you. The real thing is out there; just don't buy into everything. If you have a healthy level of scrutiny, you'll find the real deal.

What if you find the real deal and the entity acts violently; how does a non-physical being attack a physical being?

If an entity attacks you or if you're in a situation where you're really afraid, how you think or react will be the difference between affecting an entity or defending yourself. Can you physically fend off a very powerful entity? The answer is, "Yes, you can." The real question is, "How is that possible?" Think like an energy being and not like a human being.

You have an organic body; your body is a machine; it's really not you. You're an energy field co-existing with this organic body made of living organisms. You have to think of yourself as being energy that's moving around this physical body. If you can see auras, you see the energy. It's an energy field. If you extracted all of that energy from the physical body and you moved the body to the left, and the energy to the right, you'd be an entity. You're just working within this physical body that's interpreting this dimension for you so that you can understand it as an energy being. If you smell, see, hear, touch, and taste, turns into electricity. Your body is like an ATV exploring this dimension because you're an energy being trying to interpret this dimension.

If an entity hits you, it's not hitting you physically. It's hitting you with its energy and your physical body is reacting to that. In other words, if you were to stick your finger in an electrical socket, you're going to jump twenty feet through the air because the electricity will cause an instant expansion of your muscles. It's the same way your hand opens and closes; it's electricity stimulating those muscles to react in such a way.

When you get a pulse of electricity, everything expands. This creates a thrusting effect. An entity is a very select frequency. When it hits you, it's just as if it's hitting that physical part of your body and the muscle knots up. If you get a knot in your leg, how does it know to tighten up? It's because your nervous system is reacting, making it contract so tightly that it's painful. That's what an entity does. It hits your enegy field and your muscles react to it.

Are there ways of dealing with a hostile entity?

The first thing you need to do is become calm. If you're calm, your muscles will relax. Just breathe and remember your energy classes. Use the *Higher Balance Meditation* material; calm yourself, and breathe. If you maintain a good tonal, your frequency will be so powerful that no entity can get near you. If you're emitting that pitch, it's very difficult for them to approach you. So when you're meditating, it's unlikely that any entities are going to approach you. It's almost as if they cannot.

The next thing is to *think in energy*. There is a method of becoming one with the environment to the point where you're not really using your five senses. All of a sudden, you can plug into the room. When I say to you that an entity becomes part of what it is, it's very difficult to explain. If you put an electrical wire into a pool, the entire pool of water will be charged like an electrical field. You're not going to stick your toe in it, no matter what part of the pool you're near.

In the same way, you become part of the electrical field of the house, and you can feel the entities moving in you. You're part of this bigger thing. By just feeling your body, you can feel the walls of the room so you know the location of these entities. You don't necessarily open your eyes because your eyes can't detect them easily; unless you see auras. In that case, you might be able to see their body moving around. For the most part, they are moving so quickly it's hard for your brain to interpret that frequency.

So, close your eyes and you have to trust your instincts. You can literally reach out and touch them, but you can't reach out with just your hand. You have to feel and think about the energy and vibration of your hand and the aura around it. If you just swat at them while thinking of your hand as pure energy, you have the advantage because you're in both dimensions. If you think about your energy, your energy takes on a structural size. So when you hit them, it's like being hit by a five hundred pound bat.

There are other ways to affect them: you can actually grab their energy and breathe it in. Breathe in through your hand. They're shrouding themselves with a kind of energy. That's what makes them able to physically move in here. It's like clothing. When you inhale them, you're not going to take them in as in *possession; rather,* it's like you're almost pulling their clothes off of them or revealing them. They're vulnerable and naked and they can't touch anything anymore.

You're grounded in this dimension, but you also can move in their dimension if you think about your energy body. So you just pull it. Even the mildest thought is frightening to them. They're coming at you as a big bully and you just turn around and become this giant dragon that's going to snap them in one bite. It will throw them off guard. You just pull their energy in with a breath, using your hand. Breathing synchronizes the body with the mind. So when you calm your breathing, your mind slows down. When your breathing picks up, your mind speeds up.

Use your breath in energy movements. Take their energy away by reaching out and imagining breathing through your hand. You're sucking them in. In many cases, that is going to end the situation in a very fast, dramatic way. It's just difficult for you to imagine because you are so intimidated. The intimidation keeps you from concentrating to do it.

Think about your lessons. Think about what you learned from my other books. Think about calming yourself for a moment. That's when you do your best *Kung Fu*. It will come from you; you just have to let it go and trust yourself.

When you're in that tone, you're letting the Force, or God, move into you. You are an absolute force if you can just trust the Universe to come into you to take care of this. Your intent is, "I need to deal with this." You don't have to think about it. Just let the Universe move into you and it's going to take care of the problem.

Is there a specific chakra we should focus on?

Chi is the closest energy to physical energy, and it is also spiritual energy. So, you're actually using your chi energy to combat entities. There's a massive number of things you can do. There are times when I've gone to places and people have said, "There are crazy, evil, bad entities in this place. They are horrible and people are being physically hurt and thrown across rooms." I'll just go into the room and put my hand on the wall of the entrance. I don't have time to go chasing the spirits out. I just change the octave of the house so they can't stay there and it blows them right out the doors. I just go into my meditative state, pull the Force into me, become one with the Force, and feel this higher love. I say, "Okay, it's time to change the vibration of the whole building."

Then, I project this frequency into the building so that any entity with a negative intent is just pushed out. They are literally pushed as if a giant snowplow slams into them. They're shoved right out.

When you meditate, this is the vibration you're creating. This is why entities with any ill intent can't come near you. You're literally pushing them away. You just don't understand you're doing that. You can project energy if you learn how to do it. If you compassionately have intent, your emotion and love will keep bad things away.

You're filling the walls, the floor, and the carpeting with this vibration. There is a connection between every object, energy-wise. You're thinking of filling the house, so naturally it fills that area. The amount of energy you have is going to decide what you can do. An average person isn't going to come in and blow out a whole house like me. Most people who have a good spiritual sense and want to help by replacing the bad energy can work a room or an environment. They walk through the room with their positive energy and their intent to push it out. As they move their hand, they visualize this moving energy.

Anybody who has seen auras realizes how expansive the aura can become by projecting energy into and using your hands. If you just move this energy, you're going to push the entity through the house. If you think about spiritual shamans, whether they are from India, America, Europe, or any other place, you will consistently see their method for broadcasting energy. They might do it with sage or smoke. They might do it with prayer. They might do it with holy water. But in their mind, they are projecting out energy with an intention. That's what makes entities react.

Energy reacts to other energy countering it. This is what these purification rituals are about; they're done with a good intention. I'm simply stepping out of this ritual process and getting directly to the source. That's what makes it very powerful because I can magnify it and I have a very good understanding of what is behind it: *pure love*, good intent. It's intent that's very powerful and cannot be destroyed.

Why chase a spirit off? Why not just bathe it in God's absolute love? That's enough to awaken it and to remove its anger. Love can make sense to it instead of trying to negatively control its mind. If its will is stronger than yours and you're not spiritually evolved enough, or prepared to handle it, this can be a challenge for you. Find that place and the Universe becomes one with you.

When God is within you, there's nothing that's impossible. You can deal with entities. You can fight them. You can work with those scenarios if you use the Higher Balance teachings. It will help you to understand energy and give you techniques to harness and work with it. If you understand that, you can incorporate it into anything; it's multi-dimensional. This is just another dimension. It's what enables you to do these things.

There are other things you can also do with spirits or ghosts. Maybe you're having problems or feeling very uncomfortable. In many cases, ghosts just show up one day. Hauntings just happen. I know atheists who have accepted the fact that their place is being haunted and want it to stop.

Nine times out of ten, this equation always works. I will say to them, "Have you done anything differently? Have you moved the furniture around at all? Have you bought anything new recently, like a refrigerator or something?" They're probably wondering, "Where is this guy going with all of this?" The answer usually is, "Yes, we brought a refrigerator." Or, "We moved the furniture in the living room around." In some rare cases, people have vacuumed and moved furniture around and that was enough. Again, it's like buying a lottery ticket and taking a chance.

It could be the springs in the chair, electricity moving through the walls from the wiring, or telephone wires. Who's to say? If you capture a frequency, energy, or electricity by arranging certain objects in a very specific way, it creates a gateway or an arc.

Enough energy begins to vibrate to create a dimensional portal which allows spirits or entities to come through because they're attracted to it. In their reality, they see what looks like a flashing light. They're curious so they move towards it and come through to the other side. To them, this is an interesting place.

The energy in the room is multidimensional at a certain distance. They can see you but you can't see them, or you can see them and they might be able to see you. It's as if something makes both realities become one. All of these unusual paranormal things are happening because these two worlds are touching one another. It's a fluke of the positioning of things, like the positioning of the couch. Something is hitting the right frequency.

When things like this have happened to people and they contact me, I'll ask them, "Do you want it to end?" And they often reply, "Yeah." I'll say, "Okay, just start moving your furniture around. Reorganize your house." Then they will do what I suggested and, instantly, like magic, the spirits, ghosts, entities, or whatever is bothering them stops.

Sometimes they want to re-create it again, but they can never get it to happen because, even if the couch or the TV was moved just a tenth of an inch, it has changed the energy in the room. Sometimes, something will happen for one hour, or one day, and it never happens again. It's because somebody moved an object and collapsed that frequency or energy field.

There was a case of paranormal occurences that I once worked on in California. I went inside where there was a priest, some mystics, and psychics. I asked, "Well, do you want to solve the problem?" The home-owner asked me if I could and I said, "Yeah. Just reorganize the furniture. The problem's in the kid's bedroom." Then she acknowledged, "Yeah, we just put the bed, the bureau, and several new things in there." I said, "Well, it's coming from that room." She said, "You're right. That's where most things happen." She said, "I feel that myself." I told her, "Move the room around." She asked, "How's that going to help me?" I replied, "It'll solve your problem."

She later told me that it worked like a miracle. Everything stopped. People are funny. Later, she said that she wanted it to happen again. So she tried to make it happen again, but she never could. She tried to move the furniture back but there were five objects that had to be exactly in the right place to recreate the same effect or frequency, and that's what allowed it to happen. It's a million to one chance that you can re-create the same scenario.

In many cases, if you feel that you have spirits, enti-ties, or vibrations in the house that you don't feel comfortable with, it's kind of like a feng shui thing. The Chinese have it right. You don't hear a lot of stories about hauntings from their culture, at least never anything in a negative way. It's usually very positive.

In that culture, they take the roof off the house eve-ry few years. There's no roof, just an open sky. Then, they put it back on again. They believe this flushes out all the spirits and energy. There is a level of truth to that. It moves the negative energy out.

At one point, I owned a very, very old house. You might think that it would have a creepy effect or strange energy, but it didn't. The roof was all re-done at one time, and I've often thought about that. I never felt the vibes from all the people who must have lived there. I'm not just talking about the shingles. They took off the roof and built a new one, moved all the objects in the house and changed the energy. It certainly had a profound effect.

My aunt told me about a married female friend who had a lot of children. They lived out in the country near a state forest in a large Victorian house with a big porch. They awoke in the middle of the night after hearing a loud bang, as if a car had hit the house. When they went to check out what the noise was, they saw a huge mound of dirt with grass growing out of it in the middle of their living room.

They felt that there was a portal that came through the ceiling, which is very interesting. They asked if there was anything that I could do. They were so afraid that it might sound crazy if they mentioned it to anyone else. Maybe the authorities would want to take their kids away, thinking they were nuts. So, they asked me instead.

You can't explain what happened in normal terms. So, I stayed at their house, and I decided to sleep on the couch in the living room. They were also concerned about something coming through the portal and were afraid for the safety of their kids. That's why they wanted it closed. I wanted it opened. I wanted to crawl through it to see what was on the other side.

I remember hearing some sound and turning on the light. There was an Indian moccasin. It was just the beading and leather, but it was very unique.

On another occasion, an old-time watch fell through and it actually functioned. From time to time, I could see what looked like ripples of water on the ceiling. It had that same fluttering look in blues, purples and other colors. It would come and go.

This was the time that I really began to learn about the effects of moving the furniture around. I kept asking them, "When did it happen? What happened? How did it happen?" Eventually, we realized that they had moved the furniture around in their living room. We decided to rearrange it back to the old way. The phenomena completely stopped. This is how I caught on to the idea about moving furniture.

Is there a reason why ghosts, entities, and paranormal occurrences are usually experienced at night, or is it just coincidence?

Instinctually, we feel safer during the day than we do at night with the lights on. It's probably because we can see better during the day. We sense that we're safer during the day than at night. Also, in the same way that human beings sunburn, the photons from sunlight disrupt the entities' dimensional body or their energy body. It's like they know that they should avoid it. It's like heat for us. They retract from it. That's why you always sense entities in the shadow places, but never in the light.

When I lived out in the desert areas of Arizona, I could never find any entities. I had a very hard time scanning. I wanted to find entities to use to teach and work with students. I normally find all these haunted places to train students because the best way to learn is to have experiences. When I was living out there, I knew that I would have to find places, and I had a very hard time finding anything. The sun is always shinning. It's constantly pounding the environment. What entity would want to be there?

Two thousand years ago, Christ dealt with some very powerful entities, but not what I would call spirits or ghosts. He dealt with tough, powerful entities, ones that could survive in that kind of environment. They were very few, and far between. In places where there's fog, or heavy rain, just like the folktales say, most of the entities exist. That is where you'll find them.

So, hauntings are connected with the weather?

Yes, you always hear about great hauntings in England. It's the environment. There are more variables behind it such as rain creating ionization. Ionization has a lot to do with entities. It's the same reason there are temperature drops or smells associated with hauntings; these can also be caused by ionization. There is a connection between electrical storms and rain-creating energies, and hauntings. They are able to come and go from their dimension and mingle in ours in certain places under the ideal conditions.

We know that an entity or a ghost haunts a house because when they die, they are in a dream loop. They're trying to reconnect with the most familiar place to them. They will go to their home or a home where they might have lived once in their childhood. Because they're in a dream state, they're not thinking cognitively.

All of a sudden, you might find a ghost in your house. It could have been somebody who died at the age of eighty and just showed up. They're haunting the most familiar place to them. This is why ghosts are sometimes in graveyards. It's because they want to get back into their physical body. In their dream state of consciousness they think they'll wake up if they get into their body. This is why they're drawn to their physical body and this is why they haunt.

Is there more involved in the process of waking them out of their dream than simply telling them to "go to the light?"

To free an entity or a ghost from haunting, you have to get their attention. You have to convince them that they're dead. You have to convince them why they're dead because they won't believe they're dead. In your dreams, you don't realize you're dreaming until somebody wakes you from your dream. To finally convince an entity, you have to keep their consciousness on you long enough. It has to make some sense to them, somehow, whether you talk to them emotionally, or verbally. Then, you can get them to snap out of it.

If they awaken out of their dream, not only do they remember who they are, but they remember their lives; it's a frequency. Currents move a bottle thrown in the ocean to its destination. There are energies moving through time and space. If someone is not very strong, spiritually, when they die, the current moves them in different directions so they know what they need to do. It makes sense to them. It's like knowing to breath or gasp for air if you've held your breath for a long time.

Why do entities sometimes choose to haunt abandoned houses?

It's because ghosts or entities sometimes want to isolate themselves from human beings. They can feel human beings, but they can't communicate with them. They're frustrated trying to get their attention to communicate, so they isolate themselves. They're just tired of being in a loop, trying to get out of this reality. They either just don't want to deal with human beings or they're angry. So they find places of refuge from light, like a house, forest, or a cave in some cases, so that they can have refuge and withdraw.

Since they are energy, time is not the same for them. A day for us feels like a moment or a minute to them. They don't remember what happened over time. It could be a hundred years, but they don't ponder on that hundred years. They are not old or decaying. They do not feel physical pain because they're energy. So it's a very different reality.

I don't believe that most people have souls. So when most people die, their consciousness goes into the Gaia mind. If spirits or ghosts are interrupted in their routine by someone, they may realize they're dead. So they awaken to their consciousness as an energy being.

Let's say that everybody has a soul. You reincarnate and there's seven billion people on the planet. That changes every ten years. You have to compound all the people who lived from thousands of years. If you compounded that, you would now have trillions of entities and you only have seven billion bodies to incarnate into. It would mean that all the entities not currently reincarnated must hang around. It just doesn't equate.

It makes much more sense that they become part of a greater consciousness. If my grandmother dies, is it horrible to think that she didn't have a soul? It's still a beautiful thing because her memory and her existence were not in vain. We don't want to let loved ones go because we're selfish. My grandmother's life and her memory are still very much alive, every little piece of it. If you go to the Akashic Records, or what I call the Gaia mind, or into the matrix, and you choose to find them, you can actually pull all those fragmented pieces of energy together again and have this being sitting here and guiding you.

It often reminds me of the first Superman movie when he becomes an adult and he had these green fragments from his parents. He throws them out in Antarctica in the movie, and they build this place and he goes there. They hold all the memory and knowledge of his parents. So the parents show up and they're holograms. He talks to them and they teach him. But it's not really them. It's their essence. It's the same thing. Every living being's essence exists forever. It's just not in the terms that we might want it, but it's still just as profoundly amazing. It's as if their soul is always here, but part of something much bigger.

The difference is that we see ourselves as individuals and we don't want to lose our individuality. This is the difference between white cells and red cells. White Cells are people who really worked on their energy to become independent beings that keep evolving versus Red Cells who didn't work on it very hard so they become part of the Gaia consciousness. All of their memories become that.

Is there not a song that lives in your head and every memory of your life is still alive in you? In a way, you're a microverse of the Gaia mind. All the things you've ever experienced, all the people you've ever loved or known are still very much alive within you. You just think that the only way you can reach them is through your touch, smell, taste, sight, and sound, and that's not the case. It's the way you are interpreting it because it's the only way you can understand it.

Chapter 4

REFLECTIONS ON THE PARANORMAL

Most people see themselves spiritually evolving through their meditations, so to them, it seems odd to look so intently at the paranormal. However, there is a good chance that when they pass on they could be an entity, ghost, spirit, or demon. But you will not likely be in that same boat. You are going to be able to move on spiritually, whereas, the beings in those forms are there because of some kind of problem.

When you accept the idea of entities or spirits, you're acknowledging your fear of death, that there is something more than this. In an indirect way, when you deal with entities on a subliminal level, you also have to acknowledge that there is something more beyond this life. This greatly benefits you as a spiritual person in your pursuit to evolve your own consciousness. You need to acknowledge this in order to have larger spiritual breakthroughs.

It's a catch-22. By confronting spirits or entities, you are going to conquer your own inner fears and affirm the concept of life after death. It also conquers the Babbler by releasing yourself to a higher state of consciousness.

I have been recording the voices of an entity that has been traveling between our homes. We can hear the entity speak on the recorder but not in person. Why can we hear it on the recorder but not live?

A recorder has magnetic properties. I believe that dimensional space and other realities are largely based on magnetic fields. Recorders tend to capture magnetic fields or other dimensional places. I don't want to say that it's necessarily another frequency. I'm not a scientist, but I can tell you from personal experience that this type of phenomena is more likely to be captured through a recorder.

The human voice basically runs on propelled air and this is what creates sound reverberation. It's an outward projection. You would not expect to be able to hear a cell phone conversation without a device to translate the cell phone signals into a format that you can hear.

An entity is no longer a physical being; it doesn't have vocal chords and it doesn't have lungs to propel sound. It is a different being of energy rather than an organic being like you. Therefore, because it was human at one point in this life, it understands the spoken word. So it's trying to communicate vocally.

The source of the sound is not from a mouth. It's not words as you would perceive them. Therefore, you can't hear it with your organic ears or eardrums; it is of a foreign nature. I believe that the tape recorder has properties that allow it to capture bits or pieces of that communication. That is my perspective and my take on it.

There are reasons why only certain statements or phrases make it through. Instead of someone energizing their voice, they power up their mental energy and it's caught on the recording. This is a mental projection. In most cases, you'll get the more dramatic pieces. Although many of the recordings out there are not genuine, I think it's feasible to get bits and pieces off of AM radio talk shows. If the sound is slowed down or sped-up, you have distorted sounds that have a creepy effect to them. There are times you might hear a familiar commercial and just dismiss it as Sears, or J.C. Penney's. So a lot of people dismiss what they hear and it is never communicated, so the general public isn't informed about those particular recordings. The only stuff that actually gets reported, circulated, or acknowledged, is the more dramatic information or recordings.

Do we all have a spirit guide? If so, how can we talk to them? How can we distinguish whether the information we receive is our imagination or from a spirit guide?

I generally go against the grain of the popular spiritual beliefs that are out there. I don't believe that most people have spirit guides. I can't tell you how many hundreds of thousands of people out there believe that they have spirit guides. I'm not trying to disrespect that, but let me explain this from a different perspective.

Spirits and entities are intelligent, just like you. Can you imagine having to be in communication with another person 24/7, four weeks a month, twelve months a year, for years and years and years? Wouldn't you get bored? Wouldn't you ever wish to do something else or go somewhere else?

I think spirit guides may come into one's life for a brief time period. That is probably going to be a couple of hours or maybe a week here or there, and then they move on. They've got better things to do; they have their own growth and personal development to look out for. These beings also have their own lives and callings.

They've perhaps worked with you for a short period of time, but the concept is that they're always out there or there's a spiritual 900 number to call to find yourself a spiritual guide. With all due respect, you've got the answers already. Forget the spiritual guides. Just apply your own intuition. That's the bottom line. I just think that it's a bit crazy to say that everyone has a spirit guide. Most people don't want to believe that they're alone, on their own, or that they're vulnerable to other spirits. They feel more comfortable having a spirit guide or someone to advise or direct them.

When you evolve spiritually, you have to be the leader. You can't depend on outside sources to guide you anymore; you need guide yourself. Until you put yourself in that position, you become reliant on the concept of a spirit guide. So I don't think just one answer is the correct answer for a very broad question. I don't think there's one size fits all. As a general rule, I don't believe most people have spirit guides.

I believe that most people are capable of tuning into the Force, or an aspect of the Force's consciousness that they interpret as a being. But, for the most part, these beings have other things that they need to do. It would just be inconclusive to prove there is a spirit guide for somebody for years and years; I just don't agree with it.

Hollywood has done an injustice to the psyche of the population because "spiritual" movies sometimes propagate the idea that a guide talks to you just like regular people do. Certainly, they have to do that in a movie; this is called sensationalism. It's a way of reaching the most effective amount of people who are trying to understand what's happening in that movie. I've never met an entity or ghost that had vocal cords, or one that had lungs to propel sound, or eardrums to hear what I'm saying, or retinas to catch the reflective light which gives me vision. They are energy. They are of a different kind of energy that has a different design.

You might ask why an entity or a spirit appears as they do, looking like beings. Well, they're translucent for starters. That should be a hint that they are not exactly physical. They project their most familiar body shape as their image. So at times, they seem human to us; and at other times, they don't. To them, it's the most familiar shape that they've had. When they try to communicate, you don't hear anything. You're not hearing something audibly.

Sometimes when you do hear something audible, I think it's caused by fear being built up in you. You perceive it, but it's not necessarily what is being communicated. To communicate with a spirit or an entity, you have to use your consciousness as the conduit. *Your mind* is designed to communicate with your brain. For all intents and purposes, your mind is a soul. It's a spirit within a physical body. You have an organic brain and a mind that is communicating, which means you have the ability to not only communicate with yourself organically, but you can also leap over and communicate with other beings. You're going to do this internally.

When you're saying it out loud, you're also project-ing it mentally and emotionally which is a level of communication that an entity can understand. They're not hearing you say those words. They're feeling a broadcast of information that is emotion which is asking, "Who are you? Why are you here?" They can feel that. A spirit cannot hear you talk. They're not designed the way you are in this physical dimension. But, because you assume that everything communicates the same way that you do, you talk to it just like it's another physical person. That's the first error.

For starters, practice what's in my first book of this series, *Meditation Within Eternity*. Clear your mind; learn to control your mental vocalization, your Babbler. Learn to communicate or think on a different level. Then you can learn to receive impressions, empathy, or emotional communication from other beings or other persons telepathically, which is further explained in my book, *Silent Awakening*. You can refine yourself to such a level that you can get very complex communication as clear as one person talking to another.

In order to communicate with a spirit, you have to do it on an empathetic level. That means you must learn to broadcast your feelings. You also want to clear yourself and calm your mind so you're able to receive incoming impressions and know what they mean.

Every single object has a recorded feeling in your consciousness. If you were to look at a cup, you would know what that cup feels like without touching it. That's actually a coded feeling. If you look at your cup, you can sense the structure of the cup, the temperature, the ceramic feel of the cup or whatever it's made of; you're aware of all those things.

Well, if you open yourself up and you receive the feeling of that cup, you would think, "Cup! I know that's a cup." How do you know? Did the entity say the word cup? No. You know it's a cup because there are other identifying properties to it. This is how dimensional beings often communicate. It's very foreign to us. It's not what we're used to doing day in and day out but, you must remember, they're in a completely different reality than our dimension. Therefore, things function and operate dimensionally different. When you try to bring together these two worlds that aren't designed to work together, you really have to be creative with how this information is received and communicated.

So, go into a meditative state of mind, maybe in a place that has a spirit or entity. Clear your mind and broadcast your intention. If you say, "Why are you here?" There's a feeling of curiosity. And if you create that feeling of curiosity in your heart chakra area, you send it out almost as a gesture with your hands outward. You breathe it out like it's an emotional breath coming out of you, then you wait a moment. You may get an impression that says, "I'm lost. I'm angry. I'm frustrated."

Of course, logic or the Babbler is going to say, "Well, how do you know you're not creating that on your own? How do you know this is not your imagination?" This is why you train yourself to clear your mind. As you get better at it, you can discern more information. You'll be able to interpret names and visual impressions of what the person looked like. You'll see it in your mind. You'll see different information, and then that person is trying to express their name and you will suddenly know who they are. It will just become clear to you, but you won't know how you know. It's because your mind has *amazing*, amazing properties to communicate this information.

At this point, you don't completely trust it because it's not your 'normal' state of consciousness that you are using right now. It's not what you understand and are familiar with; it is something totally different. You'll learn how to recognize it, how to work with it and develop it. And it's pretty amazing stuff. So, that's, *'How you communicate with an entity 101.'* It is just the beginning stage. Obviously it gets more complex, more detailed, and more profound as you progress.

Is there a meditation technique that can make your awareness more sensitive to ghosts or paranormal activities?

Absolutely, it's in the *Higher Balance Meditation* technique. Most people begin to use it, put it into their daily practice, and experience great results with it. They also work on developing other areas with it. As long as you have a good understanding of the basic technique in my book: *Meditation Within Eternity*, you can take it and utilize it for other things too. It's Daniel's lessons in the movie, *The Karate Kid* - wax on, wax off. You learn more things than you can ever imagine.

Sit down and clear your mind just like you do in your meditation. Use the meditation skills that you learned in *Meditation Within Eternity*. Instead of going into a full-blown meditation using music, you're going to redirect and broadcast these same emotions. That's how you can utilize your training; by modifying it to a certain degree. You realize that you have more skills from this training than you thought. Other modules, like *High Guard* (Chapter 4 of *Igniting the Sixth Sense*), or the previous chapter of this book, *Energy Beings*, expand on it or refine it. You just need the desire to get even better at this. For the most part, you have the core abilities and instinctively it's there. Now it is up to you to look at it more intuitively within yourself.

So, when you ask if there is a meditation technique which would make someone's awareness more sensitive to ghosts or the paranormal, I need to explain this to you. If you go into a haunted house or a 'supposed' haunted house, you've already established your intention just by entering the house. An intention is very, very important. Intention is that unwritten feeling or vibration of *motive*. You don't have to say, "I'm here to talk to spirits." Your energy is already broadcasting your intention. That's what they're receiving from you. The entities already know you're there to talk to them. Whether or not they're able to make that contact with you or choose to do so is a whole different subject.

If you go in there, you now have the intention to communicate with a spirit. Sit down, start your meditation process, relax your mind, clear yourself and then inwardly broadcast the feeling of, "Are you here? Are you open to talking?"

You're going to be able to put out what you want. Then you're going to wait a moment and see what you receive. The receiving aspect of it will probably be very mild for you to relate to; it's going to start off weak. You're going to be wondering, "Well, am I really getting something or am I creating this?" Don't second guess yourself.

Don't worry about whether it's your imagination or not at first. Analyze later. When you have completed one hour of trying to communicate with the entity or spirit, then you can analyze whether it was your imagination or a real experience. That's the only time you should ask yourself those questions; when you have reviewed the data or the information you obtained from the session and compared it with the owners of the home.

Look at the history of the house and try to find information that you received. That's going to confirm your information or not. But, if you start to question yourself during the process, you will minimize or marginalize the potential of this kind of communication because it's very subtle at first. It starts off subtle, very mild; you think you're getting an impression, "Okay, I feel this. I think I feel that."

As you open yourself more, like anything else that you do consistently, you are going to improve. By the time you've done it for at least fifteen minutes, a half hour, an hour, or you go back the next day, you'll find that you have become very proficient with recognizing that inner communication that's not you. It's almost as if you're using your body as a device to communicate with something. You're using some part of your organic self that you weren't really fully aware of before – like a cell phone capturing information that's being broadcast. You are able to translate it. So, use the meditation that you already know. You can adjust your awareness to make it more sensitive to ghosts and spirits.

When does an entity contact or communicate with the searcher?

There are dozens of ways that an entity can initiate contact. This is where you get into violent entities, angry entities, positive entities, or helpful entities. There are as many varieties of entities as there are varieties of people. I think the vast majority of them are all pretty sensible, but it's just a matter of how you approach it.

The conditions are universal; a haunted house could be a condition. You go in there and there are all sorts of crazy things happening. You may not hear the spirit or entity trying to communicate with you, but if there are objects falling or you're hearing little sounds, this could be the entity trying to communicate.

Remember, an entity does not have the means to communicate the same way that you do. Having said that, there may be a select few entities that have developed a way to communicate, but I assure you that is extremely rare. I wouldn't necessarily say they are ghosts or spirits. They are probably more like alien dimensional beings.

Entities are greatly misunderstood. Let me expound on that: Imagine Helen Keller. She couldn't hear or see you. Her reality was very different. In the beginning, she was very crude. She would knock things over. If you sat down at the table to eat with her, you would find that her manners were atrocious. That was because she was very frustrated because she was trapped in a world she knew existed beyond her, but she didn't have a means to vocalize what she wanted to say. She wasn't able to say, "I hate tomato soup! I don't want it. Why do you keep giving it to me? It's horrible!" Instead of being able to communicate that, she threw the tomato soup and smashed things and got it all over the place. Her reality was different than the reality of the people who sat with her at the dinner table.

In many cases, when people think that an entity is aggressive, shocking, or intimidating, their reaction is fear because it's being chaotic. There are many entities out there that are misunderstood. I don't want to sound like some kind of therapist by saying they're all misunderstood. But they truly are because they can't talk to you.

They want to talk to you; they know you're there. They know you exist. They may not even be able to physically see you the way you think they see you. You may just look like an energy glow to them, but they know there's something there. They want to communicate, and when you're not being receptive to them or you're ignoring them, they're going to have conniptions. In many of the cases that I've come across, they're frustrated.

That's why you need to clear your mind and go into a meditative state beforehand. When most people talk about spirits, there are fewer good spirits and a lot more bad spirits. Of course, we fear what we don't understand. That's why we perceive that many spirits are bad, malicious, and have bad intentions. This is how I feel about it. As long as there are bad people in the world, there will be bad spirits. As long as there are good people, there will be good spirits. I believe in the innate goodness of all human beings. I don't care if you're a mad biker or a murderer; I think that they all look for forgiveness in the end, or some degree of love. They've done horrible things and that needs to be dealt with. As you grow older and more intelligent, certain things become more mundane or commonplace. You perceive differently as you grow older and you become wiser.

A spirit, an entity, or a ghost, or at least the ones that are maintaining some level of consciousness, don't have bad intentions. I think that they're people just like everybody else; they're in a predicament and the predicament is causing their frustration. The best way to deal with an entity is like a child or somebody who is having a tantrum. You don't react angrily because it just escalates their behavior. You try to patiently calm the person down with soothing words and get them to listen to you.

You hear about entities that are violent, but the reality is, that's about 1% of the cases. Most people will probably never come across a really powerful, negative entity that's *hell-bent* to hurt you. I'm not saying it can't happen because I've certainly experienced it on several occasions, but then I stick my nose into stuff I probably shouldn't. That's part of the adventure. So the vast majority of spirits are misunderstood and frustrated. They're in anguish because they're trying to communicate and they're not being received. They're frustrated. That's just the way it is.

Why is it that I cannot see spirits in my home but I can hear them walking in the halls and stairways?

I spent at least a decade heavily involved with ghosts and spirits as I was developing in other areas. In the vast majority of those homes, noises actually came from the house itself. You really have to be sensible and research it so that you're not wasting your time assuming that it's a spirit or a ghost. Now, I don't know your particular case personally, so I can't say if I really think it's legitimate or not. But, this is what I tell any student of mine, "Come up with *three* explanations for any situation."

The first one should be, "I believe they are entities and spirits." The second one should be a logical answer for these sounds or these phenomena that are happening, which is the expansion and retraction of the floorboards. The third one should be a reason besides the house settling or entities. For example, are there kids? Are they just trying to be tricksters?"

Some of the infamous cases in the history of paranormal investigators were people communicating with spirits that turned out later to be fraudulent. For more than a couple of decades, the Fox sisters held séances and communications in their home where people would hear rapping noises. The guest would ask a question, "Give me a sign or two raps," and there would be two raps. They ended up taping their hands and legs to their chairs to make it look like they weren't making the noises themselves. Then they'd shut off the lights. Later the sisters confessed that they were double-jointed and could click their hips. They really fooled everybody.

So, you can never dismiss the motives of other people. A good paranormal investigator or person who communicates with entities and spirits doesn't ever want to be fooled. Walk in highly skeptical. *Spirits do exist.* I believe that. But you have to walk in with a very cynical, skeptical perception before you openly accept that everything you hear or see is a ghost, spirit, or an entity. The vast majority of them aren't ghosts or spirits. It's very rare to come across the real McCoy.

There is a Higher Balance video (see Appendix) about seeing auras that basically teaches you to see the aura in five minutes. Well, this is also a wax on, wax off technique. If you can see an aura using that technique, you can see entities and spirits using the same technique. Your energy is essentially your soul - your frequency - that's emanating. It expands outside of your physical body to a certain degree. Remove your physical body and what are you going to be left with? You're going to be left with an energy structure or what looks like your body only it's energy. It's translucent.

Often people will say that they saw something move out of the corner of their eye or thought they saw a person walking. But when they looked, there was nobody there. You see at a higher frequency out of the corners of your eyes because of its curvature. It's like a prism bending light. It captures light and separates it. You are more likely to see an entity out of the corner of your eyes than to look directly at one where you see at a lower frequency. The higher frequency is a band-width where these entities are perhaps more visible as they move into this dimension.

So, if you practice seeing auras through this method, apply the same method when you visit a haunted house. Look at the energy of the furniture and walls and become conscious of it. Be still again. Clear your mind like you do in meditation. Do it in a standing position. Clear your mind. Be conscious of your breathing. Don't be surprised if you see something move your way. Don't panic. You're just seeing what's always been there.

How can I make myself more aware to connect with ghosts? Both of my young daughters are highly sensitive and have seen ghosts in our house, but I have only heard them when they have spoken to me. I feel helpless when my stepdaughter calls to me in fear of what she is seeing, especially when I can't identify or begin to comprehend what it is. How can I raise my awareness to the same level that she is experiencing and help her to understand it better?

What develops psychic ability the best? Fear! Fear is the emotion that humans have relied on to develop their

GUILD OF PSI

psychic ability. It goes back to survival in earlier times. It was a necessary sensory that human beings developed to sense whether a lion or wolves were being predatory, because they didn't have spears or weapons at that time. They were not as evolved as we are currently. Primitive man used the same instincts as dogs and cats to sense things. Birds follow magnetic fields.

When children are young, they are obviously more open and vulnerable. They feel more vulnerable. They are afraid of many things because their instinctual organic body's survival mechanism tells them that they're small, vulnerable, and need the strength and protection of an adult.

Children tend to be more psychic because the fear level in them still has not subsided. As you grow older, you build comfort levels by habitually experiencing life. You learn that there's nothing to fear because you've seen it happen twenty times and you know what's going to happen now. But, when you're young you don't have that experience, so the primitive instinct kicks in and your awareness and your sensory is much higher.

When an entity or something that's not explainable moves into your environment when you're young, nine times out of ten you can feel and sense it. That psychic part of your brain has not recessed yet. Some people are obviously sharper than others, so that is why they react. They feel it and sense it. It's a very real thing to them. I'm sure that if you think back to your own childhood, you're going to relate to the same sensory. But, we forget about that as we grow older and our perceptions get molded into this reality.

Their sensory, right from the beginning, is different than yours as you've grown older. You've gotten calloused; you're not as sensitive. Mentally, we're more

REFLECTIONS ON THE PARANORMAL

influenced by the doe or the Red Cell world, extracting ourselves from this other dimension that is there trying to reach out to us. We change our frequency to a deeper level of doe, and that's what separates us.

The previous chapter, Energy Beings, will help you greatly in that area by teaching you the skills, knowledge, and understanding that you need in order to cope and communicate with it. If you feel threatened by an entity, Higher Balance teaches a course called: *High Guard, the Art of Energy Defense.* You can find it in the 4th chapter of my book, *Igniting the Sixth Sense.* *High Guard* teaches you how to deal with entities if you feel that they have bad intentions.

The answer may not be so much about how you can develop yourself to help your children because it's going to take time for you to redevelop those skills. Perhaps you should educate them to not be so fearful.

What is the best way to help a trapped spirit move on?

Here's the million dollar answer. This is the absolute secret, the information that prevents you from understanding. A person who has the ability to stay out of Red Cell mode has probably achieved a White Cell level of being in a previous life. However, in this physical life they were not able to awaken properly. When their physical death occurred, it was like waking up in a dream. They didn't believe they were dead, so they believed they must be dreaming. This is a state of consciousness that may be induced upon you, so you accept it as your reality, your inner truth, or rationalization.

You've probably had a dream where you're running and someone was chasing you, meaning to do you harm. In your dream, you run and you realize you can't run as fast as you should be able to. There's a part of you that realizes that you're dreaming. You have this consciousness now in your dream and you can react and interact on a more aware or conscious level. All of a sudden, you fall back into that dream world again and you forget that you had control of that awareness. You forget why you're running slowly and that it doesn't make sense. All of a sudden, you run slowly again but it doesn't occur to you that this is odd.

For lack of a better word, the dream world is half-baked. Your consciousness, or your mind, is not able to fully perceive correctly. Time takes on a different continuity, a different structure. As energy, time is really irrelevant because, in a sense, you're not under the same natural laws like you are in the physical dimension. There's no deterioration. There's no aging. For all intents and purposes, you're immortal. So, there is a recurring process. It's a recurring dream. You don't stop and think that you've been to this place over and over again in your dream. Each time you go there, it's like a whole new experience. An entity or a ghost is repeating time. They're repeating their memory.

The best way to help a trapped spirit move on is to awaken them out of the dream. Gain their attention while they are in the dream world and explain to them they're in this dream and they've physically died and have to move on. Unfortunately, that's a very difficult thing to explain. Hence, the problems with making it simple and making it happen. If it were an easy thing to do everybody could just go out and do it. It's very tricky. It's very challenging to keep the entity's attention because it's just like they are on hallucinogenics or drunk in a way, only not fumbling around. Their mental faculties are not able to focus as well.

Now, the same dream can also explain why they're being violent. In their dream reality, they realize they're stuck in something and they're trying to get out of it. They see you and they're desperately trying to talk to you before they lose their consciousness again and fall back into a loop of repeating some other part of their dream.

You may wake up in your dream and think, "Okay, this is crazy! Why can't I run faster? I know this doesn't make any sense." Well, that's what's happening to them. So the entity has this moment of reaction and then it just stops. You don't know where it went. It may not happen for a definite period of time. That's because they've gone back into this loop state of consciousness. It sounds horrible and, if you ask me, it is horrible. But, it's no different than being in a stasis. Once they wake up, they don't necessarily remember that they've been repeating this for a hundred years. It feels like only a moment to them. Again, they don't age.

So, the best way to help a trapped spirit, once you acknowledge it using the three rules, is to ask yourself, "Is this a conscious spirit? Is it unconscious? Is it in the sleep state?" Once you've done that, just try to hold their attention. Try to give them a sense of well-being that they're in a good place, that you're a good person, and that there's no reason to feel fear.

As much as you might be afraid of an entity, they were humans also. For the most part, they have very similar thought patterns. That is the mode that they're in from their previous life and they may be intimidated by your presence. You might think, "Well, that's silly.

How can that be?" You might be surprised. There are motorcycle bikers out there who look pretty tough and grizzly, but then when they start talking, you find they are some of the nicest guys in the world. It's all a matter of perception. It depends on what you're used to and if the entity is from another culture or not. It could just go on and on and on. You should have very unique and fresh approaches when you're dealing with entities.

Can psychic attacks become physical attacks? If so, how do you defend yourself if you can't see what is attacking you?

In my book, *Igniting the Sixth Sense*, there's a chapter called *High Guard: the Art of Energy Defense*. Read that chapter and you won't have to be concerned with it ever again.

Since the topic is entities, I'm going to assume that the psychic attack is from an entity or a ghost. When I was sixteen or seventeen years old, I had a very intense experience. This is one of many, but this particular one stays pretty fresh in my mind. This entity appeared in the room that I was renting at the time. It was a pretty gruesome and very intense entity. I'm sure that it fed off my fear at that time. It used that energy as clothing to manifest in this physical dimension.

This entity literally picked me up and threw me about seven to ten feet in the air. Of course, I wasn't as large as I am now. I was younger. It threw me onto a bureau. I believe I smashed into the mirror and it broke behind me. The mirror fell down but, fortunately, I didn't get cut. I then reacted intuitively and released energy from within me, which physically dispersed this entity.

Now, that told me two things. There are some pretty ugly things out there that can jack you up. And there is a way to deal with these entities so you can defend yourself. Of course, twenty or thirty years later, I have perfected and refined that dramatically.

In the *High Guard* chapter, there's a great deal of information. When you think an entity is trying to physically attack you, smack you, hit you, bite you, or pinch you, these may not be evil entities at all. For the sake of this example, let's say you're dealing with a very bad situation. *Everything I teach is interconnected.* There is nothing that stands-alone or serves just one purpose. That's the brilliance of all this material.

Don't think in terms of fighting an entity physically because, right away, you know you can't do it. How do you fight something you can't touch, see, smell, or taste? And when you do, it's on top of you. Don't think in those terms. Think in the terms of being multi-dimensional. You are not an organic being; you are multi-dimensional. You are a dimensional being standing within a physical body.

Think in terms of energy. Think about your energy field. Think about your aura field. Think about breathing in Prana and expanding your energy field and making it stronger. See the expansion, believe, and empower it.

When you feel this entity is making a move on you, push from your lower chakra. *High Guard* teaches you all of this. Literally, you can push your energy right at that entity and you're going to jack it up. It's going to feel another energy field matching its frequency and it's not going to like it at all. You are ten times more powerful than it. You are only powerless because you are thinking in terms of dealing with it on the physical level. It has not occurred to you to think of yourself as an energy being and that you should be able to deal with this in terms of energy. *You are energy. You are made of energy. Think in those terms.*

The reason that you are ten times more powerful is because you are not combating it in its dimension. It's in your dimension, your realm. Don't surrender the position of power. It's on your turf. That's the first thing you need to realize and that might not occur to you. They're more afraid of something they can't comprehend. They're in more of a fight or flight stage and it's more like, "I'm getting the hell out of here."

If you really think about it, you are physically rooted in this dimension because of your physical body. For the most part, it's trying to affect you in this physical dimension. You can channel your energy to push out a spiritual frequency, emanating from a very powerful source in this dimension - you! You're the conduit.

So, if you really need to, you have the ability to project this energy at entities. You don't have to let them bully you. You can even fill the room with it if you want to really intimidate the entity. Sit down and create your energy field around you. Use the technique in *High Guard* to create a pyramid and just expand your energy to fill the room. All of a sudden, you switch to your heart chakra. *Now the entity has to conform to the dominant frequency (love from the heart chakra) of its environment because it is energy.* In the same way, you have to conform to the physical objects in this dimension. For instance, you're not oing to be able to walk through a physical wall. If it's there, you're going to walk into it and it's going to hurt.

If you want to dominate an environment with an outward moving energy, just feel yourself pushing outward. It creates a wall that is as real to the entity as a physical wall is to you. It's all a matter of perception and bridging your personal belief system. It's hard for you to envision that because you're so grounded in the physical dimension. What you do day in and day out is what you relate to. So now, you have to start functioning on another level in order to relate with or deal with this entity.

So, a psychic attack can come in many different forms. It can be energy that affects your organic body. It can also be energy that affects your emotional self, but you don't realize that it's depressing you, making you ill, or making you feel suicidal. It is not your emotions; it is coming from a different source and that is definitely a psychic attack. Your brain cannot rationalize that it could be coming from somewhere else, so you accept it as your own emotion because you feel it in your body. You think it must be you and you react accordingly.

Your body will start secreting all these chemicals in order to balance your organic brain. You are going to react to it as if this was something that you actually experienced or have seen before, even though you haven't. It's a foreign vibration that is influencing you.

There are also other forms of psychic attack, and your body will naturally react to these things. Your mind will also react to these things. It depends which way the psychic attack is being imposed on you, but I'll give you a really quick fix to this. The fastest way to deal with any entity that is messing with you, or any person that is messing with you psychically, is to think about your lower chakra. It's that fast. Done! Your lower chakra is very structural. It holds that energy in and converts it into something useful. It doesn't rationalize. It's just energy. It's like a bull. When it runs into a car, it doesn't think about it as a car. It just decides it's going to trample it. And it does. Your lower chakra grounds out almost all kinds of energy.

Everything that is psychic or not of this physical dimension comes from an energy dimension that incorporates into this dimension, this frequency. When you focus on your lower chakra, you crush all of this imposing energy that comes at you. It's a very quick fix until you can get your hands on *Igniting the Sixth Sense* to look at the *High Guard* chapter and learn about energy in the *Ties that Bind* chapter of *Meditation Within Eternity*. So, this is a way to defend yourself right now.

Another tool to use is meditation. If you really think you're under attack, the *Higher Balance Meditation* is very helpful. It's just a matter of converting what you have learned to what you need in the moment. So you sit down and go into a meditation. Then, go to your heart chakra. Beam that big horse-tooth smile. Feel it in you and kill them with sunshine. Broadcast it so bright that the whole city lights up dimensionally from within you. You are the sunlight coming over the horizon of the Earth. You're as bold, beautiful and brilliant as you choose to be. Be the conduit of God, the Universe. Use your "Aummm." It is so powerful; you have no idea. And those entities are going to head for the hills. I know because I've done it. I've trained other people to do it. I've cleaned out more hardcore entity houses than most people have hair on their head.

It's all a matter of perception. You just have to open up your mind. You're reading this because you are a

White Cell. White Cells are warriors. You are searching to awaken, to discover and fulfill this inner purpose that you feel. That's who I'm talking to. I'm talking to YOU, very clearly, very to the point. YOU. You have this power within you. Rest assured. All you have to do is simply choose to awaken it. Use the materials I have given you to educate yourself. Recognize what you want to isolate and when you're doing it so that you can manifest it even stronger and build it outward. It's there.

Can entities influence us, whether good, bad, or indifferent, in this physical realm?

Yes, they absolutely can. If you don't want to deal with spirits and entities, simply don't think about them. Don't enter that arena. Don't pursue them; don't look for them because then you're tuning your intention, psychically, to bring them to you or to find them. If you extract yourself from pursuing those kinds of thoughts and choose to pursue meditation, or higher consciousness, or any of those things, then that's the direction you're going to move in. Spirits don't necessarily come looking for you. Nine times out of ten, you're looking for them, whether you're consciously doing it or not. There's something in you that's actively seeking it out. That is the only way I can explain it.

So, it's a choice. The best way to not deal with them is to ignore them. Ground yourself out in the physical reality and this lowers your tonal energy so that you're not in those higher realms where they're communicating or able to sense or feel you.

They're going to sense or feel you if you're projecting yourself in higher frequencies actively seeking out that channel. That is the only way I can explain it. When I had experiences with entities, it was always because I was actively interested, thinking about them, pursuing them, wanting to understand them. When I finally got to the point where I moved on to other things, they were no longer on my mind. They were in the background and that was it.

So, if you want to experience entities, you have to put yourself into a certain frame of mind in order for them to present themselves to you. Some people will say, "Why do some people experience ghosts or entities in a house and the people standing right next to them don't?" It's because the person who senses them is more psychically attuned and aware of vibrational and psychic energies. The person who's not able to sense them simply hasn't developed this sensory. They're very much grounded in a lower energy.

Let's say there are two people who are looking at a piece of art. One has a natural instinct, an inclination, towards art and can appreciate shadowing, color, and contour. She can appreciate natural skin pigmentation and the direction of the stroke of the brush by the fine lines. She can compassionately feel something that's been encoded, as an emotion from the artist, as a complete symphony of visual proportions. So, she is brought to tears by its beauty.

The other person can't decode that. They say that it just looks like some guy lying down with bird wings and a bunch of people standing around him. They don't know what it's all about. Either you are developed, have the skill, or you haven't yet attained it. But, you can if you choose to.

I also feel very strongly about the *Magnetic Pill*. Its main ingredient, magnetite, develops psychic ability and enhances this sensory. From the research that we've gathered, almost all animals, from dogs to migratory birds, have magnetite in their brain. They sense magnetic fields. They seem to have this psychic ability.

We now know that human beings also have it. It's now been discovered scientifically. Some people naturally have higher amounts of magnetite in their body and other people have lower amounts. This is why some people naturally pick up on all of this stuff and other people are not able to feel it. They do not have the chemical properties to work with what would develop into a sixth sense ability which taps into all of this. So, there are several reasons why some people are able to experience these things and some people cannot. That's the bottom line.

So, try *Magnetic Pill*. It's phenomenal stuff. But, you have to apply yourself also. If you just take it and expect stuff to happen, it's possible, but you'll get the best results by incorporating it with your spiritual activities and your sensory. It's going to develop those neurosystems that are hotwired, naturally, to seek out the magnetite to put it to use.

Chapter 5

SIMPLE COMPLEXITY

I constantly strive for new ways to teach the concept of programmable energy to my students. Recently, I was watching a program on TV about a new invention that, to me, is a great way to explain this elusive concept.

Scientists have developed a shirt with electrical wiring within it, made specifically for people who want to play air guitars. It was set up in such a way that when you pretend to play the guitar, the wiring would sense your arm movement and would play the music through a speaker system that is plugged in to the shirt. As I was watching this, I thought, "Well, that's it!" This is a great way to explain what programmable energy is all about, and maybe my students will be able to do what I do if I make this connection for them.

You can see the emotion in a person's face whenever they play an instrument. It's as if they can *feel* the music when they play it. To them, the instrument is like a new body part. It's as if they're creating and broadcasting simultaneously. They're making love to this musical instrument, but they're also making love to you because you're receiving the product of their creation. The musician *feels* it, but if you only hear the sound of it, it will not take you as deep as if you were to listen with an open mind and heart.

My point is that I've seen these people on the TV program with the air guitar shirt playing it with the same emotion as a musician with an instrument. They are projecting, or communicating, but they are using music to do this. Ultimately, they are creating words, a language, a feeling, through the music.

I'm doing the same thing when I create and project programmable energy, but with no sound or musical instrument. My instrument is my spirit, my consciousness, and I am broadcasting that out for people to experience and receive.

It's a revolutionary thought: create that music inside you and project it out as if it was sound. If you asked me, "Well, how do you project it out?" I would tell you to pretend that you have an air guitar. Pretend to project it out, see it visually in your mind like that and it will project out of you that way. That's how it would be done.

You were saying that you don't think about controlling emotions. For me, it's almost impossible to not think about it, what would you suggest I do to subdue my desire to control it?

Okay, let's use the example of the music again. I think that a great musician does not think about controlling the music when it comes out; it flows through their intention and desire. Personally, I go into a place of creation with the intent of communicating, and it comes out of me. *If you think about controlling it or directing it, then you're using your organic brain and it isn't going to work.* It's reasons like this that cause me to contemplate how to communicate the process. If you do it without trying to control it, there is a moment when you feel like, "Got it!" and then you can go there.

The downside is that you have to deal with the Doe even if you do achieve this, and you will forget about it in a few minutes. However, there is a way to keep fighting for these achievements: *just contemplate what I am saying over and over again.* Listen to my lectures, watch my videos, and read my books. If you stand in the rain, you get wet. Just keep letting the knowledge sink in and you will succeed.

Back to my point however, you can't think about controlling it. *Control* is a negative word, both psychically and spiritually speaking. You can control it but you have to take the implication of the word *control* out of it. You can call it *influence.* Influence it, but don't control it. If you influence it, it will do what you want it to do.

Think of it as smoke. Let's say you have a puff of smoke; could you control where the smoke goes? Could you make that puff of smoke move across the room, over to another person, and stop right in front of them? What would you do to move it? If it was just hanging there like a little cloud, could you physically wave your hands without it scattering? Probably not, but logically you know that it could be done if you had the ability to do that. You might go over to the little puffy cloud and gently blow some gentle breaths. It would be enough to move it in the direction you wanted it to go. Then you could manipulate it in other directions. If you put enough thought and effort into it, your goal can be achieved. Effort is a big word in spiritual teachings. That's what it's going to take.

Try to remember how difficult it was for you to learn to walk as a child. What a monumental task to learn to move your leg forward without falling and to keep your balance as you attempted to take the next step. What about the people who get into accidents and lose their memory of their body functions, and then they have to learn how to walk all over again? They have full consciousness in their head. They lived for maybe 40 years but they have no control of the body now. They have to learn it all over again. It is frustrating and they get angry trying to do it. They get mad, tired, and frustrated, but they have to learn to walk again because they need to get off the couch to put food in their mouth. There is drive! There is a reason to do it!

As a student of spirituality, you need to really push yourself to learn.

There isn't a survival mechanism that drives you to practice projection of energy. If you can't walk, you are going to have to learn to crawl, you're going to get on your knees, and you're going to eventually learn to stumble, and walk, and hang on to things. It is that intense effort that eventually develops your abilities in the physical realm. It's the same thing in the spiritual dimensions. The difference is that you've got to have the discipline inside of you to continue to work at it. You must put in the effort and have the desire to develop that ability to where you want it to be.

I think people just assume that they should be able to do these things; they've forgotten how much work it was to learn how to walk. Now that doesn't mean that everything, spiritually, is like walking or movement. Sight comes naturally. However, you have to remember, there are different levels of sight. People may forget that sight is not just the ability to see things.

You can acknowledge contour, visual texture, color, shading differences, or variations of light density; like looking through flames to see the different levels of color and depth, or looking through water yet still seeing a reflection on its surface. These are all things that you can learn to develop as an artist, and can also be applied for the spiritual student.

If you think about your five senses and the abilities of the human body, there's a certain level of achievement. But I think physical movement is the hardest to achieve. I always say the sixth sense is an extension of the five senses; all of them can be quantitatively distinguished by levels of effort. You have to give them thought and some practice with some more so than others. The sense of smell is easy; however, to discern the difference between pine burning or a tire burning takes practice. To somebody without this knowledge, something burning is simply that with no definition. You have to understand that you must treat your sixth sense like it is a skill and say to yourself, "I need to work at this or that."

Like anything else, if you don't work at it, you lose it. It will come back faster if you're able to know where you're going with it because you have been there before. If you've been down that road, you can find that road again a little easier then someone who's never been down there before. When I drive somewhere, I always say it takes forever to arrive. But on my way back, I know the distance and it seems to go by much faster. It's the same thing.

You have always said that fear pushes the sixth sense forward. In this modern day, there are so many distractions, so much TV and all that. How do you find that spark to motivate yourself?

Well, that's why people go to retreats or isolate themselves from others. Humans are so sensory operative that those types of distractions must be overcome first to move forward. Truthfully, it's hard for people to even want to get away for any length of time. But I think that it can be done. The dependence on your normal five senses is like any other addiction. If you were to isolate yourself from all of those distractions, after the first few days you would go stir crazy. I mean literally stir crazy from boredom. Then after a while, your intellect would be forced to work on those other issues. You might turn to nature for your entertainment and it becomes your teacher. And then, if the information and the data that you're carrying is put to good use, you will exist within and you'll start decoding the secrets of nature all around you and engage your sixth sense.

The reason is that you will become bored with all of your other five senses rather quickly. You'll know the smell of the wheat grass out in the woods, the smell of trees, and the sound of the bugs. If you stay out there in isolation, you're going to want to stimulate yourself in some way. That's what you are doing on the internet, or when you are scanning through the TV channels or radio stations looking for something to stimulate yourself. When you're isolated, you'll want to do that as well. In those moments, what you are going to turn to for stimulation are your teachings. That's where your real training and decoding will kick in.

How long do you recommend that people go on retreat or remain in isolation? Let's say I want to do some self-reflecting, how long do you recommend doing that?

Everybody's different. You could go for a day and get something out of it, or you could go for several months. The thing that you must not forget is that you are trying to engage this dimension, in this century, with this technology; so you must not go for too long. By extracting yourself and going to a place where you are removed from others for too long, you'll defeat the whole purpose of existing in this day and age.

You have to be careful because the organic body can be trained by accident also. By isolating yourself, you may train yourself to become an isolated person and withdraw from society. This is an opposing goal for a spiritual person because you are needed to become part of society and part of the neural system of the matrix in order to affect it. You have to be very careful. If I isolated myself for a long time, I think I would become a hermit or like a Buddhist monk, and I would become selfish. Selfish by extracting myself out of society and saying to others, "I'm on my own enlightenment cycle and I'm extracting myself from society." I don't think that's the right way to go because it defeats your purpose to be here at this time on Earth.

Some people might argue that they extract themselves so they can come back into the world to share their experiences. But a lot of very spiritual people do not share. They enjoy the life they've chosen by themselves without social contact. I don't want that to happen to me, but on the same token, I do crave it often; however, not in the way most people think that I do.

You have to ask yourself, "Do you serve your higher purpose or do you create yourself? Are you more spiritual because of your isolation, and in that process of finding more spirituality, find that you can no longer interact with mankind?" That brings us right back to the same question, "Why are you here?" You're here to serve mankind. You're here for a purpose: to help usher in a kind of enlightenment. By extracting yourself from it, are you still doing your job?

Can you still contribute in some way without attaining a great awakening? Will it still have an effect? I know a lot of people are wondering about that because, obviously, not everyone is going to make it to that awakening stage. Are you still going to be able to contribute if you do not awaken in this lifetime?

Absolutely. You can have a conversation with a person and you may not know that you're affecting them, but five or ten years later, they have a breakthrough from reflecting on the conversation that they had with you, or something that you showed them, or something you imparted to them through your energy or your consciousness. I believe that if you heard me speak, there is a fiber of me still there.

If you speak to a person, there's a fiber of you left in them. And what is that fiber? What does it do? It's a frequency. It doesn't even have to be a profound statement that they had memorized. Knowledge is frequency. That means there's a chance for it to spring into life. It's like seeds. You can have seeds on the shelf for a long time and still plant them and they will come to life. Take plants in Africa for example. When Africa has a dry season, everything becomes parched; there is a sense of death and nothing seems to be living. Then the rain comes and those plants come out of hibernation and bloom.

I believe you have to consider the fact that every person you touch and communicate with has that same potential. I don't believe you have to be enlightened to affect others. I believe every White Cell naturally has that ability to pollinate mankind. I think it's our obligation to pollinate, to communicate, to share and assist humankind. However, I believe it should be done without being rude, forceful, or disrespectful.

You mentioned that this type of knowledge is alive, that it's an organism, and it feeds you. If the organism gives you what you need to function, to create, and to pollinate, is this organism the Force itself or is it just an intelligence that helps you connect to the Force?

It is the Force; it's a dynamic part of the Force. To ask if it is exclusively the Force, I would respond by asking you "Is your hand all that you are?" Or, "Are your eyes all that you are?" It is a working part of the Force: It is the will of the Force; it is a living thing. It is just alien for us to conceive that.

I always have to be thinking about the words I choose because students draw images instantly, and they do not always see things from my perspective. But if I were to use a comprehensive term, which in this case may carry negative connotations but still accurately describes the concept, I would say it is like a virus, a computer virus. Use your new technology to help interpret this information. When you talk to somebody, it is like a virus. It spreads like a cold.

In this particular case, it's not a bad virus; it's more like the immune system that activates to fight off a virus. Hyper dimensionally, it's like turning something inside out. This organism just thinks in a different way than you do. It's coming at everything from an opposite perspective. It spreads, but it's more like turning something inside out.

Its intelligence is very different than your own. And because it's coming from a different dimension, all of its reactions are not exactly how you would expect them to be. That's because you expect the reaction to be a certain way and you are resistant to it when it is different than your expectation.

There are other teachers who use material that is different from yours. Does that become a separate `virus' separate from your teachings?

This is where I have to be careful because people can be very judgmental and critical of what I say. They either misread what I said, or they respond to one specific part of the discussion instead of taking the entire subject as a whole to reflect upon.

I think there are a lot of other teachers out there who are teaching different dynamics of the Force, albeit necessary dynamics. I specifically teach a dynamic that is critical to White Cells. I do not dismiss the teachings of other teachers. What I am saying is that each teacher offers a particular school of thought. You should research and study with several different schools rather than isolate yourself by studying with just one. Of course, there are situations when you already know your particular calling and what works best for you. You will gravitate towards that.

I think most schools teach that love is infinitely the highest level you can attain. I teach my students *what love actually is*, not just tell them that love is the highest level attainable. I am not in favor of presenting this concept as a physical thing, but perhaps it will help you to understand better.

It's like observing the purpose of a clock or a watch; you can tell time with it and understand the concept of it. You might even have some understandings of its mechanics. The difference is my students have a driving need to dissect the inner workings of the clock. My students want to know about the spring. They want to know the purpose of each gear. They have a craving for a better understanding of all the complexities within it. The reason for this craving, after having dissected all those working parts, is what they're really after – it's the very Source. And the Source comes down to the hand that's winding that watch, the unforgotten beginning of the mechanism. What my students really want is the truth!

They're trying to find their way to the absolute truth instead of saying, "Read this book and follow this recipe. This is what love is and how you act. This is how you do things, and how you pray. This is how many beads you count, and what you chant." My students seek the absolute truth of the *meaning* of love, and in that process, they totally get and understand that each gear of the watch is a representation of many different kinds of factors that make up the whole watch.

Most people would just see the watch or the hands of the watch, but it takes a unique understanding to recognize that all these little pieces are the dynamics and aspects of the watch: hence the "love." All of the parts have a certain and critical importance to the whole. I think that many other teachings operate on a simpler concept. But I also think some of them have profound knowledge within them. The difference between my teachings and the rest is that I'm speeding up the process of teaching through my ability to quickly and rapidly take this watch apart and explain it in a way that students can better understand which accelerates their awakening process.

All I'm saying is that I've decided to take a more progressive route. I just think it's time to push the envelope. I believe that certain individuals will gravitate towards this approach, all of those who can relate to it. You may feel some resistance with this statement, but I believe this is a weeding out process. What I'm trying to get across is that my teachings will find the right people for this particular path, and those who feel differently will find their own direction.

Of course, I think this is the best path! That's why I'm on it! That's why I'm going after it. I'm not saying that there aren't other paths where you can find truth. What I am saying is that White Cells, in our particular quest, feel it and know the truth of it.

**Why does it take me a few seconds to realize that?
I see the graphics, or hear your words and
automatically know that I was looking for YOU.
Why do I feel so connected and so sure of it?**

The reason is that it's not really ME you were searching for. It is the frequency that resides within me; it inter-fibers with the tone, the texture, the voice, and its meaning. How do you know you like or dislike a certain song after only hearing a few seconds? How do you know if the song is going to be a hit or not? You know which teachings speak to you the same way that you know the best music for you. It's the same way you know when you hear my voice, my tone, my pitch, my words, the stringing together of the vocabulary, how it dances and paints a certain picture in your mind and also your dimensional heart area. It is different than it would be with another person; therefore, it elevates you. Inside you are saying, "Wow! I like that sound! I feel it!"

Inside of you is a reflection, an echo, of the part of the group, family, or tribe that you belong to. That's the White Cell vibration. It's the fabric that we're made of. Not all fabric is the same in the sense that it's identical. The thing that we all share in common with everyone else is that we are all made out of organic material.

Regarding your readers and students getting very emotional about you; they have dreams about you and there has been a lot of talk about those dreams. Can you comment about it?

I'll give you the *"million-dollar"* statement. When people tune into me, they hear me and pick up on my frequency. They pick up on my energy and know it's the connection they are looking for. It's an important part of their destiny, per se. It is not that *I* am their destiny; it's that I'm an important *mechanism* within it.

People connect with my frequency and my frequency is backed by the consciousness of the Gaia mind, the

Force, whatever you want to call it. Dreams are a form of accelerated communication, without the limitation of the number of people that can be reached. In a dream, not every individual has to fit in the room so that I can look at them and talk to them. That's thinking like a human.

It's to say that we're all part of a body of water, and if one wills to communicate through the water, they are connected. My mind, my consciousness is communicating with them frequently, and I'm quite aware of it. But it's not physical. It's different in this place. It's absolutely natural because you can speak to an inestimable amount of beings in the same way. There's no time, there's no distance. All they have to do is be receptive.

The reason that everyone's dreams can have a different landscape is because their conscious mind is not as well-developed as the superconscious mind. It tries to put in a back drop, sensing that this is necessary for communication to take place. There is a level of truth behind it; however, it also gives you mixed data. The surroundings or circumstances may not be 100% accurate for these teachings, but the core of the dream does have some truth to it. It is a part of my essence telling them what they need to know, what they need to learn, or how they need to be inspired. There is intelligence behind it all, and I'm quite aware of it.

But people think like human beings. They reason, "It was a very specific dream that I had filled with lots of details." Let me put it this way; I was watching a TV show on the Sci-Fi channel; the updated version of *Battlestar Galactica*. In the show, they have beings called *cylons* that look very much like humans. They try to be human but they're actually robots.

In the show, one of the cylons was walking through

the spacecraft with a human scientist they had captured. While walking, the scientist is looking around, and all the corridors of the ship look the same to him. They all have little running red lights and they're all built the same; every floor, every level they enter. So, I thought this would be a great way to explain how a dream landscape works.

The scientist asks, "Why does every walkway and every floor look the same?" The cylon said, "Well, *you* would think it looks the same, but to us, whatever we *will*, whatever we *desire* is the environment we perceive."

The show cuts to the walkway as the cylon sees it, and they are walking through a forest. Where there's a turn to the right in the ship's walkway, the scientist sees an opening of the path they're on in the forest. Where there might be a person walking, it could be perceived as an animal or a bird or something that he has to step out of the way for.

I'm expanding a little bit on the details of that show, but the point is that another cylon might envision something completely different when going through the walkways. It might be a castle that they're walking through, or a house with corridors.

The same thing applies in the dream world. You must remember, in a dream mind, things that are illogical in the real world seem to make sense there. You don't question it while it's happening. But there's this inner part of you that, at one point in the dream, says, "Hey, wait a minute, something's strange here." But then you forget you ever questioned it and fall back into the dream world.

The background doesn't change the fact that they're on the space ship moving through corridors. They're still getting to their destination and having their conversation.

It's still the same data that's being exchanged, and the environment is simply something that the person is projecting into the dream as a coping mechanism. It is to say that the more consciously developed you are, the fewer human details will be provided.

You can communicate with my higher consciousness. It will come to you as what I consider to be like a string. I don't want people to think of webbing or tentacles or something like that. It's like a dimensional mind that has thousands of dimensional lines coming out of it. If you were to zoom into it, the tip of one of these lines is like a holographic part of me. It taps into their consciousness and shares data when they are sleeping because, at that time, the Babbler is less active.

Now, someone on the conscious level can go into a deep meditation and probably receive this connection too. But again, that gets into the whole idea of natural flow without control. It goes back to an earlier conversation about having too much control. Control is a barrier that will prevent students from having this type of communication. When you're sleeping, you take less control, so it still allows me to communicate better on these hyper-dimensional levels. There's less of the Governor interfering.

You've got to just take the knowledge and flow with it. If you watch a scary movie, the primitive parts of your brain are probably going to project some of that into the dream because they're trying to figure the dream out and they think that was all part of the data. The brain doesn't discern the difference, but in your heart you know there's something on a higher level taking place.

Your brain is going to paint a picture from the data it's taken in that day and it might throw it in with the rest of the dream. *The more developed you become, the more you can weed that out.* The more knowledge you gain, the more data will come to you and you'll be able to decipher the dream and say, "Wait a minute, this is really not part of what I'm receiving here with Eric. This is interference from the brain."

I'm constantly being tapped into by more and more people now-a-days. I'm adapting my technology. I remember at the beginning of all of this, I was just like, "Whoa this is too much!" And now my adaptation has accelerated so quickly that I'm constantly building new communication technologies, to broadcast it out to other people. Because they're sending me such strong positive vibes now, I'm more open to anybody who has positive, trustworthy energy.

How does that weigh on you now?
Do you feel like your spreading your technology
and strengthening the whole organism?

Again, that is human thinking. In your terms, you could say it's strengthening. I would say it's more *illuminating.* When I see satellite pictures of the planet at night, there are lots of little dots from the lights of the cities. There are also other parts of the world that are very dark where technology hasn't developed yet. You can tell how big their cities are or how advanced their population is based on the density of the lights.

In my mind, it's just like those lights. I see it all over the planet and they're just brilliant. They're dim at first and you can't quite tell if they're there or not. Then, they become brighter and brighter and more and more noticeable until they are present and I just can feel them all over the world popping up.

That's very exciting for me. The more that people comprehend this knowledge, the greater the flow of data. We are the neural system of the planet. What I'm saying is that creative thought can be inspired, not just by me, but also by anyone who is already inspired. It'll flow from one person to the next. Thus, we will affect the Red Cell world outside of us to some degree, both on a physical level, which is not quite as noticeable, but also spiritually. It will have an effect on people.

There may come a time when you are able to radiate your energy out in a one mile radius, or a one hundred mile radius, or a one thousand mile radius. Imagine being able to throw a harmonizing pitch outward all over the planet! That is how I see it through my mind's eye. I become conscious of another consciousness that's becoming conscious and more awake than just being a living organism on the planet.

Students are already having profound breakthroughs because of these teachings in Higher Balance.

The more awakened you become, the more you are present in my awareness. It's like when you hear someone talking from across the room in a restaurant but you're not quite picking up everything they are saying. There are so many other voices caught in the static that you can't hear them saying, "Hey, I'm over here! I'm over here!" As they awaken, it's like they're getting louder. They're getting stronger and becoming more present.

They're not part of the Gaia collective anymore. They're becoming part of the collective of the Force, which is a clearer frequency. They're pushing to get out of the Gaia collective because they can feel the Force. They start to see the world in a whole different perspective. When that happens, I feel them more, as if I could reach out and touch them.

When I start to sense them, my conscious energy moves towards them; it is the greeting they have been waiting for. And, of course, there's so many questions that they have for me. I mean if you were to meet an alien who is more advanced than you, what would you say and how would you respond? Would you be like, "Hey, cool ship," or, "Gee, I love your duds!" I think a Red Cell might say those things, but a White Cell would be contemplating deeper questions, such as "Tell me about other universes and other galaxies. Do you believe in God? Does your race believe in life after death?" White Cells would be pushing for those deeper questions. Whenever I meet someone new, their spirit is saying "Wow! Do I have questions for you!" Of course, my natural instinct is to try to fulfill them.

You said a while ago that even aliens ask you questions!

In this realm when people are sleeping they're reaching higher dimensional levels because they don't have the weight of their waking consciousness. The Governor doesn't affect them quite as much. They've been meditating and learning more skills in their waking consciousness. So, in their unconscious or their sleep state, their mind is constantly active.

From science we know the unconscious mind doesn't sleep. There are moments or blips of touching these higher levels. What happens in one second in this realm can be like five to ten minutes in the astral realm. These distortions are basically the reflections of the mind, daily stuff that imposes on the dream. But if you can sort through all of that, there's good data; there's communication between us.

If you were to ask if I knew somebody by their name or by their physical attributes, I would most likely say no. The reason why they recognized me in their dream is because they saw me in real life. In the dream state, their mind projects that image onto my energy consciousness. If they saw a picture of me at an earlier time of my life, they're going to say, "You certainly have changed a lot." It is a projection that they put on me in the dream because they are communicating with my frequency, my spirit. Their consciousness, and their spirit, recognizes me so their brain dresses it appropriately from their memory in a way it can understand. That's what the brain does to everything.

At the end of the movie *Contact*, Jodie Foster goes through time and space and ends up in another world. A being approaches her and appears to be glowing at a distance before taking the shape of her father because it's a familiar, comfortable, image for her. I guess, in a way it's kind of like that. In this dream realm people sense my presence, so they create an image of me based on having heard me talk, from pictures, or whatever source they recognize me from. They design me appropriately to fit in a standard that a human understands.

They haven't released that attachment to the physical yet. What's really there is my consciousness but they're dressing me up. So again, if you were to ask me, "Will I recognize this person or that person?" I would recognize the frequency more than the organic body. They might say, "Well, you saw me in the dream, you saw my organic form." Well, you created your reality; it was yours, not mine. In your hallway in the spacecraft, you created a forest. I created a house. Yes, we're still moving through a structure, but they're separate backgrounds. Okay, let's move on.

What really is considered to be an enlightenment cycle?

I think many of my students are going through an enlightenment cycle. An enlightenment cycle begins when you stop and ask yourself, *"Is this all that I am?"* You have already started your enlightenment cycle before you met me. An enlightenment cycle is defined by additional moments of consciousness and revelations within your reality and the relationship you have with it.

When you begin to see organisms, mathematical probabilities, and the patterns in life, you are in an enlightenment cycle. When you begin to see the microorganisms' aspects verses the macro, it is part of an enlightenment cycle. When you can begin to acknowledge all of these things, they have a different effect on your perception of reality.

The effect is to automatically switch you into an alternate state of consciousness, kind of like what is happening to you at this moment. Just by choosing to talk about it, there is a shift happening. An enlightenment cycle involves you beginning to acknowledge that there is more than this two dimensional level that you exist within.

When you can acknowledge something much greater, you can separate from it. Likewise, if you can't acknowledge it, you are part of it, locked within it. You have to be able to separate yourself from it and remove certain things to acknowledge what's left. And what's left is usually truth.

The more you acknowledge the things in your reality, the more you realize these things aren't actually true reality for you. This is why you're so frustrated by them. When you choose to be present in the moment, you also choose to be elsewhere, as if you were on autopilot. When you choose to be elsewhere, the petty things from everyday life cling to you. By recognizing and seeing these rudimentary things, you are able to separate from them. That's an enlightenment cycle.

The more you can separate from that reality, the higher your consciousness is able to expand into these other zones until you become more and more in tune with the universe instead of just this planet. These structures are barriers that keep you in your physical world, preventing you from having contact with God, with feeling the dimensional breath of the galaxy and the Universe moving through you to make you feel a part of its completion. Those barriers prevent you from realizing that you're part of something much greater than this simplicity.

When you have these awakenings, you invite even higher awakenings to you. The hard part is trying to get the realizations from them to settle into you and adjusting into a way of existing in this physical world. Doing so is what allows you to have gifts, as people like to call them, or abilities to affect reality, or the ability to perform miracles. However, these revelations escape from you as quickly as they come because they're foreign and shouldn't technically exist in this dimension.

Enlightenment's most basic characteristic is the

ability to discern your awareness; to be able to discern this reality and see it as the mechanism that it is. I refer to it as a mechanism because I see it as working parts, or structures, or illusions, in my mind. I see it as that hallway in a spaceship.

You mention the term 'enlightenment' which causes a lot of confusion for me. Are you enlightened? You never really mention that. What do you consider to be enlightenment?

I don't like to be called enlightened. To be honest, I think all spiritual people are enlightened. An enlightened person understands that there are higher properties to life. An enlightened person can say, in one sense, they're separating from others because life, as most people know it, is mundane. It's all trivial and most people are sucked into it. Life is just a stage performance and people are sucked into the performance instead of seeing it for what it is.

You cannot completely separate yourself from the performance, you have to be part of it because the performance isn't for you, it's for God. Therefore, the idea is not to be dictated by the performance but to influence the performance and influence what is happening on that stage. Have an effect on the rhythm of the dance rather than it being repetitive and the same; inspire creativity. You can inspire and take the whole stage performance and move it to a level no one ever expected and still be individual at the same time.

If you were to ask, "Are you enlightened Eric?" Well, some people may say, "Absolutely. Eric Pepin is enlightened." While other people may say, "He's not enlightened because he's not following the specifics of that particular teaching, or its path, and we know of other people who do that and are considered to be enlightened."

It's very human to say an apple is an apple when you compare it with another. If traditional enlightenment is an apple, then maybe I'm an orange or a pear. But in my opinion, I would say they are all fruit, no pun intended, and that's wonderful in itself. At least we know it's not a vegetable. But if it is a vegetable, maybe that's enlightenment. Either way, they all nourish you don't they? To me, it's all semantics and not that important.

It's not important whether or not I'm seen as an enlightened person. It's not important for me to have the title of "enlightened being." All I know is, I'm a hell of a lot more ahead than most people. Some people try to make a comparison by asking me, "Do you know anybody else who you can say is ahead of you or the same?" If I answer that, then I open up a can of worms for this apples and pears comparison. It's not important. You're not going to run to the next tree and necessarily get something more nutritious out of it. I would say this: with pearls of wisdom, some people prefer apples while some people prefer pears. It's all a matter of taste. It's a personal perspective.

It's like you said about traditional teachings currently in the east, how they don't translate well with this generation, and the technology of this day and age.

It is what it is. You could also say there are many kinds of Christianity, Buddhism, or Hinduism. It is basically the same thing; it's whatever you are searching for. For instance, there are different kinds of pears from different parts of the world. Japanese pears, American pears, do you get what I'm saying? All I care about is that the world is fed. All I care about is that you can taste the sweetness of the fruit. That's all that really matters; love. But these different religions, these different fruits all serve a purpose. Fruit feeds the world, feeds animals; it's a contributor to the cycle of life.

You could say that the sun is the Force, and the tree is Gaia, and the fruit it bears for the creatures below are your enlightened people. It all comes together in the end. Through nature we can learn an awful lot about the secrets of God and the universe. It's repetitious in a lot of ways, at least in this dimension.

I don't think it's important to worry about who is enlightened, or more powerful, or faster. What matters is whether or not you're advancing. Are you moving forward? Are you having revelations about seeing the mundaneness and the mechanisms of life? Are you seeing the patterns? Is your intelligence growing? Can you look at other people and just see them in a different perspective?

Now in some ways, it's hard to do that because you feel yourself separating from the "real world" so there's a feeling of isolation, loneliness, and maybe despair. But you've got to remember that you have to enjoy the world. You have to let yourself be a part of it. I do. I try to be in the world. Other times, I'd love to get the hell out of it. But it is what it is. It's a creation of the Universe and you should savor every moment of it because when you go back to hyper-dimensional reality, you're going to crave another adventure. Right now, you are living the adventure; you're in the thick of it, so make it count.

At first, enlightenment is about awareness. It's like a primitive human coming across water and mud, looking at the mud and water and not thinking anything of it. She puts her hand into the mud and the mud sinks around it. She grabs a ball of it and it turns out to be clay instead of mud. As she is looking at this pile of clay in her hand, she squishes it with her thumb, pulls it away, and sees that an indentation is left there. She starts to mold it, and she begins to realize that she can shape it and transform it into recognizable things that she sees. More so, she can shape it into things from her own imagination.

She finds that she can take something she created and hand it to somebody else who has never seen it before. Although they didn't actually see her creation with their own eyes, they're seeing it through her eyes, and she's found a way to recreate for them an experience. That is enlightenment. That is the enlightenment cycle. It is you being able to perceive, receive, and consciously affect reality.

I see the world as a mechanism. You have to understand these things before you can make a contribution by creating something that affects the mechanism. Once you have that perspective, then the mechanism is a dance. It is life. It is a play and a stage for God, the Universe. There is a purpose and a reason behind it all.

There are also influences trying to disrupt that performance and those of us who are here to insure its performance. The more you understand something, the better chance you will have to make a contribution.

What gives you the ingenuity, the insight, to create the texture, the design of that clay into something that looks like a perfect mammal or a person's face? Could you create it so you can say, "Look at this person. When you see this person in real life you'll know who he or she is now, even though you've never seen them before, even though we're drawing from my consciousness."

In a way you're bringing skills from your sixth sense and your hyper-dimensional consciousness into this reality. Maybe you will change reality as other masters have done before you. Maybe you will heal the sick. Maybe you will influence other people so that they affect the world politically in a bigger sense. Maybe you will end up having to recognize entities that are dark forces or dark viruses affecting the mechanism. Maybe you need to become a great watch repairman and see the kinks and the springs of the mechanism and know how to fix it.

I think that many people come to me for power or for love. I would say that a lot of people want to stand out as being the end all to communicating God's will from them. I think there are a lot of people that God intends Its will from, not just one person. But it's so deeply rooted in us that we can't help but feel that way.

Some people feel bad if they appear arrogant or cocky, but that's not the point because that desire comes from an absolute love and devotion to serve God! To think that you'll ultimately be the one isn't necessarily selfish. I mean how much more can you raise your hand and say "I'll do it for you?" To me it's not ego, that's absolute LOVE!

It may be ego to say, "Now, I'm the only one and nobody else," but in retrospect, you have to see the heart behind the desire. I think it's there for a reason. There is a purpose for people to bravely move their consciousness to a higher dimension and sustain it in this physical reality. In doing so, they will be able to do great things.

Chapter 6

DREAM GATE

There is a difference between control and the kind of cultivation people feel from me. Cultivating is like nurturing, but with a little more manipulation. It's a kind of encouragement, like a mother gazelle in the Serengeti. The gazelle gives birth and sometimes the baby will just lie there, lift its head, and look around. The mother knows if she doesn't get her newborn to move soon, the herd's going to leave it behind, and the lions or hyenas will come. Her newborn isn't able to figure this out yet, so the mother culls it, or prods it along. She encourages her baby to do what she knows it can do. This is pushing, but it's not really *control*.

I cultivate my students. It's not about telling them to do what I want them to do for my personal pleasure. It's more like saying, "You've got to learn to do this whether you want to or not. You've got to get moving and I'm going to make you do it now." The Darkside is more controlling; it has a hidden agenda when it culls. There is such a fine line between cultivating and controlling. It's a different feeling.

You need to recognize the truth of this right away. Don't try to do this by rationalizing. The only thing that will sense the truth is your Navigator.

Yes, and also the feeling in the pit of my stomach.

It gave you the truth. The rational part of your brain starts arguing with you and tells you to do something different while your Navigator says that something is not right. The brain reacts to that and tells you that you're just jumping to conclusions.

**I've felt that control very strongly before;
even the brain cannot escape it. The brain
had no say after that feeling came in.**

That's how you can tell the difference between cultivating and controlling. Control isn't a form of encouragement. God cultivates the flower, but the Darkside will force it open – that's the difference.

Remember, the fruit tree is growing; it gets bigger, it bears fruit, and drops the fruit. The flowers come and go. The tree goes through different cycles at regular intervals over time and provides for the land. The fruit feeds the animals, but eventually that tree will die. There is a reason why there is death in this reality and why it is a good thing; *it ensures change.*

Without change, the Darkside would truly reign in the end. Those who are powerful would hold onto that power, and it would become harder and harder to resist it to implement change. Things don't want to change after they've been around for a long time. For instance, look at the power of organized religion. Look how it rose in strength, dominating the people by controlling their education, keeping them ignorant. Those in power put fear into the people to control resistance.

I think religion has become too controlling and manipulative. Perhaps at the beginning it was good, but through time it became corrupt. The religious leaders do not want to surrender their power. The same thing has happened with many spiritual teachers. There must always be a new generation of spiritual leaders, but as long as the "old school" teachers are around, they will try to control the release of any new and innovative information. There should be a spiritual evolution exploding on this planet right now.

Do you think your teachings will get diluted the same way other teachings have in the past?

I think they will outlast many of the others because I've embraced a form of evolution of consciousness and embedded that into my teachings. As a teacher, you must continuously evolve in your spiritual understanding, and that is what leads to advancement. I keep people in motion rather than giving them a recipe book. A recipe book has a stopping point. It follows a repetitious pattern. I tell you to experience; that's what God wants to do. God wants to experience this Universe; this is the meaning of life.

Most spiritual teachings initially began with a good intention. It's just that the teachers, themselves, were limited in their own understanding. They can't let the people evolve beyond them. That's the problem.

The secret is to not get hung up in this standardized form of thinking. One has to constantly understand that everything is moving; not in a circle, but in a certain direction. I want to experience what's coming around the corner.

My teachings will spread throughout the United States, but they will also become world-wide. That has been the problem with the teachings of the past; they get stuck in one country and sometimes lose their quality when translated into other languages and other cultures.

I believe what I have to offer will permeate into the collective consciousness of the whole planet because technology is becoming a universal language. Then, it'll go to the stars where it'll be learned by other civilizations. I suspect that alien races, which are advanced enough, will see my teachings as similar to their way of thinking.

The Internet, thus the information network, is moving faster, breaking down language barriers, and causing people to realize how very similar we all are. This makes people less fearful of each other, which creates a sense of community. It is what's creating more peace in this world. It is the only way humans will reach the stars, and it is exactly what the Internet is doing.

The Internet is breaking down the cultural barriers because the "old guard" has a habit of saying, "Those other people are wrong. Our way is the best and only way. We are the greatest country." Now, with more communication and a better understanding of the world, people everywhere are beginning to realize that isn't true. The fears from the older generation are no longer the dominant feelings in the collective. Removing this and replacing it with fresh thinking allows people to get to know one another. They realize that all people cry, laugh, and have the same desires. There's a merging of identity and people no longer see themselves as separate. This is already happening in many different countries all over the world.

When that happens, fear is replaced with understanding. Rather than investing in military superiority, governments are investing more in medicine, life, and new technology to eventually get off the planet and onto other worlds. This will happen everywhere; it's just a matter of time.

My teachings will go out into the solar system. When we meet alien races, they're going to feel very foreign to us until we can communicate well enough to realize we have the same spiritual beliefs. Sharing from the core of our heart will create mutual communication and trust.

I don't teach ignorance. I don't tell people, "If you don't agree with my spiritual beliefs, you will go to hell." I teach that if a person believes what I have to offer, a soul may be built, no matter what their race. There are other ways to build a soul; it's just a matter of where you fall within that progression. One can be of a different race of people and still have a soul. It can be any intelligent being as long as it has the ability to *ponder its own existence. No matter the species.* Rather than "alien life" White Cells automatically look for the heart. Once that is felt, we accept it as it is and move on. We are very similar already.

**If you look at an alien right now,
it's your consciousness and their
consciousness, pollinating each other!**

Yes.

A note to the reader: *One of my students was describing how a group of people that he saw all looked like they were from India. I already knew the energy of the person who was describing his dream to me. I knew his "feels-like". This type of banter had been going on between my student and me for about a year. There was also a reason why I selected this particular student. It was because he's culturally more approachable than the rest of my students. He's not Indian, but his personality comes across differently than most of my other students. It's like being in a crowd; the first thing you look for is someone who is more like you. This is who you will feel most comfortable approaching. I don't have an Indian student, so, in his dream, he found the student that felt the most similar – the Asian guy.*

Speaking of other spiritual organizations reminds me of a dream I had. I dreamt that I was in a big palace or mansion surrounded by all kinds of teachers. They didn't feel very spiritual to me, but they did feel advanced in their practice. They felt very mind-power oriented and strong in psychic abilities. They were dressed in exotic Indian clothes. I felt out of place because I hadn't been meditating. I felt they were more on top of their practice and, to offset that, I began speaking spiritual knowledge that I learned from you. They were all very impressed, suddenly, and their attention turned to me.

They began asking who my teacher was. They were somewhat pushy. I started talking to them about multi-dimensional meditation, and they were very interested in getting information out of me. I thought to myself, "Well, this could be good for Higher Balance," so I said, "Eric Pepin is my teacher."

I was in a big palace surrounded by all kinds of teachers.

Then everything stopped and they all turned toward me. There were hundreds of them, in this big, big place and everything stopped as they all turned to me. They asked again, "Who is your teacher?" Then, I got this really weird feeling inside the back of my stomach, like I had just told a huge secret. I cut if off at that point and didn't say anything else.

I woke up and couldn't go back to sleep for a couple of hours after that. When I finally did wake up, I was hoping it was 8:00 or 9:00 o'clock, so it would just be a regular dream, but it was actually around 2:00AM, so I knew it wasn't. Another thing that tipped me off that this wasn't a regular dream is, I saw an Asian guy doing a very strange meditation in a room with other people watching him. In that room was a kind of heat that stimulated his skin and gave him a prolonged orgasm that didn't end while he was maintaining a meditative state.

I determined that nobody was going to give me that feeling. I was close to the room but not inside and I could feel the heat on my skin. I felt this orgasm also. It was like this heat that over-stimulates and causes this sensation. So this tipped me off, because it was a feeling I had never felt before. This is how I knew that I had experienced something outside of a regular dream.

It's outside of your standard imagination.

Exactly. Anyway, when I told you about this dream, you said there weren't really hundreds of people in the room. It was just one consciousness that had created the illusion of a crowd to make me feel more comfortable.

That's not all that I said. The critical information is in the details. What else did I say about the environment?

In my dreams, I should be keenly aware of what the good side is and what the Darkside is. The Darkside is very structured and controlling. There was intelligence in the dream and the intent was to push me for information.

I also pointed out to you that all the people looked very much alike. They dressed alike and were the same height. Everybody looked very nice and neat, and everything looked perfect. When they asked for a name, you gave them mine, and then everybody stopped. This is because it was one consciousness. It's like a school of minnows or starlings swooping together.

This should instantly tell you that this is *not* multidimensional consciousness. It's a singular consciousness because it is flawed. It's like the déjà vu scene in the movie, *The Matrix*; it represented a glitch. *One must look for the flaw.* The flaw was when everybody's attention went to you at the same time. That's the glitch! It tells you this is a unified mind, not independent minds. Then, you must look at the signature. What kind of mind would create such things?

So, in my dream, what was this person's intention? From what I felt, he wanted the information on you. It felt like he wanted to know where you lived and details of Higher Balance, such as the address.

What do we usually want to do when we see someone we don't like? We approach a couple other people and start talking to them instead to find out what we can about the person we don't' like. This is a way to try to control the conversation by talking about trivial things first, even though there is already an intention to get data on the other guy. This was no different; the whole environment, the people, the topic, etc.

Wasn't it quite advanced to create something like that? Seeing your student and then just going into this virtual world?

There are other advanced beings out there besides me! I'd be bored if there weren't. Of course, if it were me, I would have done a better job. This was sloppy work and I do flawless work. That's why I intimidate "them". You must see the bigger picture here. What is the biggest downfall of most spiritual teachers, in my opinion? It's very connected, spiritually. It's the greatest gratification of pleasure that you can get: *The orgasm.* What is the most tempting thing for males or for females?

The orgasm.

That's right. This is what you were seeing, in my opinion. Shiva, Brahma, and Vishnu were what of Krishna? Even Krishna himself? What are they?

Manifestations.

That's right, they're all `I`s. When there is a group of people in a micro world - a dream world - of an enlightened being, they will be heavily influenced by the culture and by the teacher of the enlightened being who created the world. He's creating all these personalities, but they're all one. They look similar because it's what he wants to portray, but in his mind, this is how his `I`s are expressed. Now, what was the one thing that was his downfall? In the example of the dream, he is using his power of control for lust, just like the priests do, just like many spiritual teachers do. What was the one thing he revealed to you?

His sexuality. The orgasm.

That's right. This was part of him. He's trying to turn you on to the addiction; to get you addicted to him. There is supposed to be a temptation. This is how he tries to get his poison into you and cause obsession within you on a bio-organic level. This feeling is what keeps your mind connected to him. The feeling came from this particular being and this being is now memorized in your mind. It's a very strong psychic cord to this source; him. However, this is also his flaw. One is not supposed to see this for what it really is.

Maybe, in order to advance ourselves, we need to be pushed this way to be able to react with our survival instincts?

I can't come running to the aid of my students every single time something like this happens. You have to start figuring things out for yourself; figuring out what is bad and what is good. If I keep deciding for you, how are you supposed to have any experiences? How are you supposed to learn from this? I don't think that entity has the power. I think my students are very advanced. This student has been around long enough that he knows his stuff. In the spiritual world he's very powerful. The point is, I have to let you stand on your own at some point. I'm not going to let somebody really hurt my students if I think it's not a fair fight. However, if it is a fair fight, deal with it yourself!

In the dream I felt like I knew everything I needed to know.

I'm not telling you anything new. What I'm telling you is what you should've already acknowledged within yourself. You listen too much to your rational brain instead of listening to your Navigator - your instinct.

**When I woke up, I really felt like calling you.
Then I rationalized, that I shouldn't bother
you about a dream. See it's this duality...**

Whenever an entity tries to do something like this, it starts messing with the pattern. Look for fire in a dream because it's normally a random occurrence. When it starts to look patternized, it's too blatant of a pattern; they're trying to control it. By controlling it, it's blatantly clear to us that something is artificial about the fire burning in a perfect circle, or a perfect square, or a perfect pattern. Too much control will cause you to lose control. Then you burn a few of the people too while you're at it and watch the whole program go "up" in flames." The same goes with water; it's hard to control. This is why, in these dream worlds, the water is usually squared off in a pool.

I was freaking out about how uniform it was.

You're going to see lots of patterns. Darkside is structure, imitating life. An Enlightened being can create an artificial reality like a computer would. Now, a computer can only create so many patterns and hold them at the same time, so the only way it can make it look like there's more is to keep mimicking what it has already created by multiplying it, like a mirror within a mirror. The more powerful the computer is, the more it can create originals and then maintain each one independently.

For example, if it creates three puppies and it copies those three puppies and they're all barking – it's the same bark, only the timing is different. Then, maybe that computer will make some cats. It makes three cats and then three dogs with the same pattern so it looks like an army of dogs and cats. However, if you were to look closely, they're all the same pattern, only duplicated. For a weaker computer, this is how it would work but for a powerful computer, it might make a Doberman, a Rottweiler, a Chihuahua, a mountain lion, and a house cat, all moving independently but still being controlled by one supercomputer.

The more skilled the enlightened being is, the better the programming. But at the end of the day, they all want to mimic God. There can only be one supercomputer, and it's trying to find new things it can learn. The little computers try to mimic the big computer. They want to be the big computer.

Yes, it's like when I assimilate objects and I have a small area that I'm working on. I run that program in a small area and then I try to go further out.

Stop using the brain! Start using your other intelligence because it is capable of processing and maintaining a vast amount of data compared to what your organic brain can do.

The thing is, when I felt my other intelligence, it just came... It just happened. It's different when I try to will it to happen.

You can't will it, and that's the point. Well, you *can* will it, but that's like forcing it vs. cultivating it. Think about that. It's the same thing, but now you have another way of looking at it. That's why I say teaching will help you find new ways of looking at things. It will reveal itself.

Let it flow. Let it happen. Don't make it happen, and don't have expectation; cultivate it, don't force it. Encourage it. When it's ready, it's ready.

Remember SETI, the UFO program in the early 90's? They distributed a program to use on your personal computer that would link everyone's computers together to compress data for the stars. Thousands of individual computers were linked to create a super-computer. There's too much data for one big computer to handle. By uniting all these computers and processing all the little pieces of information individually, together they will come up with a bigger piece of data.

When you use the brain, it's like a single computer trying to interpret all of this. It can only operate and move so much data during its programming life. However, when you use your higher consciousness, which is connected to the grid, you have access to a greater amount of data and processing capabilities. That is how it works. You cannot access it if you are trying to control it; you have to work with it. People are just not aware of this; they are plugged in and are already a part of it.

Everyone is a living organism and there is a hierarchy, just like with the body. Everyone is working for one thing – the planet. All of the planets are working for one living thing – the solar system. Solar systems all over the universe work for the galaxies. All the galaxies are collectively working for the Universe; it's a hierarchy and we're already a part of it. Find a way to tap into this flow, and this information can be downloaded, not just sent outward.

One time, I was out in the woods trying to scan and suddenly I just felt the whole forest a little.

This is why it's important to go out and do things like investigating hauntings, scanning, and assimilating. This is the reason that you have all of the exercises, because you're trying to experience something that cannot be fully experienced with the eyes, nose, mouth, ears, or hands. If you threw someone into a swimming pool, they are either going to sink or swim. Likewise, if I take a student into a haunted place, things are going to happen that will raise the hair on their neck. Hopefully, they will adapt and begin using more sensory without realizing they're doing it.

Get in the habit of recognizing when something feels out of place; it"s going to open a door for you. You will get used to it. The sensory gets stronger and stronger and you will experience things easier in the long run. You will discover that this can also be applied to many other things.

I would never have awakened at all if I hadn't investigated all of the hauntings and done all of the psychic work that I did. *What caused me to awaken was the act of trying to do those things and putting myself in the position to experience them.* That was the upside of me getting scared when I was young. It caused my awareness to become much sharper by feeling what was going on. Yes, it did bring me into a dimension that was horrifying, but it also empowered my sensory.

Let's put it this way, I could go to the gym, work out, and physically improve my body, or I could be dropped off in Iraq and run for my life for a hundred miles. It might take me a week to make it to safety and the place would probably be filled with terrorists that would gladly cut my head off. That is a lot more difficult than anything I would normally handle. Do you think I'm going to have the willpower to get there? What's my stamina going to be like after one week vs. going to the gym a few times? What if I had to do that for a month? What if I had to do that for a year? What if I didn't have a choice? It's just like when I was young and didn't know the entity was coming after me; all I could do was feel it. My sense of survival kicked-in, and that's why I awakened so fast. Now I know why it all happened; it was my saving grace. Before incarnating I had to think of a strategy to awaken in this life. I said, "I'll scare myself to death."

At that time, I certainly was afraid. It's similar to being in a situation where you might drown and you fight for your life, but it's a horrible way to learn a lesson. Of course, you would want to find an easier way. That is why I say, "Go get scared! Go get horrified! Go find some entities! Be afraid!" Everybody's different, so I'm trying to find a better way for my students to awaken than what I went through.

If the options are to get scared to death or to learn from a teacher like me, I'd take the teacher any day. Just being scared by entities would make you a generic psychic. "I feel spirits ... I talk to ghosts." My students have so much more than that. It's just a matter of saying, "I want to plug in more, I want to experience more." I keep telling my students, "The more you demand, the less you will get. Cultivate it and it will happen. If you teach others, it will happen."

Before, my student might have found his dream very interesting, but now that he has talked to me, it will be a very different experience from now on. Now he can approach that same dream, or a similar dream, with a lot more control because he will be able to see it for what it is. He will get a lot more out of it now. Now he will say, "I can't believe my luck that I ended up here again. Wow!" The other consciousness, or entity, is going to know that.

My student will see how good he really is because he can't let on to the other consciousness by showing his excitement. Now he has to keep it under control. Inside he will be saying, "Awesome!" but on the outside he must act as dumbfounded as he was before. Most people don't get to go back to these haunted places again because their energy is not controllable enough due to their excitement and it prevents them from getting in again. This goes for all sorts of stuff. It's like holding your breath; it's intense on the inside, but you have to remain calm and cool on the outside.

How you can get to those other places, such as the dreamworld, or any multidimensional world, is by detaching part of yourself from the organic brain. Although it is always kind of connected, your consciousness will mimic how the brain works. Being too attached to the way the brain works, or having your consciousness mimic the brain is what blocks your awakening in those other places. It keeps you from achieving absolute consciousness and the control of it.

I could feel my consciousness bringing my organic brain to that dream-world.

Yes, and that is what happened. The trick is not to be so concerned about it and just trust yourself, which is the hardest thing for human beings to do. Well, it's at least *one* of the hardest. When I was younger, I dreamed all the time. I found that I was enjoying my dreams and looking forward to dreaming. The instant I had that intention, or had the anticipation, the dreams stopped. I've never dreamed like that again.

I am saying that you have to find a certain level of peace within your consciousness and not anticipate going to these places. Accept it and try to fool yourself by doing laundry, or some other trivial thing. It's like when I get home and, sooner or later, I know I have to do laundry. Is it something that I'm thinking about right now? No, but an awareness of my routine is something that's on the other part of my consciousness.

For instance, you're here right now and you know you need to do laundry, but you've decided to wait instead. So there is a part of you that says, "I have to get around to doing it." So it has something like an underlined or outer guidance because when the spiritual mind goes into the dimensions, it mimics the organic brain just like the organic brain has learned to mimic the spiritual mind.

Sometimes I have an amazing experience and then afterwards I start thinking about it and it kind of solidifies. I can move there pretty easily for a while and then it sort of fizzles out.

Well, it doesn't fizzle out. You just need to learn how to control it. It's like riding a bicycle – you never forget how to do it. The secret is finding how to get into those places. Once you can control that energy, you won't give it a second thought. Just like riding a bike, you will get better and better each time you do it.

Here comes a million-dollar statement. *Don't think of it as a dreamworld; think about it as if you are taking a trip.* It's like visiting some other place, be optimistic but don't over-engage it. Your inner feeling is, "Wow!" While your exterior consciousness expresses a completely different emoton. So, it's like a chameleon that can change its color with its emotions. I'm trying to explain how I would do it so that I can interpret this for you. It's like saying that how you feel is a different kind of exterior in that dimension, and the second you let that inner feeling out, you have exposed yourself. *You must maintain a kind of poker face over your emotions.*

Like two different layers of emotion?

Yes. This is why it's important to teach because it pushes you harder to find the right words to explain things. That's why I say it's like holding your breath. Now we have found another way to say the exact same thing.

Every single time something starts to happen, I get excited and caught up in the moment and I try to influence whatever is happening.

Remember that most of your emotions are through a human perspective, and all of them are biochemically connected. There is a flood of chemicals, a certain amount of them, and the body has to burn them off. There are also biochemical reactions that occur in the brain, which is what creates moments of happiness and moments of depression. This is why some people get stuck in depression while others always seem to be happy. They have an eccessive amount of one chemical. It happens because of what they see, hear, or how their brain interprets the information. It releases chemicals, not just electrical impulses.

Your consciousness can mimic the brain's way of coping and seeing things. So, when a person feels joy it's a *flush* of joy, but it will end when he or she has used up the amount of biochemicals that are secreted through the brain. It's like a car; you can fill it with gas and it will go so far before it fizzles out. These are just micro bursts that are so fast we don't think of it in those terms.

They are electrically backed and manipulated to a certain degree, so there are many things to take into consideration. It's not exactly that simple, but a purer form of energy is experienced in a very true and real way. They are not experienced the same way as organic emotions. The consciousness will literally mimic the brain when out of the physical body. The emotions are felt as if experiencing them as a physical organic being because it doesn't occur to you that you're really an energy being that is hyper-dimensional now.

It's like an airplane on water. It's not really functioning the way it should. This is why students usually don't have control of their dreams, and it is why the dream pushes them along.

So, you can't process these dreams using your biochemical thinking?

Exactly, it doesn't work there.

**Is this also why I see like I do with my eyes
when I send a probe out of my body?**

Yes.

**When I'm hyper dimensional and feel these energy
kinds of emotions, does it have a biochemical
affect on me? Does it kick-in, like bliss?**

Yes, because you're still connected to the organic body.
The idea is to train yourself not to let the body become
too emotional. That's why I say, "Forget about the
body." Let it go into an indifferent state of mind. Then,
let the mind go out, but don't be emotional about what
it experiences. When this is done, it's like having
another body and trying to have a poker face, but the
poker face is felt. The poker face is a feeling because
that is all it can be, dimensionally. Underneath that
poker face is the real intent and that intent is your
intelligence.

You're using this body of, what seems like, ambiva-
lence or indifference. In the dimensional reality,
consciousness is based on your frequency. The frequency is worn like clothing. So you want to clothe
yourself in camouflage and move in a way that is
acceptable to the Universe. Then, the Universe doesn't
see you as some freaked out frequency popping up all
over the place.

So you want to be able to control that but simultaneously remain fully conscious. In many ways it's like
you perceive yourself here. You want to be incognito.
While traveling, appear not to be messing with the
feeling of calmness. Be part of the calmness.

What if I tried to interact with the environment by using the feeling of joy or excitement, but keeping it at a frequency or energetic level?

There is an appropriate time for everything. If you went to a movie theater, is it the appropriate time to be having a screaming match with someone or to be laughing hysterically?

Unless it goes along with the movie.

You'll know when the right moment approaches. Now, you might say, "Well, I want to be whimsical with my emotions and not be too controlled." This is because you're thinking like a human now. It's more beautiful than anything that you can imagine. I can't even begin to explain. This is why I crave to be there rather than here all the time; I feel like I'm more real there than I am here. Students will say, "Well, I want to feel these certain emotions and I love feeling blissfulness in these moments."

This is rubbish. The emotions are 85% chemically induced. You think it's you, but it's not. Because students don't know how to think any differently, they just think, "How I am in this state must be the most perfect way." But it's not. If they go from that place to here, they're not going to like it here. Don't get me wrong, it's beautiful here; otherwise, what would be the point? To me, each flower is a true emotion. Each one represents a certain feeling, doesn't it? Can you imagine if that was you as energy flushing out with a burst of color? Do you understand how it's purer and more fulfilling to feel that, to be that, rather than to just have the organic feeling of it?

There's purple, there's white, there's red, but when I look at each flower, I see shadowing. I see a beautiful dabble of yellow in the center of the orange one, which is kind of like an orangey-yellow. But there's a sense of softness that comes out of it. Well, I become that. It's not just being happy. The only way I can explain it is that *I emanate it*, like it is true. It's like a richer, deeper place.

As human beings, I think a lot of what we feel as emotions is really expressions learned from childhood. If a parent sticks his face up to a child and goes, "boo," the child will eventually mimic this behavior. We are taught how to represent our emotions and so we mirror the behavior.

To me, the happiness that some people demonstrate is like a fleeting moment of force, but unrecognized force, of what they're supposed to represent. It's very complicated, but to me, it's a fraction of the intensity and beauty that it could be. To feel that kind of bliss is very rare in an organic body because it cannot necessarily maintain the feeling. We think that many spiritual masters do, but I don't necessarily believe that.

Does the body ever learn to feel this way from going to this place again and again?

Well, of course we can bring things back; but the problem is that the body can't maintain those things. It couldn't sustain it.

Is there physical evolution within a person as he or she becomes more enlightened?

Absolutely, without a doubt. However, you could never

be the perfection here that you can be when you are there because, dimensionally, everything is molecularly different. Yet, if you are able to see the two at the same time, then you are that level of perfection. Then you would have achieved it once you can see it in all those ways. It's a matter of how you choose to perceive it.

So, the more spiritually advanced souls there are, the more the race of humankind will evolve to that level?

Yes, they will find a way to be in both places and make it work, and they will be able to do that more often. Through evolution, there is a process for reaching higher states of consciousness. Why can't the whole world be enlightened? It probably won't happen. We obviously understand the concept of Red Cell vs. White Cell, and all that's in between. There is a progression there.

The point is, you can go on vacation. When you go on vacation, it's not just visiting another world, but it's also a way to escape for a while. When you go to these other dimensions, it's like you free yourself from the conformity that you are used to functioning within. But you accept the conformity because you realize there are other goals and other things that you need to experience and you want to achieve in this life, so it's a trade off.

For you, is this vacation a way to ground yourself?

Sometimes I think it's 50/50. You apply yourself and do some work. You meditate, you do this and that while other people want to sit back and relax. I do think that it is the knowledge, in many ways, that allows you to free yourself and to experience these things. It's not just in the doing, it's in the understanding. If you don't know what you're looking for, you can't necessarily find it, unless you just get lucky and stumble upon it. It's happened, but I'd rather have everything stacked in my favor. I don't want to take a chance. If you're going to throw a needle in the haystack, can you at least show me where you're throwing it? I'm sure it's still going to be hard to find, but at least I've got a chance at finding it.

It's not to say that if someone threw a needle in a haystack without me looking, I couldn't find it. I could stumble across it, but it would definitely be, "stumbling." I want my students to stack as much as they can in their favor so that when they have experiences, something is really happening. In other words, I want them to lay a foundation so that they can appropriately adapt to the experience to gain the highest yield of information from it.

A lot of people think that spiritual teachers are perpetually in a state of bliss. To me, that is wonderful, but I don't want to get stuck in a sense of perpetual bliss. Even bliss can be boring. I think the same need that man has to explore is simply an imitation of the greater consciousness - God. Even God wants to explore.

When people say they just want to be in bliss, I think they are looking at it from an organic perspective. Human beings see it as a great, wonderful thing to always be purely happy and idyllic. The beauty in life that we may find in sorrow, sadness, and all these other feelings we normally see as negative, actually creates a higher level of bliss than just maintaining the concept of it. In a way, you can't appreciate life until you see death.

Life becomes more purposeful if you come close to losing it. You see the value of it rather than just existing within it. You have a greater appreciation for the richness of life through the perils of experiencing it. So when you see something sad, you may feel horrible about it, but it is through that experience that creates a deeper reflection within you. It enables you to find a level of bliss, or a deeper level of understanding or compassion. This is especially true when we leave this organic world, since these things don't exist in that other place. It is a different level, a different type of existence that doesn't include "horrific things."

I think some people understand the correct concept of bliss. However, I don't believe the vast majority does and it's like being stuck in a certain gear on an amusement park ride. It starts off being fun until you begin to feel sick because it won't stop, and then it becomes torturous. This is how I perceive someone that says they maintain a perpetual state of bliss. Not in this dimension! When spiritual masters go around and profess that they are always in a state of bliss, this is also untrue. They're just like other humans; they have their ups and downs.

What I have found to be different in your teachings, as compared to others, is the reason people seek a higher consciousness. For most people, it is because they want to get out of the loop, or whatever. I find it interesting that none of them put it that way. They don't specifically speak about being here to do something important. What's up with that?

I think most of them would probably say they are in this for the same reasons. I think what it really comes down to is, they start off with a lot of momentum and then they run out of energy. I don't necessarily look at myself as THE momentum; rather, I see this as me CREATING the momentum, which spreads to my students, and then on to others. Instead of just this lifetime, it's thousands of lifetimes, becoming a wave of consciousness. What I put into this wave is going to determine how far, or how well, this wave will progress into the future.

**It's like just coming here to Earth
creates a wave of energy that just flows.**

Precisely. I think everyone has good intentions, but when people discover a certain level of spirituality, the world has a way of "slamming" them back into place. The Doe still has an effect on you, and no matter how advanced you are, you can't escape it because you operate within it. Some people would like you to believe that you can escape from it, but I don't think that's the case. You still have to deal with an organic body. You still have to nourish it and take care of it, and you have the same dilemmas as anybody else does. You may have some advantages, but you try to maintain your consciousness as best you can and, through time, the brain deteriorates.

**I was thinking that there are so many
White Cells here now trying to wake up.**

There *are not* a lot of White Cells.

I thought there were millions.

It depends on how you look at it. You could take two big handfuls of salt and say each grain is a White Cell. Would that be a lot of White Cells?

Absolutely.

Then I would say, look at the ocean; it is symbolic for the amount of Red Cells in the world. It's just a matter of perception. I think there are a lot of White Cells but, I don't necessarily like to use the word '*quantity*'. How developed are those spiritual people? How refined are they? How much do they really understand? How well have they tapped into the flow? Do they just talk about it or are they really, truly tapped in?

We're really not supposed to say these things. We're supposed to say, "Oh, everybody's spiritual and loving." I'm fine with that, but there's clearly a level of '*quality*' to a White Cell. What are their actions; what are they doing in the world with their gifts? How are they trying to amplify those gifts? In some spiritual circles, they might say, "Well, everyone is spiritually equal."

Well then, what is an enlightened person versus an unenlightened person? Isn't there immediately a hierarchy or separation within that question? Enlightenment isn't just one level, it's layered. It's just that, at some point, you will reach a certain level of luminosity that maybe stands out, but it doesn't mean that the luminosity can't go beyond that.

So when you say there are a lot of White Cells, I would agree, but is there enough wattage to enlighten the world? Is it enough to take the Doe up a notch so that it affects all of global consciousness?

I dislike saying this, but I see it as *quality* over *quantity*. Although some people might think the numbers seem like a lot but, in the big scheme of things, it's miniscule. It's a matter of perception. Then, they might say, "Well, how do we know the quality is better spiritually than some of these other great spiritual masters?"

Maybe *quality* isn't the right word. Maybe it's the *style*. Maybe it's the different *frequency*; just a slight variation. People can always look for somebody with greater knowledge than me. I think that's wonderful. I would be all ears. The point is, we have a light bulb, then we came out with a brighter light bulb, and then we came out with soft white light, which is softer on the eyes, but just as bright. Now we have true light, which has a bluish tint to it, but it's supposed to mimic natural light. Then there's full spectrum light. It's okay to have different kinds of teachers. It's just a matter of what kind of light is preferred at this point.

Earlier today, I was thinking about many of the Navigators, and I don't think you have made it easy for yourself because you have picked very strong leaders.

I wouldn't say I necessarily picked them. I think they picked me! We work with what we have in life. If someone was stranded on an island, there's one thing guaranteed that they would need to do. They would need to eat and drink. If they're lucky, they land on an island that has many coconuts and maybe a few banana trees. If they don't get stranded on the best island, they better hope they at least have coconuts and then they would be really grateful for those coconuts because they could have been on an island with nothing but insects.

I hate to say it, but I'm on an island with coconuts, spiritually speaking. I'm working with what I've got to work with and I don't regret it. I see the potential in everyone I come across and I go find him or her. Some find me before I can get around to finding them. So be it. The bottom line is, I love uniqueness. This is what I see as being something different about me compared to other teachers. I think a lot of teachers try to mold everyone to be the same. I don't like patterns.

I am pretty chaotic. In a sense, I put out the information, but I don't tell students they have to look a certain way, like everyone needs to shave their head and wear this kind of clothing. This is how I see it. I believe everything is about 3's. I take what I have as being 1, and then the student is number 2, which is the personality, the identity, and the consciousness. I say let's merge them. Let's put them together to create the third.

I gain from it, too. Don't think I don't because every time I give, I get. I don't care how it is. Sometimes I get a big headache. The point is, it becomes the byproduct of that which I spoke about recently. That is what you're after. It's a good thing, and I would rather go after something different than try to mold everything like a cookie cutter.

Yeah, then they will appeal to different audiences when they go out to teach.

That's right, but I also think some spiritual people go out and know exactly how they want their garden to grow.

They follow a strict set of rules and beliefs; they go by the book. Then what they have is a beautiful rose garden. There's no doubt that some of these religions create beautiful rose gardens. I'd rather have a jungle. I'd rather have a forest. I think there's more beauty in a forest than in a rose garden. It doesn't mean that I can't appreciate the rose garden, but I love uniqueness. I love the mystery of what each person can become rather than shaping them to what I think they should ideally be.

I don't want to know what the student will become. All I know is, I want him or her to become something good, something strong. I'm excited to think about the potential of what is going to come. Is it going to be a mighty oak tree? Will it be a blueberry bush with delicious blueberries? Will it be a blue spruce? There are so many possibilities and they're all intense.

Give me a giant forest with some sunlight cutting through the pine trees and the sudden smells of wet bark moving through the air. Then, let me walk over a hill and see a meadow with a field of flowers. There is my rose garden, but it's not roses. It's not my job to define or say this is what this student will become, spiritually. Be a warrior. Be a healer. Be this. Be that. I don't know and I don't care to know that.

There is a design in the student that is between that student and God. My job is purely to help nurture whatever seed is in them, and they already feel it there. My job is to help bring it a little bit of water, a little bit of good soil and help make sure that the sun reaches it. Then, I make sure it is strong enough to keep the hyenas from digging it up, and to keep the birds from flying off with it or eating it, even though that could be a good thing. Maybe that is a bad analogy because I could say I see the purpose in that, too.

I see purpose in everything. My job is to nourish the student and get them started; I think they can become something greater than I. I hope they do because I'm interested in the same mysteries as God. What will this be? For some people I can see where the beginning and the end is, but I never know the person I'm going to meet. I know there's potential, but I get very excited to see how much potential. I mean, how big is a seed for one tree? It could be a tiny seed and then it fools you. We think the biggest tree would grow from the bigger seed, but not necessarily.

I don't try to anticipate in that way. I just say, "Here is an inquisitive mind. My job is to feed it. That's all I care to do." When I find a student, I feel a mother's instinct toward him or her and I think every student who really gets to know me knows this. I'm like a mother or a father; this is how I've become. I want to shelter, protect, and nurture them. Most of all, I'm excited to see what they will be one day. I see everyone as being different. I don't think there are any two students that are extremely alike and I don't try to make them alike.

I deal with the problems that I see and I try to let the good parts run on their own. If they weren't flawed, I wouldn't want them. The perfection I want is beyond most people's comprehension in this world. It's simply to be who they really are. Life is too short.

Chapter 7

CROSSROADS OF AWAKENING:
DIMENSIONAL JUMPING

Note to the reader: *The following content took place during an advanced retreat in Hawaii. The information was valuable and important for your continuing studies, so we left it as Eric presented it.*

I'm quite emotional right now because I had an experience a short while ago. There's only one thing in the Universe that could even humble me – by making its presence known and saying something to me. I had just finished eating and I started to weep. I tried to hold it from the people around me, but I couldn't. I just want you to know that it's not pain. It's not sadness. It's weeping for joy. I don't know how else to say it. I wasn't expecting this to happen, so I'm just trying to pull myself together.

My mind is very dimensional. My mind is at a multiple frequency layer now. One foot is trying to stay here while the other one is in a much higher frequency. So I'm doing what you do when you shift. I'm gasping for air because, for me, it's so profound. So, if it's profound for me, I think you might have an idea where

I am and why I'm trying to come back down. I'm going to try to do this now, but it's like translating an alien language. Talk about being tested! You think you've got it all down. Then, of course, the Universe says something to you, and even I am humbled by this being – God. And I am nothing ... Nothing!

I don't want to sound like an evangelistic preacher. It's so not like me. So the first thing I want to say is:

Let me look upon your faces.
Let me look upon your souls. I cannot tell
you how proud I am that you are here.

I've been searching for you for ten thousand years. Time is very different in that other place. Time is very short, but it feels very long here in the organic body. I don't need to tell you how much I've suffered because I know that I'm preaching to the choir. I know that you too have all suffered. You all know what I mean. Being here in this dimension, in this world, it's a choice you made. It's a choice that you all made when you were in a different place, in a different time. Like *Star Wars*: In a far, far away place. All of you! To give you a little more of the riddle that I've carefully tried to dance around for a very good reason; the Universe asked me to find the very best - *the very best!* When I'm asked by God, the Universe, I don't ask why. I just say, "Okay."

The Universe asked me to find old souls – White Cells. These old-time White Cells are not your everyday spiritual people. They are ancient, old, old, old beings that were on other worlds in the Universe. And God asked for them to come here to do the work for these other worlds, for these other places ... that were FAR away. Ten thousand years of searching. Ten thousand years of journeying and coming into worlds like this, organically, in this dimension. And having to approach other enlightened beings and saying I've been asked to come here in person to ask you to come to a certain time ... a time ... a certain place ... a certain moment. And that it would be perilous, and I have to ask in person because we're trying to fly under the radar. *Under the radar!*

I've kept an oath of secrecy, not able to really, truly say what for or where. I knew that the old souls, the ancient ones, would know and understand. But I had to ask you to come here, and be part of the world. You had to come here and bury the knowledge by putting it deep! It's like asking yourself to die.

Not one of you questioned this. Not one! By merging in, you became part of the organism. You could not bring full attention upon yourself so that you were not struck down. I'll call it the *Darkside.* So, there is truth in this. Take it for what you want. I can say it now. I can show you certain things that you need to know now. *This is holy ground.* The Island is holy ground. It is Gaia's heart chakra. The Force is at its strongest here. We're not of the Earth, per se. So, in one way, this is a little unusual for us. Yet, we also fully understand it.

I can speak my mind because the Darkside is too tempted and intrigued, just as you are, to know my next move. So it won't do something to me at this point. It has a lot of curiosity about what I'm up to. What's its concern now? Holy ground. I made it to the base. *We made it to the base.* If you had known this before, you never would have made it this far. It's too hard for this state of organic mind that you are dealing and coping with every single day. The joy of knowing that I'm going to start unveiling some of this would have emanated from you. I hate to sound like Star Wars, but don't underestimate the Darkside, the dark force.

Sometimes we cannot control that temptation. Our hearts beam because of God. We beam at the mere thought of the Universe. How can we contain such intense joy, love, and loyalty that we have for this being? So we have to be silent and move under the radar. It's like holding your breath, suffering. And all of you do it willingly. I do it willingly, too.

So, I want to look at you. Let me look upon your faces. Let me look into your souls, because I am in need, finally, of the company of my friends. I'm in need and, like you, I'm tired. I need that company now because I can finally say it without the consequences of having to fly under the radar and what it might do. I've pushed certain borders. Everything I've taught is the true ancient knowledge. It's clean and interwoven with the knowledge, not polluted by human consciousness. Everything I've given you is clean. How you want to internalize it, that's up to you because I know you're going to pull it from that higher place. I didn't want clones. I wanted ancient beings that are damn powerful - the finest from across the universe!

It's like we're drawing the line. You might ask, "Well, why this planet? Why is it going to be Earth?" It's here. It's now approaching. It's not some kind of cataclysmic event. As I've been saying over and over, if it shoots straight and you can figure it out, then it isn't what it is. It still will move to the side, and you'll think, "That's funky!" So you must keep one foot here and one foot there.

There's something that you need to know. I like movies in this dimension. Sometimes the Universe talks through movies. I remember watching a movie but I can't remember the name of it. It was about an Asian family who had a daughter. So they're at the table, and the mother was saying afterwards, "Why don't you pick this? Or do this or that?" The daughter was arguing. She's very meek, very gentle, and the mother finally stops and says to her, "I see you. I see you. Don't think that I don't see you."

You know, there are certain things I can do and there are certain things I can't do. There are rules. Last year was tough because there are a lot of rules that even the Darkside broke to try and break me. It knew it was coming. So It threw all the stops and then threw in the kitchen sink and everything else at me. That's fine. I'll take it all. You can't stop it now. You can't. All I have to say is that I'm in good company. I'm in the company of powerful friends! I will say it to the Darkside now, "Step Aside! Step Aside!" That is good company.

I've been working very hard and I wanted to share a few things that were very interesting - things that I need to get off my chest. First of all, I typically teach more men than women because this is a "man's" world and they typically have more advantages than women. In this dimension, the women got the 'short end of the stick'. Women have to give birth and take care of the children. Meanwhile, men have a certain freedom where they can move towards their spirituality. When a woman gives birth, their love is given to the child. But this is an organic world, so this is still an organic child with a soul, too.

There are diversions, but I never focused that much on the women – until now. All I cared about was setting up some kind of line before I'm discovered by the Darkside. I needed to work as quickly as I could. And I thought because the feminine mind, in this dimension, moves into subject areas and interest that's not in line with the knowledge I have to give them because they move with their "gut" intelligence. It's different than how a man uses their intelligence. *When I say intelligence, I don't mean brains. I mean spirit. I mean frequency.*

I'm so humbled ... so deeply humbled! In my arrogance, never did I think that I would find such powerful women! *Powerful!* You don't even know your potential! I need you to know that. Believe me. It has to do with your work. I will teach you. I will empower you. I will do whatever I can. *But I thought wrong. I'm willing to admit it. And I am honored and humbled to be in your presence.* So much - you have no idea. So, here is to you! I wanted to straighten that piece of business out. No one can tell you any different now because it came from the Source.

There is so much to tell you, but where should I begin? There are certain techniques that I want to teach you. I'm also excited to share information I've never shared before. There are full pieces I want to give. It's not about holding back. It's about timing. I get very upset when people say that I'm holding back certain knowledge. Would you give your five year old a buck knife to go carve sticks and trees? Is the child going to argue with you if that's what it decides it wants?

So, let's get right to it. The *tones* are something that you become very familiar with in Higher Balance. The tones are a pitch; a high pitch tone if you tune into it. The tone is frequencies that I call the sound of God. As I've said before, God is not going to talk like I'm talking to you now. God is not going to say, "Hey, what's up?"

God is this presence of being that is beyond our imagination. There are things in an organic body to reawaken us and help us to move in those places, if we want to work in those higher levels. Then there are little things that are hidden for us to discover. The pitches, or the tones, are that little something. They are one of many, but one of something.

Don't think with the forward organic brain. If you listen, you will hear a high pitch sound. If you concentrate on it without using your brain, you are allowed to go deeper. But the instant you use your brain and you think upon it, the high pitch sound is suddenly whisked away. It's gone. So now you've got to clear yourself, concentrate and bring back the high pitch sound again. When you clear your mind, you can go deeper. All of a sudden, you're going to hear another tone. So it's now a bar. And it's making another high pitch sound. The more you let yourself go, and let this other consciousness move into it, the louder it can get. It can be deafening. *Deafening!*

So take this bar and just listen to the high pitch sound again. You can feel the pitches. You can see them, but it's not sight. It's not really feeling. It is coming from this other place where you exist as a dimensional being. Since you're a dimensional being, you don't have arms, legs, hands and a nervous system. But you want to go back to that because it just makes sense to your organic brain. You've got to throw the logic and the rationality out. You've got to do everything that you don't want to do. You should throw out everything that you think might be crazy. That's a threat to your organic body so it's holding you here.

So you're holding all these bars and you're controlling them all now. When the Babbler comes forward, all the tones evaporate. And you're right back to that first one so you have to start all over again. You've got to practice, over and over with it. When you get really good at it, you can lower it. You can make it come forward. You can move it in a certain direction. You can do all sorts of things with it. To your dimensional body, these are baby steps. You are learning to move in this other place. It is advanced work, so you need to practice until you get it. As you keep practicing, you're going to get better and better at it.

At some point, you're going to realize that you don't need the pitches. You can move your energy around. It's frustrating as an organic being to hang on to those pitches. It goes against everything that you want. And your brain will just throw it out if you're not careful to hold on to them because they don't belong here. As long as you're listening to them, you are moving dimensionally higher. At some point, you could get whisked away. And you're wondering what you were doing ten minutes ago. Then you realize you were doing the tones. You forget because the mechanism doesn't want you to learn.

I love Gaia, the Earth, the Goddess. Call it whatever you want. I have a friend who is very earthy and I mentioned I was going to talk about ayahuasca. Ayahuasca is a hallucinogenic. It comes mainly from Brazil, but they have taken it to other places. When you drink it, you are going to go to some deep, deep, heavy places. Other people go there and they think they know all about the Gaia rhythm. To them, it's profound knowledge. So when I say that I don't want to be part of Gaia and don't want Gaia to take me in, they don't understand. They think it's a bad thing. So I tell them that I am of the Universe.

The Universe asked me to come here to protect Gaia because it belongs to a *'much bigger picture'*. So I told *'them'*, "I will not isolate myself to the exclusiveness of just Gaia. I don't serve Gaia. I will act upon its orders, and I will protect it with *ferocity* because it is the will of God, the Universe, and I will not forget that. I will not let it slip from me that I'm so entrenched into the Earth Goddess. The Earth Goddess is nothing - nothing in comparison to her Creator. This is what people forget.

People say they remember. They feel it in their heart. It's one and the same thing. Human beings have a tendency to title and tag things. Those of you who've learned from me know what I am talking about. When you say Goddess and *the* Goddess, you can't say Universe *and* God. It's not the same. The Goddess is somehow tagged emotionally as an Earth being of energy. On Earth, she's tough. She is of nature. She's not a woman sitting here conversing. It is similar to God, but God is way more intense. The Goddess wants to create life. It wants to overtake you. She doesn't care about your flesh. Flesh to her is just part of the soil, trees, and land. It's of the earth. She wants to love you - so much. *Love you*, and you're in stasis. You're in a stasis because you're like, "Ah, love, mother, energy, creation." That's all the organic part of you. And it's love.

Unfortunately, a mother can love her child too much. That can stifle the child, keeping it at home, creating a fear of leaving the mother by being concerned about moving away. There can be too much love. The Earth has to be strong. It is in space, in subzero temperatures; it is brutal. It's getting meteorites thrown at it. Over one thousand years, maybe a million meteorites, but it's nothing to her. She constantly has to deal with stuff. She's nurturing, thriving, and wanting to grow because that is the will of God and she's obeying. She's emanating this frequency out saying, "I love God, too."

You're down in the core of it. You've been sent from another universe. You are these ancient beings, ancient White Cells, and you know what you've got to do. You've got to shut off what you know to get you through this and allow you to merge in. You know there's something here. You know that you're connected to something higher. So you sample this and you sample that – Buddhism, Christianity, Hinduism. You're sampling all these things because the Navigator's saying no... no... yep ...maybe...maybe...looks good. But in the process, you're exhausting yourselves. And you're thinking, "This isn't anything. I can't take it anymore. I love you Universe, but you've got to tell me. You've got to tell me!"

The Universe replies, "You've got it already. You agreed to the contract and signed it. So shut up now and do the job you came here to do." There are growing pains. You're thinking, "This sucks! I know I had it down. You took it from my memory, and you packed it away. I'm going to unpack it. I know it's there." Believe me, I'm helping you unpack.

So, let's get back to the pitches. The pitches... the frequencies are what are helping you to learn to move that body. I can give you data and knowledge. I can help you unravel all these knots that hold you in this dimension. The pitches are an exercise. You are going to have to fight for these tones, these pitches. They are very real. They will wake you out of a dead sleep. You'll jump up and feel like a truck just went through your head. And you'll wonder, "What the hell was that?" That is your mind slipping into those higher dimensions. When you slide into them, the organic body and the brain interpret it in a funky way. That's what it can sound like sometimes. It's not literally what it sounds like, but you are translating by electrical current through an organic brain that is trying to interpret it. It's not designed for that, but somehow you're doing it. You're taking it and you're moving it into these higher dimensions.

So, you're working with what you've got because you are building a multidimensional body. What does a person who has had a stroke and can't move half their body do for therapy? They're almost being forced to do that because there is a part of them that just wants to give up. They don't want to do it. Nobody here would be any different, including me. That's what you have to do now because you are in therapy to physically build up your bodies, multi-dimensionally, now that you are under the grid.

The frequencies are going to teach you how to do this but you're going to forget to do it. You're going to let it evaporate from your memory. You're going to initiate it and get it and jump on it. Then you're going to forget all about it. Or you're going to take it to a certain point and you're going to think, "I've done everything I can with it. What else is there to do?"

There are things you would be missing if you were to say, "I've taken it to the limit." No! You thought you took it to the limit. You really can have no mental baggage to get there. You literally have to surrender. There's something about dropping into the back of your head to reach higher. It's almost like you relax the waves. Then you slip in. The second you have a thought, the frequency shifts and you want to drop back.

You've trained the Babbler. You do your medita-tions. You know yourself, so why are you still babbling? So you go back because it's not meditation. You can play around with them (the tones), but all the skills you've learned through meditation will get you through all this other stuff that I'm going to throw at you.

I'm teaching how to beat the Babbler and how you move energy. This is how you breathe it. This is what's going on when I say this and how you're going to handle it. It's like when you start moving and your vehicle is rumbling, it's sputtering. You've got this piece of garbage that you had to fix up because you're in the middle of the jungle. You're on planet Earth and you've got to fix it to get off the island now. And you're ferociously working on it because you want to get off the damn Island. So, you've got fermented bananas to make a fuel. It is crap, but you've managed to make it work. So, you've got to work with what you got.

The tones, when you go there, are the skills you've harnessed from meditation; it is your *wax on and wax off*. When you get to certain points, and you start to fall back, you're going to use your old skills to soar! Then you're going to go right back again. It's just going to come to you intuitively.

In martial arts, you learn a move over and over again so that when something happens, you don't need to think about it. When somebody takes a swing at you, your body just reacts. You're doing the same thing. That's why you're meditating. You're holding yourself there. You're moving your energy. You're going into higher places and coming down. You're learning to control the body. So when you start to listen to the

tones and you're going into these other places, sometimes you've got to go back and look at that again
because you went through that whole place and you
didn't see a door. So you walk up to the wall and you're
kicking it and it's swinging open. It was there the whole
time. That's how you've got to be thinking. It's there but
it's hidden from you. So, when you enter the tones,
you've got to use the skills without thinking about using
the skills. You know exactly what I'm talking about.

So, I've taught you the pitch, the frequency. I've told
you it exists. I've helped you find it. So let's get back to
the airplane on the banana fuel trying to get off the
island. You're going to hit the gas, and instead of
getting up to speed, you're going to do this and the
engine's just going to blow up because it can't do that
much that fast. So now you're back at square one. Now
what are you going to find to build an engine? You've
lost all your banana fuel because you picked the whole
forest to make it. Now you've got to look for papaya
and start all over again.

So you need patience. That's one thing that most of
you don't have. Well, we're made of the same fabric. I
can tell you that much. There's no patience. I can only
warn you over and over. So if you jump into what I'm
going to show you, the reason why I haven't said
anything is, I needed to make sure people didn't jump
too fast. Now there's a big clue psychologically in what
I just said. Does anybody know one of the words I just
used?

Jump?

Yes, jump. What does the word 'jump' mean? It's like

science fiction channel. What do the space ships do? They say they are going to jump into hyper dimension. I'm going to teach you how to jump. When you jump, you are moving into that hyper dimensional place. Just because I teach you how to jump doesn't mean you are going to jump very well. That's not my problem. It's up to you to figure out how to use all the equipment. I've given you as much as I can. I will continue giving as much as I can until I can't. You are all slightly different designs. What I'm trying to say is that you're not all from the same planet. When you were on that planet, you were organic. Multidimensionally, you were not. That's why I had to intervene into this other organic world to go find where you were, and what you were doing.

Jumping is actually very simple. It's right under your noses. I wouldn't be surprised if some people caught onto it. But I can tell you already, they didn't know what they had. It's like sitting around a house and you're bored to death. There hasn't been anything to do for a month. Then you look over and the whole time there's been a TV sitting there connected to a satellite dish. I'm not recommending that you watch a lot of TV. This is just an analogy. It's been under your noses the whole time.

When you're listening to the tones, it's very simple. So, when you're listening to the pitch, breathing is your consciousness. It's somehow connected to the organic body. When you get upset, people always say, "Take a deep breath. Then, blow it out." There is something to be said about watching your breath. Your breath is the first thing you do coming into this world and it's the last thing you're going to do when you're heading out. Everybody's heard this before. Think about it. We hear things but we don't think about them. We don't reflect on it. We don't look at it. You put it up on the shelf. You don't even marvel at it.

There's stuff that I've bought in my "pack-rat" phase of life. I'll look at it now and turn it over and I'll find something about it that I never knew before. This is what I'm saying. When I say breathing is the first thing you do and it's the last thing you do, you've got to be thinking about what I'm saying. You overlook the simple things mostly because you've done it every day and night. You've already thought about it a million times. *But have you thought about it with non-thought? Have you thought about it while you're going into the zone?* What are you doing when you go into the In-Between state of consciousness? Your breathing drops. Something completely changes. There is silence and you can move the environment.

So, powerful things happen if you are careful enough to see them happening, Your breathing stops – it's almost like you're calm. Things that should be going faster suddenly go slower. Things change, but if you're not paying attention, you'll miss them.

Are you paying attention now? Big things are happening. So, remember - breathing and breath. When you're listening to the tones, take the pitch when you've got it going good. Without any thought, inhale it, and expand the pitch outward. Do it the same way I've told you to expand your energy. Breathe in like you are filling up a big balloon. Feel the energy moving out from you. It's the difference between holding it really loud and working it.

Now, all of a sudden, you're not thinking about your breath. It's the last thing on your mind. You don't want to be thinking about your body. So hold it. When I say hold it, use non-thought. Hang onto those bars. Get them nice and then just breathe and expand them. Your whole energy field is just going to go whoosh. And you're going to come back down. Even a bird needs a few attempts to fly. Don't get frustrated because you'll end up back in the Doe, back in the machine.

It's that simple. The simplest things are often the most easily overlooked. You've got to weigh out your moments. You've got to plot your course. Don't make it so you set yourself up for failure because you'll be your own worst enemy. You're going to be brutal on yourselves, mentally and psychologically, because you think you should have hit some more levels. You've got to strategize and have patience. Work on your tones before you go trying to expand it to that level.

If you haven't hit multidimensional levels yet, work on *Surrender*, breathing, the tones, and meditation skills. Start integrating them. If you mastered that class, and you worked with it, then you already would intuitively know what to do, just like with martial arts. You'll know. That's how I did it.

You have to learn things before you go jumping into them. Don't be impatient with it. Be patient with yourself. The biggest obstacle to becoming enlightened is impatience. At times, some of you feel helpless because you think your life is miserable. You have highs and lows. That's life. You have to deal with it. Master it. Find a way to work with it. So, you're feeling like a pathetic, aged weakling. You're not as robust as you used to be. You're not where you want to be either. Listen, do the things I'm telling you to do. The biggest thing that's going to hold you down is your impatience. Impatience will destroy Gods! The biggest reason why most people do not reach these enlightened states is impatience.

The second concern is having a set expectation of what it's supposed to be like. You don't even know you're doing it. That's the point. You already think, "Well, God, Eric is an enlightened man. He can probably do all of these things." Alright, so it's true. I'll admit it. All the enlightened beings can go to this fantastic dimensional yacht where we drink, whoop it up, and dance all night! *C'mon – that's not what it's like! Stop trying to figure out what it's going to be like and you might get invited in.* You want it so much, but the wanting comes from your human organic self. That creates a frequency which, in all honesty, is too thick, too heavy, and too disorganized. It can't get in because it's a tone. I don't know how else to say it. You have to unravel this.

You've got the tools. It's about having thought, but not with human thinking. It's all in the *Higher Balance Meditation*. It's all there. Think about where you've been and where you're at now. I'm not looking for clones. You don't have to be identical to what I'm teaching. I want hybrids, not clones. You need to be smart in figuring out which parts you're going to take. You've got to take the knowledge, the good stuff, and bring it in. Contemplate it and work with it. Then take half of yourself and throw out a lot of the baggage that you know you can't take with you. Then you meld them together in your dimensional self. This awakens the ancient being in you. The only thing you're really after is your true middle pillar.

You need the skills in order to get through this patch of rough weather. So I'm like your co-pilot, mapping this all out to help you get through it. I'm just trying to help you. So, you've got to stop having these unrealistic expectations.

Somebody said to me recently that what attracted them to me was that I was so real. I'm always amused by some of these other gurus and spiritual teachers. They all show up dressed immaculately. Do you think they don't fart? They're human – just like everyone else. If you're thinking that you've got to be like these people, I'm telling you that's bullshit. You're creating a set standard for your consciousness that's where you think you need to be to enter stages of enlightenment. This is weight that's holding you down. When you think this is what it should be like, you're holding yourself back. Just for the record, I have tremendous respect for certain spiritual teachers. I'm not making fun of those teachers. Keep that in mind. There are certain ones that I definitely have a lot of respect for. They have their own approach to teaching and it's for different levels of people to help and get them to where they need to be.

I'm teaching people who I consider to be White Cells. They're part of this world. They love people. They're integrated with the world. They love Earth. We have absolute love for all humanity, but there's a certain kind of knowledge that's appropriate for us. It's like you grow up. If you're Asian, you eat Asian food. If you are Asian and you come to America, you eat the American food, but what foods do you crave? You crave what is familiar to you. It's like Europeans and their chocolate. They've got to have their chocolate because the American stuff is crap to them. There's nothing wrong with Hershey's. It's good. So, you've got to realize that there's a certain kind of food from where you are from that you're looking for. This is part of searching through things and throwing all the crap over your heads.

So, that's what it is to us. I'm serving this knowledge as food for you. So, this is what it comes down to. I am not picking on other schools of teaching. I think you can come out with a Hunan dish that we would all die for. You could come out with a Persian dish or something from India. I like to sample every-thing, except seafood or fish. That will probably shock a lot of people. Seafood is slimy and icky.

Anyway, I'm trying to find another way to teach so I use a little humor. I love using analogies, making you feel certain things that you can relate to. So, you've found your food. I'm your food. I have all due respect for other belief systems. I'd be happy to sit down to hear what they have to say. I see the beauty. I see the eloquence. I see the truth in what they're saying. Then again, there are a lot of lousy cooks out there. Then there are really good cooks. Isn't that true if you look at it that way in life? That's what I'm saying. I'm poking a little fun at it, too.

In *Deep Resonating Aums*, the music is real. I'm real-ly just bringing all the different levels of this being through this body to allow this being to sustain in this flesh. This is very potent stuff. I never intended for it to be distributed; I don't know what I was doing – I was just doing it. That's the place I go to when I'm by myself. That's where I exist and I like being there. The other part of me that you see is an 'I' that enables me to teach, use the body, and work with the tones. In all truth, that's probably where I reside normally; it's a certain feeling.

You'll hear some very deep Aums from my mascu-line, more robust side. The higher Aums come from the feminine side. There's also some medium range ones. If you let yourself experience it, you can hear that balance. I'm allowing the other ones to step forward and just find a way to harmonize all those into one being. That's when you can approach God, the Universe. It's only when you've got that right resonation where they all move forward together. You can't capture that on any mechanism in this dimension. So I'm really bringing it to the edge. It's up to you to internalize it and take it to the next step.

Sometimes people have some funky energy or nasty beings around their house. Those are times you can put the album *Deep Resonating Aums* in and crank it up. That solves the problem. It will eventually ferment into your environment as you are working with it, so it will move your energy. It is a frequency, but it needs a living being to move through. When I'm coming from that place, it's now mechanized, but there's data layered in those tones. *If you listen to the Aums, you literally can move into that place with me.* If you can let yourself go, there's no good, there's no bad, there are no ups or downs; it's just *ism*. That is the only way I can explain it.

It can be deep, dark, or light. Dark places can be just as beautiful as bright places. It's not about good or bad. It's just ism. It's a good place to rebuild one's spirit, one's soul. Don't put conditions on whether you're going to be healed now or not. That's not for you to decide. Just say, "I'm here, I'm clay in your hands. Do what you want. When you are done, and you made me into a ball and it's lopsided, that must be what you want for this week." Don't set any conditions. That's the big key here.

So the album is *Deep Resonating Aums*. It's real. It was not done in a studio; I think it was done in my bedroom. There is a part of me that wants to rent a studio to start recording, but I'm afraid that if that happens I'm not going to be able to go where I need to go to do what I do. I can't just be pre-packaged. I don't know how a lot of these other spiritual teachers can. To me, it's as dry as British comedy. If they stick me in a studio, it will probably sound okay, but I am going to sound just like everybody else. When I speak, I'm letting my body move to get the energy to create this verbalization. There's a lot there if you are aware and open to it.

Chapter 8

CROSSROADS OF AWAKENING:

SPIRITUAL POLARITIES

We know that males use a large portion of their brain's left hemisphere. We know that females use the right hemisphere, but not mirrored in size. It's a little bit smaller, but they also use a little bit of the left whereas males don't use any of the right. If the scientists would just do the research, they would discover that the females are most likely using both hemispheres of the brain. However, the heterosexual society and the ego of humankind will not let them do it.

By using both hemispheres, you are more brilliant. You are better able to transcend concepts, knowledge, and theory – all the things you need to transcend, spiritually. You can lift yourself out of the Doe and build the dimensional vortices inside of you faster than having to struggle and work with the limited material.

Krishna is God on Earth in Hinduism. He was their teacher as Jesus was to Christians, as Buddha was to Buddhists, and so on. Krishna had an awesome student whose name was Arjuna. He was the fiercest warrior of warriors. He would say, "I'm going to shoot that bird through the eye." Then he'd shoot an arrow into the sky and kill the bird, shooting it through the eye! How amazing is that?

These people existed. This is not a fable – trust me on this. It was another time, another place. Now, there was a point where he and his brothers had all reached most of the levels of enlightenment, but they weren't quite there yet. They had a battle with their stepbrother. They had to go into exile and hide. *A wise spiritual man told them that they could only survive if they acted on their deepest secret and lived among the people.* Only that would be enough to protect them so that nobody would know they were hiding. Arjuna, the greatest, manliest warrior of them all, with a chestful of hair, lived as a woman. He chose to be a woman! One of the most powerful chose to live as a woman!

Think of the significance of this message. Why did Krishna say this? What is God? Is God a man? Is God a woman? Does God give birth? The answer is both yes and no. Who did God have sex with to create the universe? Was there a feminine and masculine equivalent? Who were the creators? This is a birth. It's a birth! The universe was a birth of creation. If you can't see it as a birth, your mind is limited. You could say that God created or birthed by himself. It's like God is a hermaphrodite, a being that has both masculine and feminine polarities within it. It doesn't care what gender you are because it doesn't have a vagina. It doesn't have a penis. It doesn't have the biochemicals telling it what sex to identify with. It doesn't care. *It doesn't care!* You know who cares? *YOU care because society tells you to care. And if, by the way, you happen to prefer both sexes, you're bad!* According to social standards you are! Well, this is what's holding consciousness in place and making it move along so slowly.

I should have said that sooner, but I couldn't. Like a lot of things, I had to wait for the right timing. You are trying to find a balanced polarity inside of you. The dimension for God is here. It's layered and it gets more and more balanced as you approach the core of it. When you leave your body, are you a man or are you a woman? *You're neither!* When you come back in, will you be a man or a woman? Does it really matter? Well, those of you who are women have it tougher, so you will probably have something to say about that now!

So, God is this frequency that's neither male nor female. That's how you must look at it because you are in this organic planet for it. Organically, we must create more life for the survival of the planet. So genetically, it's burned into us to make sure that our species survives.

So, if you're going to approach God, you can't just say to God, "Alright, I'm developed now." If you're wondering why you haven't had the breakthrough yet, it's because you've accepted certain rules that are interwoven sociologically. You've accepted certain rules of how you see and how you think. Even if you acknowledge it, it's still embedded in there. I can feel the problem; even with me, I can feel it. I've got the same sociological makeup as you do. It's like a fear that's been beaten into us. In ancient Greece, sexuality was not even an afterthought. People like Socrates, Plato, Aristotle – they didn't care. Look at the brilliance that came from them.

So you have to find the balance of male/female inside of you. A lot of spiritual women who are powerful are very feminine, but they also have a backbone. You'll find that creative spiritual men are very balanced. So, the point is that Buddha had feminine energy as well as masculine energy.

With all due respect, if you're a woman who is too masculine, as a teacher I'm not interested. If you're a guy who is too feminine, I'm not interested. It's too much to deal with! If you are sexually unbalanced, you've got the genitalia but you've switched your energy all to the feminine side of the brain. I don't want that. I want some balance, but you also need to keep your core identity stronger. That's what I want. It's okay to have your masculinity, but you also need to let yourself experience the feminine aspect.

Keep in mind, I'm speaking more to the feminine man than I am to the masculine woman, because I'm in a male body and even I'm doing it. I'm trying to think of what I'm missing, so I'll try to interweave it, but it's like this: if a man and a woman looked at a painting, they would both interpret it differently. A woman would generally *feel* something. They may not always admit it, but they know that men don't feel it. Usually, they won't even bring it up because they feel it's a waste of time. When they're doing that, it's not because they're being female. It's like a code. There's communication going on in that painting that a guy doesn't necessarily have the means to decode. They get it and they'll say, "It's very beautiful," but they can only interpret ten to forty percent and think they understand it all. Some women can sit there, observe it, and not 'get it' either. If you're in balance and looking at certain things, a guy may understand and the girl might miss the boat because they are using a different part of their brain. They think from a different place.

Certain things are *alienesque. You* think you would *know* that, but *you can feel it.* That's the frustration between relationship and desire. You are constantly looking externally for your opposite polarity instead of looking inside of yourself to create it.

If you look at Buddha, you're going to recognize the feminine side of him, but you're also going to see the masculine because Buddha has both sides. That's why he became enlightened. If you look at Jesus, you won't see him as just masculine. But he certainly could be tough when he needed to be. Look what he did at the temple with the money changers, turning their tables over.

With Krishna, it's the same thing. Krishna was married and had children. He was a king and he had to keep his lineage going. There was a certain amount of pressure to produce offspring. I'm not saying that he felt like he had to do that; he genuinely loved both sexes.

It is true when they say spiritual people often lead a life of celibacy, which is also why many priests are having problems with their sexuality. They don't want to deal with it, so they suppress it. They believe that if they lead a spiritual life, the people will believe they gave up sex. That's the only thing that society will not question them about. That's bullshit. They still want it. They thought, "This is what I'll do to appease them and make them happy."

So, when you look at Jesus, there is a feminine/masculine balance. Think about it! How did he have the compassion, the love, and endurance to deal with the pain of people all of the time? That's a nurturing, female kind of love. He had a balance of both. If you look at the theologian scholars, they will tell you the stuff that's not talked about. When you read the letters of John in the Bible, it is evident that they're love letters. John and Jesus were like lovers. Nobody wants to talk about that. Even inside of you, there's this voice saying, "I can't believe Eric's saying all of this." Do your

homework and see if I'm right or wrong. The theologian scolars will say, "Well, he never really did anything.
They were lovers but nothing sexual ever happened
while they inhabited a cave for six months. They were
just meditating and connecting with God. Jesus was
teaching John for six months and that was it."

If you don't like the truth, then don't listen to me. At
this point, my job is not to care whether you like it or
not. My job is to say it the way it is. If you don't agree
with me, that's fine, don't agree with me. But I can die
and say that I called it like it was. I gave you the best
that I could. If you reject it and go on another path,
that's fine, but you will not find enlightenment unless
you know this piece of information. That doesn't mean
that you have to go and have sex with someone of the
same-sex. Instead, find that resistance inside of you
and start disassembling your thought process.

I realize just how stringent I am, myself, in that area
as it's very narrow. I will recoil if a transvestite comes
up to me and says, "Hello." From a distance, I can sit,
watch, and be amused. My thought process is, "He's got
to have the gonads to do that," and I realize it's not
even the gonads because it is genetic, in many ways.

There are scienfitic studies showing when a gay or
lesbian dies and there is an autopsy performed; they have
seen there are different portions of the brain that cause
you to be more feminine or masculine. When I watch
women put on their eyeliner, if they're very particular
about it, I imagine that if they were to have an autopsy
after death with the technology that we have now, the
brain would show it's larger on the femininity side.

There are some women who don't seem ultra-
feminine. They don't feel like they have to put the makeup, blush, lipstick, and eyeliner on every day. They put

their jeans and shirt on and pull their hair backward in a knot. When they get older and they get the power that I'm talking about after menopause, they usually cut their long hair off. They don't care. They're sick of combing and dyeing it so they'll make it shorter. They've put in their time to appease everybody. That's really what it's all about in this culture.

So, what I'm really talking about is energy and allowing yourself to take your power back. When women become menopausal, they finally give up on pleasing everyone else. They are now tapping into their masculine side. This doesn't mean that they're out having sex with other women. They have found that masculine energy that empowers them and the man doesn't want to deal with it.

Something changes, biochemically. For some women, it's a little sooner than menopause and for others it is a little bit later. Some women are so psychologically subjected that they never really change even when they hit menopause. Being very feminine doesn't necessarily mean that portion of the brain is going to detract, but it does have certain advantages and disadvantages. For a woman who is very beautiful, highly empowered,super-feminine, and in that zone, she's still doing the eyebrows, lipstick, and the hair, but she's doing it for herself because it makes her happy. But other women say, "It's too much work. I'm not going to do all that." It's a portion of the brain that is made to do this.

With men, I think it's the same thing. My higher brain wants to analyze everything, so when I looked at male transvestites, I think that that part of their brain is very similar to an ultra-feminine woman. What causes them to risk being spit on and beat up as a child? Why don't they just accept it, submit, and be like everybody else? They hide it for as long as they can. What drives them to be hated and despised by society and still have to do all of this and say, "I'm beautiful. I'm going to dress up and I don't care." They can't help themselves, because it's coming from this place in their brain.

Those of you who follow the more evolutionary design are a little bit more balanced. I would like to have all of you autopsied because I think there's something already there for you to know, like 'this is it!' When you came into this body, something was manufactured from your will, your spirit. It had to design certain things to format a certain way, to make it so you could exist in this body. I believe you manipulated things on a cellular level and the rest was potluck. You get what you get so you can work with that. I'm still working with it.

If you truly are spiritual beings worthy enough to say that you are growing spiritually, you have to look at your compassionate side and not just be compassionate. You have to say, "I get it. I understand." I'm not saying that I can feel that way. I'm not saying that I could do that. I'm not saying that I would let somebody manipulate me to do that. There are certain boundaries but you understand it. This is what certain societies at a certain time could understand. This is why those cultures thrived. Spiritually, you have to look at yourself and play around with your masculine-feminine identity.

I had a person come to me for advice once, and I told her, "You need to empower yourself. You have a lot of feminine energy. If you want to take it to the next level, you need to empower that masculine energy inside of you." So I said to her, "Can you make a manly face? And feel manly when you do it. When I make the manly face, I feel manly. It's a feeling. *It's a feeling.* The muscles know it. The body knows it. The energy knows it. The spirit knows it.

So, of course, she gave me her best manly face and I said, "That's a good start." She understood what I was saying so I said, "Now you're going to strut in the hallway. You've got to walk like a man and feel like a man." So she's alright with that but I know she was thinking, "I can't believe he's going to do this to me." So, I said, "I'll go first," so I started doing my manly walk. Then she did it but she was wiggling her hips so I told her not to do that. After a while, she did a good job, so I told her to do it again and feel it. So she was starting to feel it. Six months later, she's going to be a very im-proved spiritual being. That's all I care about.

I talked to my stepfather about this subject. He's a nice guy, a man's man. So I sat down at the table to talk to him. We know each other, but he recently married my mother so we don't know each other that well. So I asked him, "What do you think the population of gay people is?" He replied, "Around ten percent of the population." I thought to myself, "Yeah, you're smart. That's good. I'm glad you're smart." So I said, "Aristotle, Plato, Socrates, and the greatest warrior of all time, Alexander the Great, a man's man." I continued on along those lines. So I said to him, "Out of all the well-known minds in history, what part of society do you think gay people account for significantly?

He said to me, "They were that way?" I replied, "Yeah, that way." I don't care if it happened to be over ten percent. If it was out of a ten percent pool in history, that's unfathomable statistically. But I'm ranking it up in the seventy to eighty percent range now because society would flog those people, killing most of them off. They were treated like Jews, or lepers – they were eliminated. *That is astonishing.* Even if they were a minimal amount, it's astonishing that the greatest majority made it into this bracket of history!

I suspect that if you look throughout history at a lot of brilliant women, many of those females; strong, powerful figures, really had short hair for their time period and wore very little make-up. They wore masculine clothing as well, instead of sundresses; they were already cutting edge. We'll never know because men wrote history. It's what you don't know that makes you ignorant because you didn't try to at least find out.

Listen, as your friend, as your mentor, your teacher, whatever you want to call me, take a hard look at what I'm saying. I definitely do not want to see any of you in drag. That is not what I'm after. It doesn't interest me and I'll cringe. Think about what you can experience when you can start turning on the other half of the biosphere of the brain. It will turn on just from contemplating and thinking about this. I've already opened Pandora's Box because you trust me and you're willing to take what I have to say seriously. You agreed with a lot of the things I said before, so you're willing to at least mull this over. I've waited a long time before I've said this, because if I said it earlier, many of you probably wouldn't have progressed this far.

God does not identify with being a gender of sexuality. Humanity thinks that way so that the organism, the planet, can procreate. I believe that evolution is influenced by a higher consciousness which is intertwined into our dimension. If you have any doubts, do your own research. When human beings came out of the ocean, they were very fishlike. As they adjusted to the land; I don't believe they had to mate. Worms have both reproductive organs, so they're neither male nor female. There's now a lizard that impregnated itself to give birth. It's called the Whiptale Lizard. It's an all-female species where reproduction is two females acting out the roles of a male mounting a female. The result is cloning! There is more of this than you can possibly imagine.

This knowledge is suppressed by some people who decide whether or not you need to know this. It is the same thing that happened with religion. Somebody decided to tell them what to know and what to under-stand. So they've edited the Bible to manipulate the people into believing certain things. That is what created this big mess with the world's religions. The data is skewed and is being shut down. The people who control this type of knowledge decide what you will be exposed to, so only little tiny pieces of information come out now and then.

One of the science channels said that around eighty percent of the animal kingdom not only will mate with their own sex but actually prefer to keep company with their own sex. They find that they're more agreeable than when they are with the opposite sex. I thought this was interesting, but I thought they better triple check their data. The head researcher had been study-ing mountain rams for twenty years. The whole time he studied them, he never knew. The researcher said if he had known they were all homosexual twenty years ago, it would have changed all his research. He had been scratching his head, trying to figure out why they were so interesting, because it's the one thing he refused to look at. It never occurred to him. It was blocked from his thinking!

Aside from being the only recorded animal other than primates to have sex purely for pleasure, dolphins take it a step further by engaging in bisexual and same sex encounters. The females don't want to deal with the males. Can you imagine? Two female dolphins can talk without having sex.

Who do women tell their problems to all the time? Who do they consult for support and friendship? Guys, who are you drinking with? Who understands that your wife is a pain in the ass because they've got one, too? There's love and there are unions. You are being given a set of directions in societal structure, and you have accepted it that way. If you have emotion one way or the other, even if it's real compassionate love for the same sex and it's not about sex, you shut it down because you're concerned that you might be gay. The females think the same way.

Spiritually, that's all I care about. It's not about sex. I'm not trying to make it about sex, but I have to go there to inform you, to bring you from a lower frequency in your thought process so that you can look at things differently. I'm not saying you have to go out and make some gay friends. I'm not saying you have to like them either. Spiritually, you have to look at your energies and your frequencies.

Since the urge to procreate is biological, that's why you identify so strongly with it. It's what locks humanity off from becoming too spiritual and separating themselves from the Earth. There must be a species that will give their consciousness to the planet so it can stay in the loop. If all the cells in your body suddenly said, "Well, we've decided to hang out with just the white cells and do what they're doing," that would collapse the entire inner universe of your body.

There's a risk. Unfortunately, that's the truth of it. If all the Red Cells switched their thinking, you would find them more spiritually inclined. They may not be nearly as advanced as a White Cell, but their tonal is going to shift in mass proportions. You would see a drop in religions, but also a potential sociological collapse until that adjustment fully stabilizes. Then it will probably rebound.

If everybody were to switch their tonal and rethink the idea of having kids, the planet would be in big trouble. So there's a certain necessity for the way things are. It's what keeps the Red Cells largely remaining as Red Cells. It's the whole process: find someone, mate, have your children, and raise them. You get a breather, but just when you think you're done and you're happy, they go and have children. Then they drop the children off with you to watch them, or you have to help them out financially. I'm not saying that you can't reach spirituality. You have an advantage. You're old souls. There's a certain drive in you that helps you find a way around it, whereas Red Cells function in the machine. They're not thinking beyond that nor are they allowed to, but some become very spiritual and make it.

Do you know any extremely masculine spiritual people? Can you name even one person like that? You'll find that they'll have a persona where you're not sure of their orientation and they're not going to tell. There are a lot of spiritual people that I think are overly heterosexual. I think it is human nature that they exploit that. This is something you have to know. Just because somebody is spiritual, that doesn't mean they're nonsexual. This is again human sociological rules. You can't believe that just because you're really spiritual, you can't desire sex and want to do those things.

If you constantly fit everything you don't know and what you assume into a mold, then it has already been locked down. You set standards and boundaries. You try to do the right thing. That's what it's about.

Could you speak about the relationship between Jesus and Mary Magdalene?

Sure, I really don't want to get into religion, but I'll touch on it. I don't think that Mary Magdalene and Jesus were in a relationship. I don't believe they married and went to France. I personally don't believe that. Research is often tainted by one's personal perspective. Often, research is a reflection of what you personally believe. So, if someone wanted to find how the science of evolution fits in a Christian box, they are going to find the research angled to justify that particular perspective.

There is a book out there called *Jesus Lived in India* by Holger Kersten. It's available in paperback. The writer is brilliant. If you want to know my opinion, this is my perspective. Kersten does not go into the sexuality of Jesus, so it's not about that. But he does present a reality check on the story of Jesus. He doesn't say that Jesus didn't exist. He acknowledges that Jesus did exist, but he additionally comes up with some amazing information.

Have you heard about the Shroud of Turin? It bears the image of Christ in the cloth. It was touted as real, so the church put it up for display. Then, all of a sudden, information was released that the cloth wasn't authentic, so it was pulled from the mainstream and it almost faded away. In 1532, there was a fire where it was stored in this chapel in France. It burned part of the cloth and they were able to carbon date it, proving that the shroud was only around eight hundred years old. So how could it be the shroud that Jesus had for his burial? So that's why the media stopped reporting about it. The church really didn't want it out there because it wouldn't look good for them, and it was too arguable.

Kersten is very smart, so much so that the Christian theologians do not want to argue with him because he can fiercely debate this issue. He knows everything: verse, chapter, backwards and forwards. When they debate, he really sets them straight. Kersten argued that the carbon dating was incorrect because the smoke was saturated into the fabric. Therefore, the carbon dating comes up with an incorrect date. So the carbon dating determines the date of the fire – not the age of the cloth. They checked the fabric for traces of flowers or pollens to see if there were any selective species that only grew in one specific area of the world. A botanist at the Hebrew University of Jerusalem discerned that the Chrysanthemum coronarium pointed to March or April in Jerusalem.

Kersten explains that the reason why the Shroud of Turin was nixed by the church is because the shroud was saturated with blood when it lay on Christ when they crucified him. The shroud was placed on him when he died. They had placed him in the tomb and prepared his body with frankincense and myrrh. He says that's another problem because that's not what they used during that time period. If you look at other historical records, burial ointments didn't include antiseptics for wounds. *They use antiseptics traditionally for medicine to clean wounds for a living person,* not for someone they're preparing for death with certain scented oils, because the body creates an odor upon death. That doesn't make any sense when you read it. Dead men don't bleed. He was taken down from the cross and his body was moved a good distance until they got to the outskirts of the city. Why was his burial area separate from everyone else's? Why was it so close to the city? Why did he have a special funeral place?

So the cloth went on his body last and it shows the location of the blood stains. *Dead men don't bleed, so his heart was still pumping.* So, according to Kersten, it means that Jesus wasn't dead when they took him down. Why did the guard lance him? Why the cut? He says that the word kept getting retranslated from the original Greek text, so eventually the meaning of the text changed into something else. So instead of a cut, it was a scraping.

When Jesus was put on the cross, his followers were going to the guards, pressuring them to take Jesus down, "He's dead already. He's dead already. Can't we take him down?" The Roman guards liked Jesus so they checked to see if he was really dead. In those days, it could take a week to die on the cross, so they were very surprised when he died after just a few hours. That was bizarre in those days. So they scraped him to see if his muscles were going to react. Even if he was unconscious, the muscles would have retracted so the guard would know that he wasn't dead yet. So his followers didn't know. They just wanted him down. The guards were probably shocked when the followers asked for his body. So the head guard lanced him with his sword and Jesus didn't react. The guard just presumed Jesus was dead and that he died quickly.

The guard went to his superior, Pontious Pilot, upon the urges of Jesus's followers. This is something which he normally wouldn't have done. Three people were crucified: Jesus and the two other criminals. So, the guard, who is an expert at crucifying people and knowing when they're dead wasn't going to screw this up. The head guard asked, "Well, did you lance him?" And the guard said they did all those things. So the head guard says with puzzlement, "He's dead already?" He had to be thinking that was way too fast. So he agreed, "Well, if you did all that, go ahead and take him down." So he was taken down after about three hours.

Do you remember that Jesus was given a bittersweet drink? There was a point when somebody gave him a drink that was bittersweet. Now everybody *thinks* it was bittersweet. They interpret that he's dying and he has some water so it's bittersweet because it's the last time he's ever going to drink water because he's dying. No, read between the lines. This was an elixir. Somebody there was one of his followers or friends and they gave him a very strong intoxicating drink. This is why it was bittersweet.

Jesus knew. It wasn't a surprise. He knew! He knew he had to make it from point A to point B and that they would be in the crowds. They knew that there would be enough going on that they could get away with it. Jesus was as strong as the two other criminals, if not stronger. Jesus didn't live in a condo. He didn't live in a castle. He was out there working among the tough people, so he was at least as strong as the other two.

Yet when he finishes this drink, he can't carry that big cross anymore. What happened? Someone else had to carry it for him. Why was he already in disarray then? Perhaps he got hit in the head with a stone, or maybe he was injured. He could have been beaten more than the two criminals. I can see the logic of it.

He was put on the cross and in a short amount of time, he quickly passed out. They speared him and he didn't react, so they were urged to bring him down. The Roman guards were feeling guilty. Joseph of Arimathia, who was very wealthy, asked for the body of Jesus. He purchased the tomb himself and gave it to Jesus it was close to Golgotha where this occurred.

Kersten said this was very strange because, in those times, there were certain laws and rules that applied to a Jewish burial. At that time, cultural opinion was extremely different than it is today. If you died and we built a mausoleum around the corner for you in the middle of town, wouldn't that seem a little odd? That's what it was like, but since Joseph was rich, and well-respected, he could do whatever he wanted to do.

Jesus was carried this short distance because he needed the anti-toxin to counteract the drug that put him into a coma; otherwise, he really would have died. So, he was given the antitoxin in the tomb in private as fast as possible. His followers had to do it in secret and make it look as natural as possible so it wouldn't draw any attention. If the rabbis found out, they would have been worse than the Romans because they wanted him dead for a long time. So they had to get him from point A to point B, off the cross quickly before his heart stopped. His heart was probably beating maybe once every four or five minutes - just enough to sustain life. So they got him in there quickly and they administered the antitoxin. Who administered the antitoxin? Who did the Mary Magdalen see? There were people dressed all in white and she said they were shining brilliantly. Right away, they had to be angels.

At that time, there were Essenes who studied Vedic teachings and Indian philosophies. They were brilliant. They knew about medicinal herbs, plants, and oils long before other cultures, especially the Hebrews. It was pretty amazing stuff.

So where did Jesus go after the incident in the temple when he was twelve? How many years was he gone? That's not in the Bible. It's as if he just vanished. In the bible, he is mostly talked about in his earlier years when he was a child, and then he suddenly disappeared. He showed up again for a brief time, knowledgable and articulate, preaching to the rabbis and the audience. The rabbis were very envious of him and thought, "Who the hell does he think he is?" Then he disappeared again and showed up when he was around thirty years old and preached for about three years.

So there's a lot of time missing – about eighteen years. Ask yourself, "Where was he?" If you disappeared for eighteen years, what would you be doing? Learning something? Trying to improve yourself? Weren't Mary and Joseph exiled when Jesus was young? Weren't they running for their lives? If you left Palestine and went southwest on the trade routes, you would eventually reach India. Kersten said that Jesus lived near the trade routes in India. So as a youth, Jesus was exposed to the merchants who brought their wares to trade with other cultures. At some point, he must have been around them, so he would have learned a few things from them.

Where did he learn all of the knowledge that he knew? What did the Hindu population believe? They believed in pacifism, "If somebody hits you, you don't hit them back." Like Gandhi said, "An eye for an eye will leave everyone blind." He learned that in India. In India, they're not out sacrificing animals. If you kill a cow you eat well, but after a while you've got a problem because there's no milk, meat, or anything. Somebody was smart enough to tell the primitive people, "The cow is sacred. It'll always give milk. We don't have to worry about the people sacrificing it then, because it's sacred. Then we all can drink the milk which will sustain us in good times and in bad."

By the way, who were the three wise men? Joseph describes them as having a strange color skin that was different from what they have. According to Kersten, the three wise men probably came from India. The Buddhists look for reincarnated masters. When their masters die, the people wait several years and then, in their meditations, they get a message that says, "Go to this place to find the child. He'll be a young boy and that will be your teacher reincarnated." They would find many of them that way because there wasn't just one.

To get back to your question, Kersten argues that the story about Mary Magdalene and Jesus is romantic and it's what people want to believe. In my opinion, it's more acceptable sociologically than the story that I'm putting out there. But I'll tell you, if you had to get down to the nuts and bolts of this, I bet you Kersten's story holds up much better. He's right on.

So, he says that even Jesus' followers were not aware of his revival. It was only a small group. He kept the Essenes separate from his other students, but there was a rumor that John the Baptist belonged to the Essenes. They had a hand code that most people didn't know. When they greeted people walking through the desert, they didn't always know who was coming so there was concern that somebody could harm them. When Jesus came upon John the Baptist in the river, Jesus greeted him using a hand signal. This was a secret society. They were educated in mathematics, on the geography of the area, and on almost everything else that the common people didn't have access to.

Jesus was very well educated. There is an old Buddhist text that talks about Jesus. Karsten talks about it in his book. The text describes him as being a brilliant student. It also mentions his teacher and how he absorbed all the teachings while rising up in the rankings. So during all of those missing years, Jesus was learning from lamas and other Hindu teachers.

When he died, the Essenes were in the tomb with him. They nursed him back to health and moved him somewhere else to continue to heal. That's why there was nothing left but a few robes. He had risen and they got him out of there quickly because the Romans and the rabbis would have executed him if they found him alive.

Then Jesus met with Thomas who doubted he was alive. Jesus said, "Place your hands in my wounds." Then Thomas touched him and he realized it really was Jesus. Thomas was uneducated and didn't know about the Essenes or herbal plants, so right away he assumed that Jesus was dead; now he's alive! That's what happened.

Eventually, Jesus went to see his followers who didn't know what had happened. Why? Because he didn't want them babbling about it! I can see the logic and feel the truth of this, but the world is not ready to yet. They want to believe what they have been told, so they don't even question the truth of it. It's just the way it is. Keep the people stupid. Fleece the sheep. If they get too smart, they're going to wander off. If they go over a hill, they're going to go to hell. There's fire and brimstone over that hill. So, there's a lot of rationalizing going on, "He's smarter than the rest of us, right? We better not go over the hill."

At this point, Jesus immediately left the area. I don't think he ended up in England or France. Kersten said that he did leave. Of course, the trail dies eventually, but they can find certain traces of him because the people from that part of the world (India) were brilliant. They were light years ahead in their writing, their articulation, and their storage of data. There were bits and pieces where Jesus is talked about.

I'll tell you another interesting thing. Do you remember when the Egyptians were chasing Moses and the big fire came out of the ground? Did you see the movie *The Ten Commandments* with Charlton Heston? God is fire, just like with the burning bush. God uses fire repeatedly to blast the Egyptians. Evidently, God likes fire. Kersten wrote an interesting disclosure about Moses. He says that Moses was a prince of Egypt. He was adopted and became a prince. As a prince, Moses governed a few territories.

Everyone assumes that, during that time, gunpowder didn't exist. Kersten says that Moses was working in the mines and he kept secret whatever they were mining. It was actually gunpowder. They took massive quantities out of the mines. If you don't know what a bang from gunpowder sounds like, just imagine what a stick of dynamite could do. If there was a blast from the mine and the people didn't know any better, they would probably think, "Holy shit! – God has spoken!"

Moses wanted to get back to his people, so he started a fight to distract the soldiers. The Egyptian soldiers didn't know about gunpowder and Moses was smart enough to have his miners go into the desert. He told them, "They're going to chase us with chariots. This is where you're going to put it. This is how it works. This is how you set it off. Let's keep this quiet." Moses set everything up. He knew what the blast would do – he was brilliant. He knew what the king and the prince would do. He was raised with them; they were like family to him. You know how your mother would react. If you've got brothers or sisters, you know the routine. I believe he knew strategically how it was going to go down. He also told the Egyptian people, "If you mess with me, my God will smite you!"

I haven't come up with an answer yet for the stick that turned into the snake. Perhaps it never happened. That's why I can't find the answer for that one so I don't know for sure, but I do know he had gunpowder out there. I know he mined it, and I know most people don't know that. So to me, it all adds up.

Chapter 9

CROSSROADS OF AWAKENING:

WATER AND ENERGY

During my childhood, there were several times when I really should have drowned. I was always in the water because I loved it so much. The first time was when I was a little kid; I remember being in this above ground circular pool with my family. I remember being under water, looking at everybody's legs and the ceiling of the water from the bottom of the pool.

I couldn't have been more than five years old at that time. I wasn't thinking about breathing, or about getting to the surface. They could have forgotten about me down there. I remember feeling like it was a very different perspective and this wasn't normal. It's almost like a different reality. Then I remember that my grandmother pulled me up from the water. We were back out of the pool again. Then I remember just being a normal kid again. It just seemed to kick in.

So I slipped out of my body while I was under the water looking around. I guess it was that shift of perspective. The surrealism of it brought my old spiritual self forward a bit. It felt different and good, but not normal. I don't ever remember feeling the need to breathe, nor did I panic or anything like that.

Another time, I remember that I turned up missing. I don't remember all of it because I was so young, but my family has told me the stories. We had a little cottage house. There were a lot of them, so it wasn't very private. It was on a very small island on a lake connected by a bridge. It had a five foot high stone wall around it. The interesting part was that the wall was flat. It might have had cobblestones or cement, but it went straight into the water. It wasn't a gradual decline. The fence was built to support these little houses. We didn't have a backyard, so everybody stood in the front yard. The family was out there; my grandmother, grandfather, mom, older brother, and everybody else.

Apparently, I had disappeared. I hadn't really disappeared, but they suddenly started wondering where I was and began searching the house. Then they looked around the property, calling me. My grandfather went around one way and my aunt and uncle went around the other. Then some other people came by.

Meanwhile, I was standing on the wall with the water behind me. My heels were right at the edge. They came around the house and discovered me standing on the wall there and started shouting, "Oh my God! Oh my God!" The water was dripping off me, as if I had just been plucked out of the water. They were shocked because they wondered who helped me out and what had happened. There was nobody there and they realized there was no way I could have scaled that wall. It would be difficult for an adult to do it, let alone a five-year-old child.

At that time, I told them that the 'light lady' pulled me out. They could never get more of an answer than that. I don't really recall what happened; I just know that water is not my problem. I wasn't afraid of it, but I'm sure I should have drowned. I fell in there somehow, some way, and was brought out of it.

The next time I was in a swimming pool, I learned all of my energy movements. It was a large pool for the apartment complex that I grew up in. There were a lot of people in the complex, so it's surprising that I always had the pool to myself. I was in it all the time; I loved being in it. There was a ten foot deep section with a diving board that came out like a boot. I was there with a friend named Patty, a freckled tomboy who was cool. There was also a female lifeguard there that day. They were at the picnic table playing backgammon.

I had a nerf ball and I wanted to hide it from Patty. So I swam down to the ten foot section wondering where I was going to put it. I looked at the drain; it should have been bolted down, but it wasn't. So I swam to the drain at the bottom of the ten foot deep pool. I got my fingers under the metal drain and I lifted it up. It was heavy so I slid it to the side. I thought this was a great place to hide the nerf ball. So I put the ball in there and it fell all the way down into the pump. I thought, "Oh my God! I'm going to blow up the pump system! I'm going to have to buy Patty a new nerf ball."

All this time, I was holding my breath. As I tried to grab the ball, the pump turned on full force and it just sucked my hand down with the ball. I kept pulling and pulling, trying to get loose. I tried everything to get my body to pull out and I just couldn't, but for some reason I wasn't afraid of drowning. I was probably around ten or eleven years old. I remember thinking, "This sucks. I can't get my arm out of there." I was only concerned about my arm and breaking the pool. I always worried about everybody else. Finally, it just went boom and I felt a shockwave through the pool as the pulling stopped. I thought there must have been a safety switch so it would be able to stop if there was an emergency.

Evidently it was a very old pump from the apartment complex. It had been there forever. It wasn't very safe and it didn't work well. So there was a big deal made over it when they looked at it. But nobody could figure why the pump stopped. It shouldn't have stopped; it was set to run for twenty minute cycles, if I recall correctly. Anyway, when I got out of the pool, I had a big red mark on my arm. You could see the little blood spots from the suction.

As for the last time, it doesn't really matter. It's all trivial at this point. I remember moving water in that pool every day, doing various things. At that time, I was with my biological father who was into a lot of spiritual things. He would haul me off to my aunt or the neighbor's houses. They sucked me dry by getting me to heal them or predict their future. I remember being led into rooms. After they shut the door, we'd sit on the bed and they would ask me, "Eric, tell me what's going to happen in my future."

I had never seen a psychic reading done before, so I gave them incredibly detailed readings – like the person's hair style and hair color, or the make and model of their car. I thought that was the norm for a reading. The first time I ever saw someone do a 'professional reading,' my mouth hung open. It was like, "A dark haired person. She's got a big car." I was thinking, "What kind of crap is that? It's so vague!"

I was around seventeen then. One of my female clients had dragged me off to a psychic fair. That's when it was a big deal at the mall. The line for me went down the inside of the mall and around the corner. All the other psychics hated me. People were bringing me flowers. Other 'psychics' asked me, "What are you telling people? Why are they bringing you flowers? What are you doing?" So I replied, "You're using tarot cards but you're not even telling your clients what they're meant for." So I realized that these false psychics were lying to their clients; that's when it first hit me. So I never did a psychic fair after that.

Water is what helped to accelerate my subconsciousness awakening. When I was first asked me to heal someone, I remember wondering how to do it. I was very young. What do you do? What's the protocol? Is there a book that tells you how to do it? What's the process? So I asked my father. He told me, "Just use your hands and touch them." I didn't want to touch them because they looked really sick. One guy had a sore on his side. I remember feeling a lot of pressure to heal him because he was very quiet, watching me.

Typically, there would be a roomful of people sitting in chairs. The room was really dark. I don't know how else to explain it except to say that it had that old Catholic feel to it. People kept telling me, "You've got to be a healer!" All of a sudden, I remembered about the water.

I thought about how I could move the water – all day long – every single day that I could. My skin must have looked like a prune. It wasn't about swimming. It was all about moving and feeling the water. I would move my body and it would push off my chest, literally moving like a gentle wave. It would hit the side of the wall. It splashed off the wall and it would come back to me. I remember feeling the subtlety of it when I paid attention to that very gentle feeling. I recognized that as something unique. I didn't swim around and splash like most kids do. I just floated like a log, but there was something else going on at a very early stage for me. It was training me how to use what I needed to get myself to where I am today.

As a kid, when I touched somebody's head to heal them; I remember reaching out and putting my hand on their head as if to pull something out of it. At that age, I wondered what I was going to pull out. My father told me, "Pull out the badness." The guy with the sore had a lot of cancer. Just for the record, I refuse to be a healer now. I will not go down the road of healing ever again, so please don't ask me. I'll teach you what to do so you can heal yourself or somebody else. I did it for many years in my youth and I swore I would never do it again.

Anyway, I remember putting my hand on his head and just pushing and lifting until I got to the point where I could get the water, like a suction cup. I could push it down and the wave would come up so that I could suction it up. If you try it, you can control it and minimize it. I literally remember pulling and feeling the weight after. I could feel the senses, and after a while I was very aware of the amount of inches that I was lifting it up. You all have this water information within you. It was recorded the first time you played around with it as children. So you just have to go back to that place within you.

When I put my hand on the guy's head, I recalled that same feeling, "I'll move it like I do the water." As I pushed with my hand, I could feel some other part of me in my chest intelligence. *So feel it in your chest intelligence, not just in your hand. There's a duality and it's important that I let you know that.* You can feel a pressure in your chest. It's a real thing but it's subtle. As I took a breath in, I pushed my hand down towards the person. Then as I pulled my hand away from the person, I breathed out. That's what I was doing. That's what was going on in my head. I do it instinctively, so it's like I did the same thing to their energy as I did to the water. I pushed down, *wanting the sensation of IT* but not in me. It was just like lifting the water, motioning my hand up and down. *If the water in him didn't ripple correctly, I knew that it would somehow hurt him.*

So playing with the water taught me how to work with energy. There's a correlation. Water is transparent; it's the closest thing between two thresholds, between what we imagine this other dimension to be. Ask yourselves, "How do you go into another dimension? How do you function? What do you do when you're there? How do you use these energies?" Everybody tells you "Move the energy out. Feel it going out."

Well, I repeat over and over that it's in the details. It's all about the details; that's what's going to get you there. For instance, if you're wondering how long a piece of cloth is going to last, look at the stitching that holds it together. Was it made poorly? Or was it woven strongly? You have to look. How did they stitch it? What kind of thread did they use for the stitches? Think about the details. The details are going to set you free. It takes a great effort for me to nail it for you, to figure out what aspect I'm looking for. First, I have to feel it and then I've got to translate it into verbiage.

I've gone into many houses that were supposedly haunted. For every one hundred supposedly haunted houses, you're lucky if one really has something in it. It could end up being squirrels, a hole inside the wall, a creaking house, water, or something else. I've seen it all. I've been bummed out and disgusted many times because there isn't anything here. The one house that does have something in it spurs you on to search another hundred to find somewhere else that's paranormal. So you really have to search for the real thing.

I can scan so well now that I don't even have to move my body, but I still do it. If you could see me out with the weather, I'm always analyzing what I do so I can teach it later. One time, I had my hand up while meditating and I was thinking to myself, "What are you doing?" In order to tell somebody what that is, I have to think about its spiritual aspects in English. You can't just do this without people knowing that you're probably messing with the weather.

So I turned and said to the person behind me, "I want to tell you what I'm doing. I'm not doing anything special, yet it *is* special. I have my hand out because the wind is a pressure that moves through you, but it's there. It's solid but it's not solid. I have this feeling that I'm reaching out to touch someone I love on the face and it's at this moment!

The first few seconds are better than the twenty seconds afterwards. There's this second where your heart feels this out and it feels good. It feels good that you're giving that love. It's like they love you back. Or they're surrendering into your hand because they know this is a beautiful affection. So I said, "I'm feeling the face of the wind," but it's like a *loop*. I don't want those first three seconds to ever end. I want to hold those three seconds forever! I just want to weep with joy for it. That's what's going through my mind.

These are the things that go through my head when I'm touching the wind. I want to caress it. I want to hold it. I want it to just lie in my arms so it's comforting me. I'm sure that you also have to feel the same thing. You're just not looking at the details; why and how come it's so intense. If I tell you, you can take it up several notches. I don't feel the wind on my leg or my arm; I feel it in my chest center. That is the zone. If you think about it, that's what you do as well.

I don't know how much you will try to grab with your hand because you will probably wonder how it's possible to grab air. There's substance there. There's weight. There's volume. There's mass too, but it's not the kind of mass that you think of in a solid object. As soon as you can get past that kind of thinking and accept that you can never fully grasp it, you can almost experience it in the chest area. This reception is just like making love to somebody, but without all the biochemical processing. If you love the wind enough, she'll dance with you. There's something that happens when you love it so much. Something or somebody always seems to knock you out of it. Usually somebody interrupts you or wants to say hello. It is almost like something spirals inside of you, if you just let it happen.

It's as if you want to physically use your body, yet it's the body that's holding you here. It's that weight in your brain. You just have to love it... love it... love it until you just can't love anymore. Then, all of a sudden, it almost pulls you right out. It's like you're out of your body! It just feels beautiful, like floating on the water. It's holding you, but it's got less mass than the water. So you just surrender to it. It's like it moves you around and, all of a sudden, it settles down and you're back in your body. You can't want for it to happen. If you want it, it won't happen for you. The second you want it, its desire is changed. It changes the texture or whatever is going on in your chest so you're setting conditions on what it should be. How do you know what it's going to be like if you've never experienced it?

You have to know it but you can't apply the rules to it. I'm telling you where to look for it and how to find it. I'm telling you when you experience it, this is going to happen. So don't panic and lock yourself in. Trust it. That's what I'm trying to say. When it begins to happen, you have an idea of what's happening to you, so don't panic. Just let the mind go like you learned in meditation. When you meditate, it may take a while to get to that place.

I know it is work, but it doesn't matter whether your meditation is perfect or not. You just have to do it enough so that you can learn these places. The second you know what's going on, you're going to recall the place that you let go because you're going to experience it at least two or three times, even if you've meditated for a year. At some point, you're going to hit those spaces because they're recorded. Everything I'm telling you is recorded in the water. When I'm talking, you know what I'm talking about; you're feeling it in your chest. Ask yourself a question: If you put your hand out to the water and you push back down, where are you feeling it? You're feeling it in your chest.

If I tell you not to say it, don't speak it with words. I want you to do the alphabet right now. Go on. Now stop. Point to me where it's emanating from. ABC. Where are you hearing the alphabet? You're hearing it in your head. You won't be able to say specifically where. When you move the water, there's a certain feeling to it. It's got an identity. It's got a name without being named. So when you lift your hand, it's almost like tension in your chest.

Get a bottle of water; pretend you're reaching out for it right now and you're just going to grasp it. What does it feel like? Can you feel its texture? Is it cold? Is it warm? Are there soft, rippled textures in it? Does the paper on the bottle feel a little different? This feeling has a name without words. This has a weight. You know every little detail already. Feel the cap. See the little ridges. Can you feel it? Is it memory or is something else communicating with you? Is it giving you the feeling in your mind? Is the bottle identifying with your mind or is it identifying with you down in your chest center? Don't worry about whether the brain is localizing it and it's moving the neurons. Forget it. I know all of that. It's the same thing when you touch the bottle. The nerves go up to your brain.

This has a name without calling it a bottle of water. It has a feeling. Name one thing that doesn't have a feeling. Can you feel a pillow without touching it? If you hold it, what it's going to feel like? Can you feel it? When you feel it, you feel it in your chest. When you feel its softness, you're feeling it in your chest. That feeling is a language. Later, I'm going to take you on a journey in a very creative way. I'm going to give you specific information that you can only decode by doing what I'm showing you now. If you try to name it, you're out of the loop. If you can hang with me and do the best you can out of what I'm going to talk about, you're going to get something that you can't get any other way - not in the physical, organic body.

So, the water helped me understand what I needed. When you see people doing tai chi, they're seeing their role and the energy simultaneously. You already know that feeling. How do you know? Is it ancient knowledge? Something is telling you that information so that you can feel it.

If you've been successful in some of my energy classes, that's fantastic. But if you only *think* that you have but aren't certain, don't lie to yourself. Students sometimes lie because they don't want to disappoint me. It's important that you're honest with yourself! I have to look students in the eye and ask, "Are you sure?" If they're not certain, I'll show them how to do it. Ten minutes later, they're astounded! What if I didn't ask if you were sure? What if I didn't annoy you and ask if you were sure because I doubted that you knew about it? You never would have known. You'd cheat yourself. Don't do it for me. Do it for yourself. Don't settle for second best.

I want you to think about water now. Your hands are underwater. I want you to imagine that you're moving the water in a circle in front of you. Feel it; feel the texture of the water on you. Imagine that you actually know how to move bubbles through the water. You're probably moving more energy now, but it's so minute compared to what you could do in a week or a month. It's just going to get stronger and stronger because the rest of the energy stops fighting.

Move the water in a circle in front of you. Use the water to help
yourself understand moving energy into a ball.

It's like your body says, "Oh, you're moving water. I understand the physics of it. I know what you're doing." You're stretching the truth and you're not thinking about whether you're stretching the truth or not. You don't ask yourself, "Is this possible? Can I logically figure it out?" First, you start with logic and it makes sense. The logical mind is going to think, "Well, you're not going to get the water to stay in a ball." So start moving it out away from you. Convince yourself of the truth. Convince yourself that you are doing it with water. Your body is saying, "Yes, it's doing that. Unequivocally, I can feel the water moving.

When doing this in the pool, if I'm still and if I'm close enough to the wall, I'll feel it eventually bounce back." This is how you train yourself to feel this. You can then step a little further back from the wall and do it again. Then wait. That's patience. That's non-thought. You have non-thought. If you're thinking, you're going to miss it. Then you take another step back and do it again. I had the pool to myself because I was out there on cloudy days. I could wait and wait and wait and be still. I remember being in the pool a long way from the wall. I could push the water from there and be really still but relaxed, like in non-thought. Eventually, I felt it subtly come back to me. There it was.

Had I not spent all those years in the pool, like a crazy maniac, I don't think I would know what I know now. Of course, being who I am and wanting to awaken, the Navigator really worked with me diligently. It was probably the thing that kept me in the pool because I wasn't off climbing trees. My mother used to think I was crazy. I had very painful ear infections every year and my mother would say all the time, "Don't go in the pool." I remember lying on the ground in pain because ear infections are the worst. If you haven't had one, you don't want it. Having an earache was like taking a little metal knife, getting it red-hot and sliding it in your ear. It is the very worst kind of pain I've ever had.

The building's maintenance budget was really cheap so they didn't put enough chlorine in the pool to kill the bacteria. I knew that if I swam in the pool, the bacteria would give me an earache. My mother had repeatedly told me what was going to happen and why. She was sick of taking me to the doctor. I knew the consequences of swimming in the pool, but I went anyway because I just loved working in the water. I remember lying out in the middle of the pool, floating and slowly letting the breath out of my mouth so I would sink. I remember just sinking, sinking, sinking like in an abyss. Then I did it over and over again.

There were points when I would just hover under the water because of the weightlessness. I would just lie there. I swam so much that I had very good lungs. I could hold my breath probably longer than I can now. I remember lingering there, away from my body, just as if I had no body. I was just free. Of course, then I would push down with my arms and I would come up for air. When I came up for air, it represented coming back into my body. As I'd come out of the water, there were all these sounds and music; people were doing things and I was immersed back into the world.

When I was in the other place, I didn't have that connection, so I could let my mind go. I had other sensations and there were other sounds but the water distorted them. So I was not intimated by things that my organic brain couldn't understand. When I switched my brain back to the sound, I came out of it because I was concentrating so much on what I was hearing. I got used to different things going on and I knew it wasn't a threat. I knew it was just part of that environment.

When I was very young, I learned how to do astral projection. By the time I was ten years old, I was very good at it. I remember two friends, Chipper and Ted, who were older than me. They had to have been seventeen years old. They knew I was really into astral projection but they didn't believe me. They thought I was making it up. I told them, "I'll take you and I'll show you these places that I'm talking about." That's how real it was for me. I don't know where I got this idea from because even today, I don't know how I pulled that off. They didn't believe me, but they were still curious enough to check it out.

I remember being over at Ted's house. I think that everybody that lived in those apartment complexes were poor. I don't remember there being a lot of furniture in that apartment. There was a bed in the room, so we sat at the edge of the bed with one of them on either side of me. Then I said, "Okay, give me your hands." We all sat there and I told them, "Just relax. Lie back and pretend we're floating in the pool. The mattress will support our bodies just like we're in the water."

I remember lying back on the bed, pretending it's a pool. We were floating and I remember saying, "Now we're going to go under the water. We're just going to let ourselves sink." So I pulled them as if I was pulling them down with me. Then I told them, "It's okay. You're not going to drown." They knew we weren't in the pool. They went with it; maybe it took a youthful mind to accept it without rationalizing it. So I sank down, then I said, "We're going up," and I just lifted them right out of their bodies!

That was my astral projection phase so I could see my body. I don't use that approach now-a-days.

I knew that I created the body. If the mind says that you need a body, you construct these things. What difference does it make if you have an energy body or if your consciousness is moving? You create the body because you need a body. How could you go anywhere without a body? If it comforts you, then work with it. If I don't say it, then how are you supposed to know? How are you supposed to accelerate? Breakthroughs inspire us to move on to bigger breakthroughs.

So anyway, I was lying on the bed and I didn't even think twice about it. It was like pulling someone to the surface of the water with me. Then we took off. They were shocked by their energy; but it wasn't vocal because I couldn't hear them anymore. There was no sound. I kept reassuring them, "It's okay. I have you. I know where I'm going." We went to other worlds. I showed them other things and they were just blown away. I remember doing it a few times. Then their families moved on.

Everybody always moved back then. I don't know why we didn't do it more often. I don't know why, it wasn't a big deal. As I reflect back on it now, it was quite profound, but I took it for granted. I moved on to other things spiritually or psychically. Of course, there was other chaos in my life, so those things brought me harder into this reality. It's like a fairy tale now, but it happened.

Water really is the medium to teach the body how to understand these energies and these movements. You don't have to know the intricacies of each movement. It isn't about that. After a while, what you need to know just surfaces.

So, when I go to a haunted house now, I don't need to use my hands to feel the energy, but I still do because I feel confident with it. This is how I'm used to doing it. I may look around with my head, but my mind isn't there. That's for the people in the house. They're wondering about the ghost or entity.

Everything has a feeling. Can you feel the chair? Now just go through it. With your energy, you can feel everything in the house - the chair, the pillows, the carpet, the wood floors, walls, paintings, and the light fixture. You know the feels-like for a chair. So as you're going through, feel everything. If you come across something that is unfamiliar, you may wonder, "What was that? That wasn't a chair, or a painting, or the carpet." It's something else. Then this something else, all of a sudden, might project, "Who the heck are you?"

They're curious because nobody's ever touched them. You're not touching them with words or sight, but with energy. They're going to feel you back because they're wondering what's going on. If you were a dead person and you were just floating around in a dream and somebody suddenly grabbed you, that's what it would feel like, but it's not physical. You're probably going to be shocked and surprised. It could be someone completely friendly but you're still not used to what's happening. This is new to your environment.

So, I go into the house and feel. It's not just like playing with the water. There's movement and I'm feeling it back. It's the texture of moving water. When I go after a spirit, there are a few that can get nasty. They're like kids with temper tantrums. They can't think straight. Their rationale is like a drunken person, but they somehow can't contain their thoughts correctly. They act irrationally. They're angry and they want to get rid of you.

If you went to a place where there was a spirit, would you want to keep it there so you could study and play with it, or would you try to get rid of it quickly? As long as it didn't bite you, you'd probably be curious. If it bites, you'll likely bump it out of there. So when you go into a house, use your hands like when you're in the water, sampling the energy. Also use your chest center and breathe the room in. Taste the air, rolling it off the front of your tongue.

Certain beliefs tell you to draw in Prana under the tongue. I don't want you to do that. Just lick the air without sticking out your tongue. When you breathe in, breathe in the room. That's where you're breathing the chair in. When you feel the chair, watch what you do. I bet you breathe in. When you try to feel it, it's almost as if you're inhaling because that tells your body to take it in, to feel it in your assimilation. If you pay attention to the subtle things, it will tell you the truth.

It's all in the breathing. Your breathing is what fools the brain, the Babbler, and the Governor, letting you slide by with something. When you do it more and more often, the Babbler starts to think this is just the way things are. It lets you do it more and more intensely.

So take one of those things and learn it. Don't try to do them all at the same time because thinking about what you're going to do is a problem. When you practice a technique over and over, just like you would a karate move, you learn to excel without thinking about what to do. It just comes naturally. When you're in a house and an unhappy entity feels you, you're going to feel it coming and you'll know what to do. You're going to hit it in the head, but you're not going to do it with your hand. You'll remember the water so you'll push it. If you don't think about the water and how it felt, you haven't got any power. You can't think about hitting it with your body.

When you've trained by working with water, you know all the programs from it already. You don't have to be in the pool to use those programs. You already know that whole pool is holographically in your head, feelings, and everything. You can just sit there, lie down, and go over all the moves. Feel it; move it; squish your hips; feel it. Then take it up a notch and go to the places that have dimensional frequencies.

Anyway, if someone urinates in a pool, it creates a hot spot. If you step into a hot spot, you know you're in one, so you know you're not in a good spot. If you're in a cold spot, it's weird because it's different. Everyone knows a hot spot is bad in a pool. If you think of the room as a pool, your tactile sensory tells you that you've got to switch it up by moving the water out of the room. So you're moving through the room. Then you're going to feel the fan. Feel it in your chest; breathe it in; feel the whole thing. Everything has a feeling. Just go in and feel the table, breathing everything in. Use your hands; your hands almost go where your eyes go. If you watch your hands, and you look for something, it's almost like your finger is already reaching before you even make the effort to tell it to reach. These are the subtle things one must pay attention to that will drive you crazy because there is so much to think about. If you do it often enough, you won't even think about it. It's like the karate move. Welcome to this dimension.

Chapter 10

CROSSROADS OF AWAKENING:

FEELS-LIKE

When I talk about feels-like, you probably have some understanding of it. I'm going to take feels-like and give it to you in a way that you can experiences pieces. Then I'm going to try to put it all together to show you what I'm describing as feels-like. I can't tell you the whole piece as there are just no words for it. You have to see, do, or experience feels-like to approach it. You can't do a feels-like if it just doesn't exist for you.

Everything should be familiar to you. Don't try to make logical sense of it. That's the worst thing you can do. If you catch yourself doing it, don't get mad and frustrated because you caught yourself doing it. If you catch yourself doing it, just go along for the ride. What's going to happen if you stand out in the rain? You're going to get wet. So don't worry about whether you think you got it or didn't. Don't be concerned if you don't think anything happened. I don't know what's going to happen with it. At some later point, you're going to sit down and meditate and some of what I said is going to come forward.

I'm giving you data so that when you meditate, it's going to come alive. That's the only way I can explain it. You're going to think about what I said and see the image or feel the impression of it. Then the rest of it is going to open because your energy is like a light bulb that runs on batteries; you are just touching the two cords together now. The mechanism is in place. You are the juice, so you've got to let it run. You will go into a certain place. You have the juice. The rest is there so it just drops down and comes to light, like you plugged in a Christmas tree. Before, it was just a tree. You couldn't see the lights before. Now it's all lit up in various colors. It's beautiful. Then it starts playing music and rotating. Don't think you're not getting it. It's not going to be what you expect it to be. And if you expect it to be anything, you will get nothing.

So, I'm just going to say whatever I can translate. It won't have any real logic and may sound like psychobabble. I just can't imagine it having any logic when I translate in my head from this place. You may want to get into a meditation position. Just let your mind go. Close your eyes; take a few breaths in and out. Do not try to make logical sense of what I am going to say. These pieces are going to pop up randomly and probably out of sync, but your minds are going to put it together and build it.

Walking up to a morning sink. A "morning sink."

It's difficult to translate for you. Sometimes things don't make sense. But you know exactly what I am talking about. I'm talking about the sink in your bathroom.

You walk to your morning sink. You're at the sink... turning on the water... the water is flowing ... hands touching water ... just still ... letting the water flow. The water has got the bubbles in it from how it runs. It's like the white water with all the oxygen from it ... and the hands are in it and it's appreciating the warmth ... and the water is moving over the hands... thin transparency to see the hands behind it ... the fingers behind it. The grooves of the finger ... the discoloration of the red blood underneath it ... and the white spots where the blood needs to move into.

The water ... the rhythm ... "sshsssssshssss." The water hitting it ... and just observing it. The water moving over the hands ... flowing, moving over the hands. It has a meaning. It "feels-like." Feels-like. The water over the hands ... the water moving over ... the transparency ... the fingers

... touching the water ... feeling the heat ... the texture of the water ... the water pressure ... not just the heat ... the feeling ... it feels-like ... the observance of it ... the watching of it ... the rhythm ... "sshsssssshssss." Feels-like! It's a good place ... simple but good.

And then stopping the water ... shutting it off... turning the dials ... turning the faucet off ... the hands reaching up wet ... The mirror there but not quite looking at it because the hands are coming up. The hands are in front of you and the water is there but it's not nearly as much. And you can see the discoloration still in your hand ... the red and the white behind the skin from the blood flow ... the fingers ... the glow ... the glow around the fingers ... the slight aura transparency. The energy around the fingers holds me ... holds me. I breathe in through the chest ... feels-like ... Feels good ... feels-like.

Touching my face and wiping the water on my face to wake ... to stimulate ... to clear the mind. Touching the face ... opening the eyes and seeing my reflection in the mirror ... my face ... my body ... who I am ... who I am supposed to be. I am looking at my face in the mirror. You are looking at your face in the mirror ... feels-like. Searching in the eyes ... looking at the eyes ... looking at the skin ... looking at the lines underneath the eyes ... the puffiness from waking ... the bridge of the nose ... the discoloration of the skin ... the pigmentation differences ... the sweat pores. Being still ... just staring. Breathing in from the chest ... slowly ... calmly ... feeling the moment ... Feels-like ... the moment feels-like.

Sitting on the stairs heading outdoors ... the steps from the door to the ground ... sitting down ... concrete ... porous concrete. Concrete is like pumice ... different stone speckles making up one piece. There's one piece of cement block to sit on ... my skin touching it ... the porous pumiceous of it. Not enough to scratch but enough to feel the roughness. The roughness feels good in a way ... cold and cool and firm and ... feels-like ... feels-like. Staring at the cement ... there's little tiny red bugs ... tiny ... tiny ... tiny little ones. And they just run around. They are just moving around ... no sense or order to the direction they are going ... no real purpose that's recognizable ... on the surface of the cement ... like mountain ranges to it ... depths and valleys. And it's running ... it's different ... staring at them moving around on the cement. Breathing in ... it feels good ... feels good ... feels-like ... feels-like.

The sun on the ground ... the intensity of it ... the brightness ... the yellow ... the white of it. The white of the light moving off the ground ... reflecting from the sun over my head ... and I'm not even looking at it ... it's on the ground. The moment is the light moving off of the ground ... not touching the ground ... just the essence of it. The whiteness of it... almost as if I was looking out now to a field and the whole area on a summer day. A summer day ... like 90 degrees ... the brilliance of it. Almost like my eyes hurt to see it ... and it's still. Everything is still. There is no wind ... there is nothing. It's just beautiful ... a field of hay ... like the white grass when the summer has dried it out ... and the summer is coming to an end ... but it's still a last summer's day. The hum of a bug in the distance. Still

... just staring at it ... staring at it ... staring at it. Feels-like ... feels-like.

Like you are moving but you are not moving. Like you can move forward or over it but you can't. You've got a body ... you've got feet ... you've got body mass. Like you're at the edge of a diving board ... very high up. You've got to dive ... and you want to dive but you are afraid to dive. It looks so far away now. It feels so far away ... the distance. Feels-like ... feels-like. And you know when you leap off ... you are going to be in it instantly ... feels-like. The approach ... the approach that you don't even think about. You just leap and you fall ... and you're moving ... and all you are doing is bracing yourself for the moment you hit it. It's the moment between ... the moment between stepping off and moving down. It is before you hit the water ... feels-like.

Children's marbles ... swirling colors in glass. Three ... four of them ... on a table ... rolling your hand around on them. Little lumps ... firm lumps of balls of glass pressing against your fingers. Moving your hands over them ... the table ... pushing from the other side through them back at your hand. Your hand pushing through the marbles ... back into the table. The space ... the space in between is the marbles. Pressing feeling rolling ... feels-like. Rolling them forward ... feels-like. There are four of them on your hand ... rolling them with your hand all at the same time in their own spots differently ... feels-like. The marble ... the swirling glass in the marble. The blue swirls with the darker blues around the baby blues ... like a wave in a piece of glass with transparent parts. Feels-like ... Feels artificial ... feels not what I want. But enough to interest me because it swirls ... it bends ... it's moving but it's not moving. It's still ... it's frozen ... feels-like.

The planet ... floating above it ... the atmosphere ... the vastness of it. I am engulfed not in the planet. I am brought in by the haze ... the haze is like a fog off the land after rain on a summer day. You can see this haze coming above the tree line. Haze ... its thickness ... thickness. And I see the planet below me and it has this haze over it. It's not a bad haze. It's moisture ... it's moisture. And it glows on one part because the sun is reflecting in the distance ... the distance ... the sun so small ... and the dark ... like liquid black ... like black ... no stars ... like ink. Almost a shimmer ... but no shimmer ... like a reflection ... like water would have on black ink ... or black ink with a shimmer. Black ink with shimmer ... feels-like.

The sun ... the earth ... I see the earth before me to the left of me ... the sun far back as a little glowing intensely small orange brilliant marble. The planet ... the haze ... the haze ... I almost want to breathe it in and breathe it out. It's life. It's moisture. It's the Force intermingled with Gaia. It is between. It is as if it is a balance between the two energies ... becoming one and solidifying ... and its water ... its energy ... its droplets ... its haze. Nourishing and feeding all around this ball ... this glowing ball of landmass I can see below. I can see oceans below the clouds. I see continents. I can feel emanating from it the "Auuuuummmm," and it's moving through me ... feels-like.

Looking at a billion stars around me now ... a night's sky ... the stars ... but no sound ... absolute deafening ... no sound ... nothing. And there is a hum that cannot be heard but it is there. It's a hum ... but I can't hear it. I want to hear it with my ears ... but it cannot be heard with your ears. But it is a sound. It is a presence. And it is moving through the stars. It is present everywhere. And if I move into it ... to somehow construct it ... it's like little waves ... thousands and thousands of waves. They're thin ... and ever not present. They are not there ... but they're just there. It's a hum that cannot be heard. It cannot be felt. But it says, "I am here." It is there. Feels-like ... feels-like.

Breathe it in. Feel it in the chest. Once you feel ... once you feel it ... it doesn't have a name. There's no connection to it. It's just ism. And it's like thousands of little static electrical lines ... billions of them. They are there but they are not there. It's like looking at a photograph. You look at the photograph ... and there's the picture. You look harder at the photograph and you begin to see little brown dots. The dots of color ... the billions and billions of them that make up the one ... the one picture ... as you pull your sight out to see the whole of the picture. You look at the stars. You look at the galaxies. You look at everything ... and it's in front of you like your hand. And you pull it all away. You pull it all away like the picture you just looked at with the little dots. You pull it all away. It's not what you see. It's what you're feeling between the moment of pulling it away ... the Universe pulling away to look at. It is the look at ... the anticipation just before it reveals itself ... for only a moment ... for a second. Feels-like ... feels-like.

Feel like it's moving ... the static lines are moving ... and the chest goes in and you don't know if it's good or if it's bad. It's nothing. It cannot be felt organically. The static lines ... the Universe, these fine thin little electrical lines ... billions of them. There's no sound. There's no feeling. There's nothing ... but yet there is a presence ... and it's going, "Auuuuummmm." It's beyond what I can do ... what I can project from my body. It's so deep. It's so powerful. It's so beautiful. It's so intense ... feels-like ... feels-like.

Feels-like floating in water ... every part of you touched ... but not pushed. Hugged but not held ... free, floating, but moving at the same time ... moving but not moving. I am here ... feeling the Aum ... the deep vibration beyond Aum ... because there is no name for it. There is no sound for it ... but again it is ever present. But when I feel upon it ... and I think what is on the other side of the Universe ... before I think what is on the other side of the Universe ... before I grasp organically the concept to think it. I know it already. And I move. I move ... and I'm on the other side of the Universe before I've had time to process the idea of thinking about it. It takes my chest and my stomach area ... and it's not there ... but it's there ... and now I'm across the Universe in the same position floating. And all around me is still yet this static charge that's going, "Auuuuuuummmm." Feels-like.

The Universe ... all of the totality of the Universe. My organic body ... the stars ... planets ... galaxies. It's all there. It's like meat. Substance ... structure.

*The frequencies are there ... and I say. I feel. I de-
sire ... before I can think it ... I know that there is
more. Like hyperdimensional shift but coming out
of some other place ... or going to some other
place. Everything just goes whoosh ... like a
transparent wave ... like a big object hitting water ... and it ripples ... feels-like. But it's not water.
It's not ripples. It's not ... feels-like.*

*All of a sudden, it bounces back and there's a
whole other dimension of galaxies ... time ...
space. Not galaxies ... not planets ... not stone nor
water nor substance. Yet, it is, "Ommmm
wwwaaaaa." And the frequency is the same but
now I know it's not the same little grid lines. It's
not the same color. But it's not a color because
it's ... feels-like.*

*The frequency lines are different ... but they don't
exist. They cannot exist ... but, yet they do. The
rational must go. Accept. Stop pushing. Stop
pushing your body against the water to get
movement ... because you can't move if you are
floating in air. There's no mass to push. There's
no body to push with. You think it. You feel it. And
before you think it and before you feel it, you are
moving again. I think. Before I can think, I desire
to know. I desire to know what can take me higher. What is beyond this? This that cannot be seen
... but yet there is stuff there. The organic brain
cannot compute it. It cannot see it. It cannot be
known, but yet it is there. How can it be denied?
You want to see it? You can see it. I choose to see
it. I choose to see it before I can think it. It comes*

from the chest ... the thinking ... faster than the brain. I think I want to see what this place is ... and I already know. This place is nothing. It's one of an infinitive amount of places that fills beyond your universe of understanding. I rest to it. I rest to it. I surrender to it. And when I surrender to it ... feels-like.

And what you see cannot be said. But yet it is there ... feels-like. It's just as real ... just as much substance ... but it's not substance. It's structure but there's no structure. It's as real as this place we are in now ... as firm as this ground. But it's not ... feels-like. It will spit you out like a seed from fruit. It will pop you right out ... if you don't surrender to it ... because you're foreign. Even as energy ... even as consciousness. You are foreign because you have too much weight. What is your weight? Your weight is the ugly parts of humanity ... of what's in that organism that does not belong. Surrender it. And now that I want to push further, I'm told no! I cannot disobey. But I want to disobey ... feels-like.

I want to show but I'm told I can't show ... feels-like. Am I allowed to feel frustration? No. Am I allowed to feel denial? No. They don't exist. If they exist, then I am already in the place of this dimension, and staying here. It cannot exist. Surrender it. I look at this static place and I want to know what's more. And I weep. I weep deeply because I want to go home. I want to go home and I know home is there ... feels-like. And when I weep ... so deeply from my chest ... feels-like.

I weep and then everything that I thought, when I wasn't going to get it, says, "Welcome. Welcome." Feels-like.

That's all I have to say.

I weep, but it is not sadness; it's joy. I weep for all of you that it may be open and you can go there. *Feels-like, don't forget the feels-like.* That is your key. You already have it. You've already earned it. It belongs to you. Don't forget that. I said so.

Chapter 11

ORIGINS EXPLORED

The leading Christian theosophists believe that over eighty percent of the Bible is embellishments. So most people who follow the Bible don't really know what is or isn't the truth. You're told to believe on faith, but when you compare the Bible to archaeology or information based on fact, you come out with an entirely different story. My belief is that if you can't rely on something one hundred percent, you should be very cautious.

First of all, I *do not* believe in Heaven or Hell. I *do not* believe that angels rebelled against God and in the process were cast out and turned into demons. I really feel that religion is filled with a vast amount of made up stories and lies. There are so many different perspectives on the story about Lucifer and God.

As you know, Lucifer was the number one Archangel, *arch* meaning top of the line, and he was considered to be the angel of light. He was the most beautiful and most respected of all the angels. In fact, he was at the "right hand" of God, so to say. God said to him, "You'll never bow down to anyone but me. You will always be number one with me. You're always going to be at the top of the line." This is the *Reader's Digest* version in modern day lingo.

Lucifer loved God. He would die for God. He fought God's battles; he did his errands for him; he even went out and spied for him. He did all of this without question because of his love for God. God was the highest, most important thing to him. Nothing was higher. And if God spoke, that's the way it is. That's going to be the way it is for infinity, because this is God, and Lucifer was the most loyal being to God.

Time moved on and in the process, God created the Earth and eventually Adam and Eve. God said to Lucifer and the other angels, "I've created humanity and you will bow to them. Humanity is greater than you and you are second to them. Humanity is now my greatest accomplishment, created in my image. Humanity is beautiful, perfection, innocence, and goodness." And Lucifer said, "What do you mean? I don't understand. You told me I'd never have to bow to anyone else. You told me no one else would ever come before me. You're God! Whatever you say is the way it is. What do you mean I have to bow to humanity? That I am second to humans?" And God said, "End of discussion, there's nothing to discuss. I'm God, that's the way it is."

Lucifer had a big problem with that. So Lucifer and the other angels got together and decided, "Well, if God says this is the way it is, then that's the way it is, but God changes his mind. So what stability is there in having faith in God, if God can regularly change his mind any time he wants? What security is there? What feeling of belonging is there when we could belong today and not belong tomorrow?"

They were angry over this; they were frustrated over this and this is what started the division. Some angels sided with Lucifer and some of the angels didn't. They said, "Well, God is God. God can do whatever he wants to do, and if God changes his mind, that's God's decision." And Lucifer said, "But this is God! This is not like the mayor, or the President, or your wife, or something. God can't just whimsically change his mind!" There was a heated argument and that is what caused the rebellion.

And they said, "We don't agree with you, God. We're not going to bow to them. We're not going to put them above us. We're not. You said we were all of this and we dedicated our lives to you." And God said, "Fine, then leave." This was their home. Where else did they have to go? And this is what created the turmoil, the battle, and the casting out.

In my opinion, these stories are just embellishments. In fact, I don't believe in the the "truth" of the Bible to begin with. The majority of it was created by humans. Are demons hideous, repulsive creatures that want to do you harm? Are they vile beings, such as what you've seen on *The Exorcist*?

Are you more intelligent with age? Are you wiser? How about when you are 50 years old? Are you wiser and more intelligent then? What if you are 100 years old? You're going to be a little wiser, right? How about 300 years old or 400 years old, 500, 1000, 10,000 years old? Are you more articulate? Are you more intelligent? Are you calmer, patient, and more refined?

How old do you think the angels are? They are ancient. They're supposed to be immortal. They were around long before the Earth was even created. So, all of a sudden, these educated, intelligent helpers that created the Universe with God's help become barbaric, hateful animals overnight? That is ridiculous. It's preposterous. Think about it. They're civilized. They're beyond civilized. They're instilled with absolute understanding of the complete mechanisms of the Universe. They're fully capable of understanding molecular structure far beyond anything science ever will. And yet, they have nothing better to do than run around the Earth possessing and killing people and making them commit suicide? That is ridiculous! It is fictional. It's all creative imagination. The Bible was written during a time period when people needed a basic understanding of life. They didn't have the education that we have today.

Suppose a Neanderthal man walked through a forest in our current times, but didn't know he was in the 21st Century. Let's say he was able to access the future and was just walking along. Then a jet flew over his head. How do you think he would react to that? He would die of fright. But if you were walking through the same forest and a jet flew over head, what would you do? Fear wouldn't enter your mind at all, except maybe from the surprise of it.

The Bible was written, created, and formulated for simple people. Of course, there were some educated people then too. They used fear to manipulate and control the non-educated people. So, the Bible was manipulated over time by well-educated, intelligent people who used their power to get land, control armies, and influence kings and queens. It was distorted and twisted in a very evil and malicious way. Demons and the fiery pit were used to instill fear into the uneducated masses to control them.

Now that we've established that, do I believe in demons? Yes, I believe in demons. I believe that there are different kinds of demons, and I think that it's much more complicated than most people understand. Is there a hell? No, there's not a place that you go where you're perpetually tortured throughout infinity. I do believe there is a kind of hell though.

First of all, when people talk about their life-after-death experiences, they were really not dead, even though they say they were clinically dead. Their heart and their breathing may have stopped. They may be unconscious for ten minutes, but it's not brain death. True death is brain death, when the brain totally shuts down. That's it, you're dead and you aren't coming back. But if you don't have brain death, then you're really not officially dead. The brain still has electrons moving. It's still doing something internally. People talk about times when they've been attacked or when they're drowning. At first, you fight and you struggle. Then your brain says, "Okay, well this is it," and you start to shut down. Your brain releases a chemical that's much more powerful than heroin, and all of a sudden, you feel the most blissful, at ease, peaceful experience you could ever imagine. Your brain is totally relaxed. You don't feel any pain. People who have been attacked by lions say the same thing. It's a chemical that's released in their brain. There's a relaxing, blissful chemical that's released into the body.

Many religious people have said, "I saw a tunnel. I saw my friends and relatives at the end of the tunnel. Jesus was there." Well, the tunnel is actually a very common thing, universally seen throughout the world. A Christian will make it sound like it was a miracle, like it was exclusive to them. That's what makes their faith the one "true religion." What they don't mention is that Buddhist monks and Hindus see the same thing.

Whoever you imagine as your savior or whatever you expect to happen at the end of your life is what you will experience at the end of that tunnel. If you don't believe in any of those, you're still going to see a tunnel, and that is your Heaven. Eventually, when you get to the end of it, the brain dies. All of a sudden, it's just like a TV without power. It's over, unless you believe in a soul, which is a whole other discussion for another time.

So, unless you are revived before you go through the tunnel, your mind will create all kinds of things at the end of your life. Suppose you took many hits of acid. You might see anything, even floating angels. You could see all your relatives, anything your mind wants to create just like you are on an acid trip. But, unless you're medically resuscitated, your brain will eventually stop. The picture's over, and you're dead!

If you are resuscitated, you can come back and talk about your great experience and now different things can happen. You could leave your body through astral projection. The energy will start to accumulate and it will seem as if you're moving out of your body, but it's really all happening internally in your head. When you feel as if you're temporarily leaving your body, your soul is not really leaving. It's energy that is like a satellite. You're creating energy to go outside of you. It happens so fast that you don't even realize what's going on. So, there are different things that can happen, but it doesn't mean there's a heaven or a hell.

In the same way that you find "*heaven*" and come back to life before brain death, you can also find "*hell*." It's not talked about much because people are terrified after their experience and don't want to discuss it. However, they really do think that it exists. I'll give you an example.

I heard about a person who died. He found himself floating above Earth. Now you can imagine this must have been a beautiful sight. He saw stars, pitch black-ness, the golden hue of the sun, the blue planet with white clouds and oceans illuminating it with light. And he was floating there. In the process of floating there, he realized there was a puzzle in front of him, and he instinctively knew that when he completed the puzzle, he could move on. He could go to Heaven, or reincar-nate. He could move on, and he knew this. So he thought, "Okay, fair enough." This was his punishment. He had to work this out, but he didn't think it was going to be that difficult. So he began to put the puzzle together.

As he put each piece into place, the shape of the puzzle became evident. He reached for the next piece and by the time he turned his head back to look at it again, it had changed. He realized he would spend eternity trying to put this puzzle together, never being allowed to leave. This is all he would ever do. So he's intensely frustrated, and he knew then that he was in Hell. And that's hell if you ask me!

Hell is something that you have to work out in your own mind, your own inner guilt. Guilt is what creates hell in your brain. You know what you've done wrong in your life. You know what you've done wrong to other people. That guilt is going to have to be worked out in your brain when you die. In your mind, what feels like 24 hours is probably less than a minute.

On older computers there was a little button that said, "Turbo." When you pressed that button, it forced the computer to run twice as fast or up to five times faster. That means what once took ten minutes to process could now be done in about two minutes. When your body shuts down and the brain starts to do everything, it hits "Turbo." Your thoughts seem to be operating naturally, but in reality, they're moving one thousand times faster. So, you could do more in your head than if you were awake and alert, and it would seem very real to you. People see their whole life flashing before them.

I was in an accident where my car was hit by some drunk drivers. My car flipped over. I was inside the car, moving rapidly down the street, upside down, waiting to hit the guardrails and die. It probably took only a minute or two. When that happened, I thought about my family, my friends, my life and my spirituality. I wasn't afraid, but I thought about so much. I remember being aware of the other cars going by. It was like slow motion, as if I was becoming impatient. My thinking was, "When the hell am I going to hit the curb?" I was starting to run out of things to think about. It sounds funny, but it's the truth. I knew when I hit the curb, and I didn't go over the edge. That was cool, too. So the brain sped up so fast that it processed thought at an incredible rate.

The same thing happens if you are at your death scene. You visit your family, walk around the garden, or grave site, and internalize it. It's because the brain is creating this inner universe of thought, and it's all about making you feel more peaceful. If you've committed sins or done bad things in your life, then it makes you go to your perceived hell. It makes you work all these things out before you actually have complete death, brain death. This is the truth about heaven and hell.

I strongly recommend that you watch a movie on this subject. It's called *Jacob 's Ladder*. It's a lot more truthful than you think. It's my concept of hell and heaven. You can have a combination of both, which is basically the story of this movie. Hopefully, you now have a better insight into this subject, and I think it's a more logical and intelligent one.

So, this plane of existence isn't necessarily heaven or hell, rather it's your own guilt or thoughts that can create it?

That's right. You can't remove guilt, but you can work it out while you're still alive. If you've done something really bad, you can work it out now instead of trying to work it out as you're going through your death scenario. But don't think for a minute that you will say, "I feel guilt free."

As for the demons, they are beings, either human or alien, that have achieved a level of awareness. They believe in life after death and practice that level of knowledge. In other words, you practice to create a vessel or a soul to leave this body so that you can exist outside of your body. They have too, but they were corrupted by the Darkside. Even though you're with the Darkside, you can still achieve certain things. The Force says, "If you're going to be evil, you're going to be evil." It doesn't say, "I'm going to zap you and kill you." It's got its own ordeal with the Darkside.

You still have individuality. You can become an evil soul, hateful towards life. You may not *want* to be incarnated. Maybe you've been around for so long that you despise human beings or you despise life. You just want it all to end because you are immortal. You can't even kill yourself now. So, there is a psychological sickness you take on that's similar to a psychopathic serial killer, if you will. Thought is thought. It's not that you have to be human to be a psychopathic killer. You can be an entity and be the same way. They have no body, but their logic is screwed up and they perpetually hate life. They perpetually hate human beings. They perpetually hate other beings, and in some ways do damage, attack, defile, or try to destroy anything in their path.

Most people have preconceived ideas about demons, but there are several other possibilities that should be considered. A demon could be a person who was once very spiritual but has taken the path of the Darkside. They have not incarnated and are psychologically hateful towards human beings. Or it could be an entity from another dimension. Another possibility is it may not be a demon at all. It is absolutely feasible to have an *alter-reality of you*. In other words, you are telekinetically moving something by willing it to move at the right time and at right place.

The mind can do incredible things. Who is to say that you don't have alter-personalities? Or that you can't project yourself somewhere and physically manifest a form of energy in the shape of a human body, or at least scratch somebody physically? When something happens, people automatically think, "Oh my God, a demon did it," but it could be another human being telepathically or telekinetically doing this to you from their dream state. You should never take the first option as the only answer, assuming that everything's caused by a demon. There are many other possibilities in the realm of the paranormal.

I classify them on a scale of one to ten. A level one entity would make you subtly feel its presence so that you know there is an evil presence around you, but it doesn't have the power to do anything to you. A Level ten entity could literally grab ten people and throw them right through a glass door. For no apparent reason, it could physically snap your neck as you walk by. Or it could make an entire wall rip out, exercising incredible levels of strength.

How many level tens are there in the world? There's probably none. Do they have the ability to come here from time to time? I would imagine it's possible. They might come once every 10,000 years. It's more likely that you are dealing with a lower level entity at a maximum of Level five with seven being the most extreme. However, that is extremely rare. As an average human being not practicing anything paranormal, the odds are more likely that you would come across a Level one entity. It's a million to one chance that will occur, but it does happen.

Entities do not just physically attack you. Since we are electrical beings, we are also emotional. Emotion is electricity, or electrons in the body, and chemical charges in the brain that produce a reaction. The chemicals are released and emotions or feelings are felt by the electrons stimulating the chemical to be released. A negative entity can have a great amount of hatred, but not have the ability to physically harm you. They can't condense their energy enough to touch you. The message they project is, "Why are you here? Get out of here! I hate you! Die! Die!"

If they're constantly doing this to you, you may react by suddenly lashing out at your mate. You may become physically violent with them and draw blood, or maybe even harm them. Your brain cannot discern the difference between *your emotion* and the emotion of something coming from an unknown source. It just assumes that it's your own emotion. The brain doesn't define what's yours and what's not. It doesn't see, hear, smell or taste anything. Therefore, the brain is very limited by human conditioning that it deduces, "Well, this must be free will."

There's always an exception to every rule. You are dealing with something that is not yet mapped out. It's a world of dimension and thinking that is untouchable, un-seeable, and unknowable. Except for certain points of study and research, there are not answers for everything. You could always say, "Every time I push this cup, it's going to fall a certain way," but there's always that one time that it will fall in a different direction.

The more aware you are, the more you are going to say, "This is not *my* feeling." If you don't have that knowledge, you cannot come to any other conclusion than to say, "This is the way I am and I'm going to hurt this person." With the right training, you say, "This is *not* my normal self." Then the brain says, "Red alert! Where is this coming from?" Then you start to rationalize and feel the entities presence. But until you start to think like this, the entity is in stealth mode. You think it's you.

There are energies and feelings from other human beings that you might feel and think, "Oh, that's bad." That doesn't mean it's coming from an entity. It could be coming from hostile energy, composed of anger or hatred, that's imbued into a pillow. It's going to compress in here. That's why everything has an aura. It's going to broadcast out and suddenly after about 30 minutes, you're going to say, "Why do I feel so bad?" But you are not aware of where that emotion is coming from.

Is there any difference between an entity that's not in a body and one that is? Isn't the one encased in a body so negative that it's the same thing?

They have advantages that one doesn't have in a human body, but also vice versa. If you're intelligent, there are advantages in every situation.

Does an entity's emotions enter your mind the same as people's emotions do?

Not as freely. Human beings don't think about forcing their will on someone whereas an entity is constantly in thought. They can't touch you physically, so they use their mind instead. Will this, will that. That's how they do things. The entity will have an advantage over you because it's used to doing things that way. It will make you go crazier faster than a human being could. It's like working muscles. If you lost your left arm, and you could only use your right arm, wouldn't your right arm get very strong? Yes. Since you are able to touch, write, and do everything tangibly, you don't use your mind to communicate with. But an entity does it all the time. If it wants to make you feel a certain way, it can easily overpower you because it's so used to communicating that way.

You are becoming aware of a kind of knowledge that is not necessary. What I mean by that is you don't need to know this knowledge in order to live your life. To those of us who are interested, intrigued, and absorbed by it, there's no other choice. We need to have this kind of knowledge. The more you know the scarier, but then also the more beautiful it becomes. We're focusing on a very ugly subject out of many positive subjects. The more knowledge you gain, the more of a threat to the Darkside you will become. So the more equal and opposite reaction it's going to create. This is your situation with entities and demons. It's a whole conversation and class in itself that falls under a different topic. Later, you'll be able to combine the two and then things will make more sense to you.

When you learn High Guard and different things about energy, you'll learn how to defend yourself and fight these things. Energy is everything. The more Prana energy you can consume, the more powerful you will be in order to do what you want to do. It's a fuel. Some people call it, "Psi." It's an energy that you consume. You can get energy from meditating. You can get energy from thinking about Prana and drinking water. Whether it's for combat or for doing anything spiritually, Prana energy is everything. It's critical. It's the core of development. The more you can get, the more powerful you will become and the farther you will go.

Now that I've covered a little bit about demons and you have a better concept of them, let's look at angels. Now you get to look at the positive side of things. For the most part, angels are also a fabrication of humanity. During the progression of time, it started to evolve from one concept and metaphor into a human concept.

Essentially, the first concept of an angel can be traced back to a creature that looks like a lion with wings and a human face. It would be at the doorway of a holy place, and these creatures were supposed to stay there to protect the entrance. It was essentially a guardian. This was the origin of the concept. It then metamorphosed into something different because all of imagination comes from one idea to the next as you evolve it. These were, in my opinion, the first angels. As time progressed, the concept changed from a lion with a human face to a human with wings. Then it became an angelic figure instead of a mystical creature. This is really where the concept of angels with wings originated.

There were prophets who claimed they had visions. They had conversations with angels or God in the desert. Let's say you think about meeting Bugs Bunny and you are determined to meet him, so you put a great deal of thought into this. You think about his weight, height, intelligence, what he would say or wouldn't say, in great complexity. Then one day, you decide you're going to go out to the desert, which can range from 125 degrees during the day to extremely cold at night, and you're out there for a month without food or water. What do you think is going to happen? You're going to hallucinate! Who are you going to see if you're bound and determined to meet Bugs Bunny out there? You're going to meet Bugs Bunny! You're going to see Bugs Bunny so real and so tangible that it's going to blow your mind.

If people go out to the desert for two days without nourishment, say on a vision quest, they will become dehydrated and see mirages. They think they see water and tropical vegetation. They literally do. This is no joke. This is not a TV or Hollywood thing. This really does happen.

So those prophets would go out to the desert for three months at a time, and they would come back with horrific stories about God, angels, and many experiences of how they battled the devil. This is what they conceived they were going to experience, much like the death scenario you think you're going to get. It's very similar. I believe this is why most of them saw angels. They believed they were going to see angels, so they went out there and had a conversation with Archangel Michael.

You don't ever hear about them having a conversation with Archangel Michael while having a drink, feeling nourished, refreshed, and positive. No, they're usually half-dead, lying on the ground, and the angels are flaming above them saying, "Hey you, by the will of God!" And you're replying, "Hello."

So, again, I don't give credit to a lot of the stories about the prophets and their experiences. I'm not saying that they're completely incorrect, but they're certainly arguable and questionable.

If aliens showed up in front of a large group of Christians and started yelling at them, the Christians are going to say, "It's a demon!" It could be the most brilliant thing that ever happened to them, if only they would just sit down and figure out what the alien was trying to communicate. It could be the kindest, loving creature, but people are generally afraid of anything they don't understand.

Since I do believe in past lives, alien worlds, and many unexplainable things, and also believe I've lived many past lives before, I will give you some hidden knowledge.

There were beings from a distant part of the Universe who were highly advanced, and appeared to have arrived on Earth at a very early time period when there were no cities, farms, or things of that nature. Humans were just at the point of becoming intelligent. Seven of these beings suddenly appeared. They were seven feet tall with very large eyes. These beings had knowledge that was heretofore unknown, and they taught it to the people. They educated them in medicine, architecture, mathematics, agriculture, and many other things.

Over time, the beings disappeared. Did they even exist? Were they ever here on Earth? Certain historical texts from ancient cultures claim that they were. There are statues carved in their image that exist even today. There are stories saying those people were on Earth. The most interesting fact is that, almost overnight, civilization was suddenly educated. All of a sudden, they had mathematics, agriculture, and architecture. Under normal circumstances it would take years to develop all of this, but they did it very quickly. So there had to have been some influence from the beings.

They were called "Elohim," which is translated as 'god' or 'gods' in Ancient and Modern Hebrew. In either case, they disappeared and the civilization flourished. There was an earthquake or a land upheaval. Many of the people who survived broke off and travelled to different locations throughout the continents and then resettled.

Around that time period, Egypt suddenly emerged and other great empires were developed. We believe that their knowledge came from those seven beings. Over thousands of years, those beings were depicted as being the archangels from the Bible. They became the Greek gods and the Norse gods. You will notice that the gods always had a certain function, in almost every case, until humanity evolved and came up with the concept of one God.

This is where the concept of angels came from. It's where the biblical stories actually originated from because the stories weren't written then; rather they were passed down by the people. Nobody was educated enough to write. There were lyricists and poets who traveled, telling stories through their words. Of course, in time, everybody had a better way of embellishing them.

In the book, *Angels: An Endangered Species*, by Malcolm Godwin, Chapter 5, page 210, it reads, *"There is a certain lazy arrogance in our modern assumptions of who we are and where we came from." "We smile indulgently when we learn of the Anglican archbishop of Armagh, Dr. James Ussher who calculated the creation of the world to have been at precisely 8 pm on the 22nd of October, 4004 BCE." "We remain amused to learn that the Vice Chancellor of Cambridge University insisted that Adam was not actually created until 9 am on the following day (Greenwich Mean Time)."*

They're making a joke of these people. It's ludicrous to come up with these statements. What do they base this knowledge on? From what point of fact do they evaluate? But people will say anything for fame. Anyway, *"Most 20th century citizens have Darwin's theory of evolution, with its vastly expanded time scale, firmly established in their minds when reading of such childish inventions."*

By having this knowledge, when you hear this kind of thing, you realize how hokey it is since you believe more in evolution. *"It is now acknowledged that any hypothesis which gives the age of the Universe as less than 10 billion years old is absurd,"* which is very true. It's actually closer to 15 billion years old now. *"Virtually, all the authorities from the various disciplines, which examine pre-history, present a comforting assurance that Homo sapiens appeared simultaneously with the last of the Neanderthals around 32,000 years ago. It was these new humans who created the awesome drawings and paintings which were found in the caves of Lascaux."*

"Orthodox theory then seems to lose track of these superbly gifted and visionary people until they turned up 20,000 years later in Jericho, the Indus Valley, Sumer and

Egypt." What happened to them for 20,000 years? First, they're in caves and then they just disappear. There's no sign of them evolving, creating tools, weapons, shelter, nothing. They just ceased to exist. *"By then, our ancestors had mysteriously, as if overnight, acquired the most miraculous skills of cutting building blocks, harvesting, storing grain, making long ocean trips in large sea worthy vessels, and working metals."* Of course, this is after 20,000 years that we just reappear! *"Every year, new discoveries in all parts of the world pushed this historical rising further and further into the past. Although there is concrete evidence that our old prehistorical view is wrong, outdated chronologies live on in our minds."*

In other words, we believe in God and the Bible instead of really understanding. Even when it's pointed out to us, we have a bad tendency to go back to our old beliefs, even though something better has been shown to us that is probably accurate and more truthful. We just habitually always go back to our old habits. *"The problem seems to be that the sheer weight and mass of archaeological opinion is about as movable as the pyramids. Too much painstaking labor has gone into the whole theoretical framework for a few curious anomalies to make any dent in the superstructure."*

However, there are a number of unorthodox views as to how primitive, foraging cavemen so abruptly acquired superb civilization in the Middle and Near East as if from nowhere. Theories of how this could have come about range from the plausible to the outrageous. Von Daniken proposes that we are the experimental product of visitors from outer-space. Charles Berlitz suggests that the legendary island of Atlantis once had a thriving and advanced culture, even before the painters of Lascaux had found their caves. Then about 12,000 years ago, it suffered devastating collapse. He maintains there were survivors who escaped to both the old and the new world with remnants of their once advanced technology.

James Churchward spent his whole life searching for concrete evidence of a lost continent in the Pacific which he called Mu, supposedly occurring at the same time as Atlantis and almost as technologically advanced. He also believed that this great civilization once drowned by some terrible volcanic upheaval which caused the land mass to sink into the ocean. The survivors spurred to South America in the east and to China and India in the west, reaching as far as the coast of the Mediterranean.

In another account, Christian O'Brien would have us believe that, *"A small band of luminous individuals appeared out of nowhere, yet had such a profound effect upon our ancestors that they remain in our memories and in our myths and legends as angels."* This is what we're talking about now. *"It is easy to dismiss those writers whose academic or scientific backgrounds do not correspond to what an archaeological expert is supposed to be."* They provide the valuable service of questioning the holy cows of orthodoxy. So that means that we're not supposed to question them. They're so knowledgeable and so great that they tell us, "This is the way it is," and we're not allowed to ask, "But, what about...?" They don't want to hear it.

"O'Brien is of special interest as he authors a closely argued case, giving a plausible and very down-to-earth explanation of the origins of the angelic host, and it is an explanation we just cannot afford to ignore. It is a classic within the genre usually labeled, 'Alternative

History.' His action centers in the Lebanon and the Mesopotamian basin. Sumer has long been considered as the crucible of civilization about 5,500 years ago. It had suddenly blazed forth in a number of closely connected centers within the valley of the Tigris and Euphrates. There was a prodigious explosion of art and artifacts which appeared with seemingly no transitional era between cavemen and the priest kings who seem to be the focus of all of this activity."

In other words, there are cavemen. Then suddenly there's art, structure, and paintings. *"The archaeologist and writer Andre Parrot has suggested this sudden flowering could only be attributed to the genius of the few. Who these brilliant integrators could have been, or where they came from, formed the basis of O'Brien's speculation. He suggests that they were a group of advanced archaeologists who physically appeared to be very different from the indigenous natives of the area. It was these great lords of cultivation who created a settlement in the region of present day Lebanon. It was this cultivated area with its extensive irrigation schemes and rich orchards which became the model upon which later scholars and priests based the various myths of paradise Eden."*

This is where Eden came from. I'll read it again. It says, *"It was these great lords of cultivation who created a settlement in the region of present day Lebanon. It was this cultivated area with its extensive irrigation schemes and rich orchards, which became the model upon which later scholars and priests based the various myths of the paradise Eden."* This is a story embellished over time. Let's say you were a cave dweller and you had never seen a garden, let alone aqueducts with moving water, and you had to pick berries by walking five miles in a given direction to find a berry bush growing wild, or some roots and nuts. Then, all of a sudden, you walked out and saw this giant field of pure vegetation with water going to each little one and literally tons of strictly food, with no random trees, what would you think?

That's Paradise.

Exactly, that's Paradise. You're darn right it is. It's beautiful, and it made such an impact on their minds that it became Paradise over time. A new story was given and given and given until it became known as Eden. Then it was written in the Bible. *"It was within the boundaries of this Garden of Eden located in the highlands near Mount Herman that we first encounter the seven archangels, their lord, and the infamous watchers who became the fallen angels. This is hardly a timid theme. Its very boldness becomes all the more attractive when we discover that there are at least two factual and relatively unadorned accounts describing this settlement and those who lived and worked there. It is a story of the building of a community which might well have been very like a modern Israeli kibbutz."* (This means a gathering of people.)

"Between the two records, we can build up a picture of its creation and its Golden Age and the steady decline when the so-called angels dispersed and left the area. What is fascinating about the whole epic is how the Sumerians, the Babylonians, and the Hebrews, all of them God-makers, managed to still embellish the original story that by the 4th century BCE, the leader of the settlement had become God. His lieutenants had

been transformed into archangels and their working assistants were now flying around as angels."

"The early Hebrew people, in keeping with their wandering nature, were habitual exiles and thus a highly eclectic people. Their scholar priests freely borrowed from whichever culture they happened to find themselves in, whether it was Egyptian, Sumerian, Babylonian, Assyrian, or later Persian, Greek, or Roman. Scholarship by its very nature, whether religious or secular, anthropological or archaeological, is notoriously inventive when describing the artifacts of ordinary life."

"The temptation to spice up an otherwise dull subject often has led to attributing great events to little happenings, and creating supernatural phenomena where none actually existed. Thus, a chair is transformed into the 'sacred throne' of a priest king, and a toothpick acquires the aura of a holy relic. In the following account, we see how such a process has probably been in action for over 5 millennia. Religious ideas were plastered over secular events, creating legendary stories."

"Over the years, these stories became truths which avidly fed upon themselves, within whichever closed or chosen community they were found. In such a greenhouse condition, even the most patently absurd ideas can become stronger and more uncontroversial with each ritual and act of worship. In this way, two very ordinary secular events could have become defined. One is the legend of the Garden of Eden, and the other is that this paradise was peopled by supernatural beings called angels."

This is the origin of angels and devils. This is the whole concept on these two topics. I've heard people claim that they believed every human being had one guardian angel. I want you to think about how many

people are on this planet right now. Consider not just
Los Angeles, which has millions, not just California,
which has even more millions of people in it, not just
America, which has hundreds of millions of people, but
also Canada's millions. What about Mexico, which has
one of the largest cities in the world, and Europe which
contains France and Germany?

You've got to look at the whole planet. Right now,
imagine our planet from outer space, with billions and
billions of human beings on this planet each having
their own designated archangel who watches over
them 24 hours a day. Hello! Give me a break! It's
ridiculous! This is like saying, "I want to be so happy
and thrilled in life that everybody has an angel." I'm not
going to pop your bubble. If you're happy thinking that
way, that's fine. I choose the truth.

Why can't you save your own life? Why can't this be
an entity or spirit that just happens to be there at that
time? It could be kinetics. It could be your parent's
kinetics or a friend's kinetics saying, "Oh my God!", and
throwing its energy out so that it saves your life or
moves you. There could be other types of energy rather
than an angel.

Could your own energy push you out
of the way as self-preservation?

Absolutely, it can. Now some people might say to me,
"Well, how come they have the ability to move things,
or how come they have such physical strength?" When
you're scared, you have massive amounts of adrenaline
surging through you, and you can do amazing things.
Mothers have picked up entire cars and pulled their kid

out from underneath it in an emergency situation. That's adrenaline; it's amazing.

When you are possessed, you don't have any thought. The brain just starts pumping chemicals out. It pumps you with adrenaline so you can do incredible things, which would explain that supernatural strength. Suppose someone were able to do something psychically, such as read your mind. They believe they're a demon, so all of their natural psychic abilities come through since the Governor is now removed. If there's no Governor, there's nothing to limit how much ability they have. So all of a sudden, they growl like a demon and they make things move. This is part of the whole process which makes it very believable.

In my opinion, angels are not necessarily the ones that have been incarnated, because anybody can be incarnated, reaching awareness. They're really the ones that significantly contribute to the Universe. The defenders of the Universe are the ones who are enlightened. They are the angels, much like the Elohim who originally came to Earth. They educated the people and they became angels through stories. But it could be anybody who teaches a profound knowledge, evolving you so that you can understand the inner workings of the Universe, not the outer workings where you can see planets and stars, but the inner forces that affect us.

By saying you need to defend life, and instill the drive to defend life, that has to be Angelic. If you are going to understand what goodness truly is, this is a part of it. Why did those advanced beings choose to be here? Why did they choose to teach you? Why now? Why here? That's something very special to feel a part of. It's something incredible and is a pivotal point.

That's what I would consider to be the angels. Now, *there* is a story.

The modern mythos is that the world is coming near an end and that the Darkside is creating dark beings on Earth to control and put it under a certain power and influence; that these Darkside beings have certain abilities to hurt and attack people; that there are old souls that are sent here to awaken people, and that these seven are the seven archangels.

It's much like the seven that were here originally who portrayed themselves as human beings or as close as they could come. *They've returned, or at least one or two of them have returned, and they're awakening sleepers.* Sleepers are people who would be considered archangels or enlightened already, but because they incarnated, they're in a sleep stasis. Their multiple personalities portray a personality, but inside they are in a deep slumber that they need to be awakened from. Through training they will awaken.

This is probably the closest you're going to come to a modern day concept of archangels and such. They're very powerful. They're somewhat like the will of the Force invoked in physical matter so that they can physically do incredible things like Christ was proclaimed to have done.

Chapter 12

OTHER ORDINARY LIFE:

ALIENS

Many people have questioned whether or not aliens, immortals, and other beings exist on Earth and there has been a lot of information written on this subject in the past. It's now time to take this subject one step further.

I believe aliens have been on Earth, have visited Earth, and continue to visit Earth. However, don't believe the vast amount of abductions that supposedly have taken place actually happened. Probably two out of one hundered abduction cases are remotely close to being true. Not all of the people who make this claim are actually being abducted. People are making up most of these stories, or they might even believe it happened, but I honestly don't think that it did. They just want attention.

Nobody was reporting anything about being abducted, or what an alien looked like until the movie *Close Encounters of the Third Kind* came out and people began to allege they were being abducted. They were giving descriptions of the same aliens in the movie, which would highly suggest that most people don't know what they're talking about.

There have been a few debates and arguments to back up their theory. A scientist who specializes in genetics would say that an alien from another world or solar system with the ability to create life in various ways would probably look nothing like a human being. People just assume an alien would have two hands, five fingers, or no fingers at all, a nose, eyeballs, and consist of a certain quantity of water in their body. The possibility is highly improbable that an alien would resemble a human at all. So, in their opinion, it's just amazing that aliens have arms and legs and look like us. This is their argument.

My take is this: all life in the universe has intermingled or will intermingle at some point. There are a million ways for this to happen, but the most likely scenario is going to be pods – like pollination of the universe, much like I've described pollination of the Earth. As we advance, we will pollinate other worlds with human beings. It is the Earth using us as its form of pollination. It's no different than sperm and eggs for humans or pollen for trees. It's a way of carrying the genetic material of one individual to another. We will go to other worlds and pollinate them with all the natural things of Earth - fruits, berries, fish. All of these things that are customary to us are the genetics of Earth and we will take them forth and multiply other worlds.

All things multiply. The point is that the universe has done the same thing on a much grander level. Vegetation and life has grown on other planets in the form of seeds, organisms, and micro-organisms. Worlds have exploded and these things are hurled as meteorites throughout the universe. They strike other planets, plunging and blasting into the atmosphere, allowing the seeds or enzymes, or the natural forms of life to polli-nate worlds, creating an existence on lifeless worlds. All the nutrients of life are there on the planet, but no life has actually been created there. Whatever feasibly lives through it attaches and creates, even if it's only a simple form of algae. A million years later, there might be a multitude of varieties of different species that have grown out of it.

Most people don't understand the concept of life. The reason we're talking about life is because we're talking about aliens and the possibility of them being here.

How did life start and were human beings actually made from aliens?

Aliens did not come down and create the Earth. There wasn't a bomb that created life like on Star Trek. The Earth was some form of an ammonia-based planet that was like ocean water, but it wasn't water, it was ammonia.

The number one contributor to life in the universe, let alone the Earth, or any universe or solar system, is the sun. The sun throws forth energy. Energy travels through time and space until it hits another object. That object absorbs and collects the energy or radia-tion. Radiation assisted the creation and effect of changing cellular structure. If you are near a nuclear plant that's leaking radiation, the bodies of the people who live there start to physically change because radiation is affecting their cellular structure.

All life on Earth was created by radiation. This is why leaves look the way they do, why corn looks the way it looks, and why animals look the way they do. It's because of a specific amount of radiation. If the level of radiation was more or less, life as we know it would look radically different. Your skin might have blue pigments. Leaves might be purple instead of green. These are all circumstances of the quantity of radiation and of the distance of the Earth to the sun. There are other variables to plug into the equation, but the major contributor is radiation, how the Earth deals with that radiation, and the quantity absorbed versus how much is bounced off the magnetosphere.

The ammonia-sunlight combination created a form of algae that could survive in ammonia over millions of years. The algae started to eat the ammonia and its byproduct was oxygen. The oxygen bubbled through the plant life to the surface and, over millions and millions of years; it created an oxygen level in the atmosphere. This changed how sunlight would affect the rest of the planet. It changed the angle of light reflected and how much energy was then consumed. As it began to change, new algae grew from the elevated quantity of sunlight because it was coming through oxygen now. This was the formulation of life.

Over millions and millions of years, new algae and new life later created different kinds of organisms. The organisms multiplied until, eventually, there were higher breeds of organisms, like jellyfish and eventually regular fish. The regular fish eventually evolved into land mammals. This is basically how life began.

So, we originated from the sun, which is the case for life throughout the universe or multi-universes. Different worlds are either closer to their sun or further away from *the* sun; accordingly, the planets are either larger or smaller. Life on those planets will evolve differently than here. Maybe their world started off in another kind of chemical, and the sunlight interacted with a different kind of algae which created life that is very different than what we can imagine. The variables are astronomical. So the chances of something even remotely looking like us with a head, eyes, nose, ears, arms, and fingers, are also astronomical.

If aliens do look like us, then there is a good chance they had something to do with us. You have to look at monkeys. You even have to look at cats or dogs. They have certain developments that also look like fingers or toes, but not as advanced as ours. This is something genetically built into man.

You could say that maybe a universe or a world exploded and it spread forth the seeds of life throughout the universe via meteorites; therefore, other worlds grew more advanced quickly. Or maybe all the worlds started off about the same time, but some worlds were just better prepared. They had better minerals. They had better creature adaptation through chance, and these aliens were able to advance faster because they had better natural resources than man did. So they advanced faster even though they started at the same time.

In either case, there are other worlds and other forms of life. Probably most of the life out there is not as advanced as Earth or the human race, but there are probably other races out there that are definitely more advanced than we are. One of the things that bothers me the most is that people always assume aliens are more advanced and superior to us. They may be more technologically advanced.

If you went to Africa and met a person in a very remote area who's never seen civilization before, and you asked him to drive a car, he would be completely lost. It would be beyond his comprehension. If you brought him to the United States, gave him a place to live, a job, and you left him for a year, what would that person be like when you met him a year later? He'd pick you up in the car. He'd be honking. He'd be laughing. He'd bring you over to his place. He'd show you how to use the microwave oven. He'd show you how to use cable TV. He'd be adjusted to all of these things.

How many aliens flying a spaceship know how to build the vehicle or even have an understanding of how it functions? You may be able to drive a car, but can you build the engine? Do you know what makes that car actually function? Do you know how the fuel works, how it creates combustion? Do you know how to control or create the ratio of the fuel? Do you even know how gasoline is created?

So the point is that you would be superior in one aspect to the person from Africa who was from an isolated area, but he also has the same capability as you do to adapt, adjust, and absorb this kind of knowledge and make it part of his life. I think alien races have scientists. The scientists create things for the general masses and they use it. There are people in the military who know how to use the equipment and fire the weapons, but they probably don't know how to make it.

So, I don't think aliens are superior to us. They may have some advanced technology that we don't have yet. Our civilization began slowly; it took millions of years for us to figure out what we were doing. Since science and technology have gotten more attention, there's been an explosion of knowledge and information unlike anything before in the past six million years of human life. This acceleration has happened only within the last 200 years. What took us maybe 20 years to figure out, we're now figuring out in a day. The technological advances of even the next five years are going to resemble things you'd see in Star Trek.

Scientists are already working on equipment that breaks down matter into molecular structure and beams it to another place; maybe not humans, but certainly matter. Certain technologies are slow to be made public, but they are there.

Did aliens create human beings?

I'm not going to say that they created human beings because I don't necessarily believe that. I think we are, for the most part, a product of this planet. There are certain indications that explain that human beings were manipulated genetically or that there was some kind of interference. There are a lot of reasons for this.

One of the main reasons is, genetically, everything on this planet pretty much follows similar patterns. Mammals have many similarities: lung, heart, two eyes, two ears, and a certain kind of structure. But the most interesting thing is the human nose. All mammals have flat noses - every single one. Human beings are the only ones that have a nose that protrudes and points down.

Now, that may not seem like such a big deal, but when you look at over 100,000 different mammal species, if you figure out the odds and rationalize this, you'll realize how peculiar that is. Humans should have flat noses, but we don't. So what was the reason behind that? And how did nature make such a big difference physiologically, let alone intellectually? We all have similar ears, similar eyes, lips, cheeks, tongue and glands. Everything is highly identical - just positioned differently. Yet the nose is so vastly different.

The development of the brain to such an astronomical level where human beings are not just superior, but they are far superior over all the other species on the planet. Monkeys don't come remotely close to our ingenuity. The same goes for aquatic based animals. Nothing comes close to us. Nothing. We are absolutely superior. How is it that we became so superior? Why are monkeys so far behind us in their development? How did that come to be?

All the other animals in the world are equal in intelligence. None of them really demonstrate anything greater or lesser as a species. Monkeys are no more intelligent than dolphins. There are two different sets of circumstances, but both show about the same intelligence. If apes are the highest form of evolution in comparison to humans, and we are far beyond them, shouldn't there be some kind of similarity to us like there is with dolphins versus monkeys? They are all in the same class of intelligence, yet human beings are absolutely superior to them all. It doesn't make any sense if everything is a creation of nature. It just seems highly unusual.

We have to really look at those things and take them into consideration. If we look further back into man's history, we know that there was Cro-Magnon, which was basically what we are now, and then there was Neanderthal. Neanderthal and Cro-Magnon were two different races of human beings. They looked very similar, but they were very different. They had a very different build than we do.

There are large caves in France where Neanderthal

and Cro-Magnon man lived near each other. They competed for food sources from one river where there were giant caves to shelter them. They left paintings on the walls of the caves of animals they encountered. Something very interesting to me is that Neanderthal man virtually vanished. They became extinct in an astronomically short amount of time. They just ceased to exist.

Is that because just the bones were found where they lived? Were the bones found in various times throughout history?

More burial places should have been discovered. The evolution of Neanderthal man, how they meagerly started off and how they differed from Cro-Magnon man was evident. The skeletal remains could be found and compared as a species. They both existed alongside each other yet, all of a sudden, Neanderthal man just disappeared. There's no more evidence of its existence. There's no continuation while Cro-Magnon survived and flourished.

Something interesting was depicted in the pictures in the caves of France. Cro-Magnon also vanished for a length of time and then suddenly showed up again, flourishing technologically. They were painting, farming, and building houses again. It's a dramatic leap, historically.

When you tie these two things together, it's very easy to let your mind expand toward other things. This discovery of the flourishing race suggested to me that perhaps there was an alien race that took a very strong interest in Cro-Magnon man. Perhaps it was an alien race that wanted to see the proliferation or expansion of whatever project or study they were working on. Or maybe they genetically altered the Cro-Magnon species and they wanted to ensure their survival so they removed Neanderthal man from the face of the planet. Suddenly there is new technology, farming, tools, and shelter in such a short period of time.

How did that all come to be?

I think a lot of it points to alien interference on some level. Scientists don't have any good answers to explain it. There's a big gap in time. In fact, there's a brief overlap with the story of the Elohim. There are the cave drawings and there was this sudden moment of progression. That's really the key, isn't it? That's what you have to look at. That's what you have to focus on. Then you need to look at other historical information.

There's the situation with the pyramids: There are three pyramids in Giza, as well as several others throughout Egypt and other places throughout the world. Almost all of the pyramids were man-made. There's no doubt in my mind about that. Many of those ancient quarries still exist. We know that the Nile used to be much larger than it is now and it floods seasonally. The banks are muddy during a certain time of year and, back then, the Hebrew slaves would drag the stones that they cut at the quarry, place them on levers – wooden slabs – against the mud slicks on the side of the river. When the river was low enough, they would make huge dirt mountains on which they would pull up the stones.

When that was completed, they would dig up the whole mountain of dirt that was probably bigger than an 18 story building. The soil was carbon-dated and it was determined the dirt mountains along the Nile were built around 2500 BCE. All of the remaining mountains of dirt are minuscule compared to the three large pyramids of Giza.

Concerning the three large pyramids of Giza, I don't believe they were human-made for one reason. Most Egyptologists estimate around 2.5 million blocks of stone were used to build the great pyramid. Some of the largest granite stones weighed 25 to 80 tons each and were transported from Aswan, more than 800 km (500 miles) away. What power could have moved these stones that far? How did they cut the blocks with laser-like precision and fit them perfectly in place? How did they lift and transport the rocks from their original position? How did they move them across the terrain, desert, water, and sand and then lift them on top of each other in order to build the pyramid?

Even if the workers had achieved the unimaginable feat of ten blocks piled up on top of each other a day, they would have assembled the 2.5 million stone blocks into the stone pyramid in about 250,000 days - about 684 years.

As impressed as I am with the human race and all the things that have been accomplished and created throughout time, I am doubtful that Giza was made by humanity. I certainly believe that humans made all the other pyramids though.

I can see the Pharaohs looking at Giza and saying to the builders and engineers, "I'm a god. I will destroy you and your whole family if you don't create some-thing like that for me." The Pharaoh wanted something to rival Giza. The engineers and builders did the best they could, so they created some amazing structures under a great level of stress.

How did they get the perfect measurements?

They used a kind of measuring wheel; each rotaton equates to a certain measurment. They used this to determine the height and width. That's how the engineers and builders came up with the perfect size for these structures. There's no mystery about it. But Giza is a mystery in itself.

There are stories throughout history of the gods on Earth who became angry with the other gods. They confronted the other gods in their chariots. One chariot is described as being a giant square and the other one is tubular, like a cigar. They hover, and they shoot lightning at each other for three days. What was this? To the modern man, it was some kind of craft, and these two worlds were fighting.

There are some stories in Hinduism, like the Mahabharata. The Mahabharata is set very early in the history of man, thousands and thousands of years ago, but long before anything was that civilized. It's basically a story of two families; brothers that were split up. There was a great battle that took place in a valley between the two families and all the kings/kingdoms, tribes, and villages who fought with them. The two armies numbered in the hundreds of thousands. It was one of the largest battle-fronts to ever take place in this giant valley.

The families and their respective armies clashed in the valley. Supposedly, there were gods involved. The gods gave certain leaders some abilities and weapons to use in the battle.

For the longest time, it was believed that none of this really took place, it was a fable, and the valley never existed. The battle never took place because it was thousands and thousands of years ago. However, a researcher investigated and found the actual valley where the battle took place. He found wagon wheels, pieces of chariots, helmets, spears, and knives by the dozens. It was very, very deep in the ground from years of settling dust. Because this battle took place so far back in time, he sent for various other researchers to come excavate. When one of the researchers started testing the valley walls to carbon-date it, they discovered that atomic blasting had taken place in this valley thousands of years ago. The radiation was burned into the walls of the valley.

I'm sure that when they looked at the stone, there were very deep fragments remaining. So they concluded that something happened there long ago, and it was far beyond the technology that should have been there. It makes you wonder who these gods were. They were probably aliens who were interfering.

My theory is, in very ancient times, aliens discovered the world and manipulated it. Then younger alien races sent out their research teams to probe the universe looking for new materials or metals to bring back to their world for science.

There are probably alien races that don't get along. We fight with Iraq, and Iraq fights with their neighbors; it stands to reason that alien races might do the same. It's all a matter of how close you live and how capable you are. What's your boundary?

When a civilization has space technology, they war with other solar systems because they get to know each other. Perhaps there are disagreements, or they just don't like each other and can't get along. There's tension just like there is between countries. I think the alien races fly out, find a world, and start digging and researching. Then there are other aliens that find something valuable and convince the human beings to do all the manual labor because they convinced the humans they were gods.

Hypothetically, when something like that happens, the different races of aliens would discover one another. They would be like, "There's the Alcarie race," and "That's Jupiter's race." They'd get together and reach some kind of agreement rather than fight and kill each other. Their goal would be to beat the other race to get the technology back into their own world. It could be gold, nickel, or copper; it could be a different metal they could manipulate to do incredible things.

In order to avoid killing each other but still beat the other race, one race would get their human workers to feud with the human workers of the other race; whoever wins will get to leave first. Or maybe they wouldn't have to agree with each other. They would just do it, or generate a mutual agreement between the races to not fight with one another. At some point, one of them would surmise, "Well, if we get our workers to kill their workers, then they can't be as productive as us."

This is how the wars began and how the gods manipulated the people. They gave the people weapons to help ensure their victory. These are intelligent beings; they're not going to kill one another. If they were intelligent, what would they do? They would get the grunts to do the work for them. They got the human beings to fight each other, thinking this is what their gods wanted. That's really what happened.

There are also other stories of aliens, like the one about Elijah going up into heaven while still living. He went up in a chariot of fire with aliens, and he saw everything. It wasn't the angels or God who did this to him. When you read this story and think of the possibility of it being aliens, it makes much more sense. Elijah was a simple person who had never been exposed to something that awe-striking, and he described something that was obviously beyond his comprehension. He didn't have words to describe a rocket because rockets didn't exist. He didn't have any explanation to describe vehicles because cars didn't exist. This was something beyond his imagination, so he used ordinary words that were very common at the time to describe something very complex.

As man evolved, I think the general consensus was, "We've messed around with Earth enough. We have to back off because they're becoming civilized. And let's say, some day Earth becomes a powerful planet. They're going to be pissed off and maybe go to war with us because we interfered with them for thousands of years. We know that sooner or later they're going to get there. Now, we'd like to take over the planet, but the ulterior race who created them or altered their genetics is very powerful. If we mess with Earth, they're going to mess with us. So it's a stalemate." I think that's what the deal is about Earth. I think there's a stalemate going on. There are other races that are interested in the Earth. There are other races that would just as soon get rid of us but don't want to suffer the consequences; so you have this constant stalemate.

So, these are all things to take into consideration. Now, you might wonder how I deduce all of this. Well, nothing is for certain and nothing is for sure. My point is, there are people out there who have done a great deal of research and believe this to be the case. Zecharia Sitchin wrote "The Wars of Gods and Men." Eric Von

Daniken wrote a book on artifacts of the Earth, which probably were from aliens. One of them shows a picture of an Aztec man inside of a rocket-type ship holding the handles with fuel coming out the end.

Those ideas would never be introduced unless the authors were exposed to a concept like that. Sitchin says there was a big galactic war when Earth was still very primitive and undeveloped, but Mars was very advanced and had spaceships. He says there was a war, not unlike the war between the Empire and the Rebellion in Star Wars. He says Venus and Mars both had life that was very advanced. There was a big war that took place and, using Star Wars terminology, the Empire won. The Empire totally destroyed life on Mars and left the *face on Mars*, which is the face of the alien race, as a reminder to all races throughout the solar system of what they are capable of doing. If it truly is a face and not an optical illusion, it is half the size of the city of Los Angeles. Sitchin believes this is a reminder of the power of the Empire, and whoever dares to rise up against it will suffer the same fate as Mars and Venus.

That's all very interesting, and a good read, but how much of it is really the truth? In the 1960's or 1970's, Sitchin was already describing what would be found on Venus when nobody had been there yet. He gave details and descriptions of what he believed were ancient alien-human communications that were written down. He had discovered some ancient texts from which he learned this knowledge. When our civilization sent a probe to Venus, the findings were identical to his descriptions. The scientist's had no idea of what they would find, but Zecharia Sitchin knew and he was highly accurate.

So aliens did intervene with human beings; it is

where Mu, Atlantis, and many other stories originated, but they are not completely true. There could have been some intervention at Giza; so when the Empire won, they decided not to educate those people and left. The alien race did not advance this civilization because the people were part of a rebellious technology; part of this other race. So the aliens just let the people go, but with limitations so they would never cause an upheaval. There are people who think that we're here on Earth to develop the planet. Once the planet is fully developed with cities and technology, the aliens will wipe us out and take the Earth for themselves because we're just workers. There are all sorts of crazy concepts out there, but the point is to bring to light all of this information.

I find it interesting that Sitchin was so accurate about a lot of his information. But the real question is whether or not I believe there was a rebellion. I believe that there was life on Mars because of its terrain. At one time, there probably were oceans and water, and where there is water, there is life. We know there is water on Mars - mass quantities of water.

The life that once inhabited Mars could have started out long before life on Earth had even begun. There could still have been ammonia water here. Did some Empire wipe them out? I don't know. I find that pretty hard to swallow, but let's say that there are alien races that did feud; anything's possible.

So Mars has water on it right now?

Yes, there are polar ice caps.

Is there an alien race that can live for 800 years? They could watch us develop in one single life time and, if we are an experiment, they are more apt to see results?

Obviously, we're under observation. Think about it. Let's assume that alien races do exist and already have the technology to get here. Wouldn't it be logical that they would watch us? It's no different than us studying the animal kingdom. We set up research centers and try to blend in. We try to be discrete. We try to be anonymous. We try to observe so that we can watch the natural process without interfering because, as soon as you interfere, you lose that natural process. That's what aliens are doing.

Is that why we're not aware of their existence?

Yes. They're trying not to interfere because they want to see the natural process of things. They know what will happen if they show themselves. I'm sure they've gone to other worlds and exposed themselves in the beginning but, through trial and error, they realized that it doesn't serve them well if they interfere. They can observe but they can't touch. They can't make their presence known.

How much are they aware of? In our classes, we have talked about entities, and we talked about different energies. Are they aware of all those things?

Absolutely, I think they harness those things. They don't look at them as being threats like we do because they have an understanding that those are parallel dimensions - that those beings are still entities. Entities are intelligent; therefore, they look at them as being intelligent beings. I believe they have a good understanding of all that. Maybe not all of the races of aliens out there, but certainly some do.

So they study every single element of the Earth?

Well, there are many cases of hauntings and, at the same time, there are UFO sightings. UFO's are known to fly over places that are haunted, so there has to be some correlation. We call it a haunting and perceive it as creepy, but that may be because of our primitive way of thinking. They may look at it and perceive other reasons why an entity would be there.

So their basic interest in preventing our development past a certain level is because we would be in competition with them?

The alien races are no different than humans; the answers can be found in nature. This also holds true of the universe. We are very competitive with other races on Earth. We share feelings of envy for being the successor; I don't think alien races are any different. They probably understand that their interference with our race would inspire technological advances; new concepts that, perhaps, have not even been thought of before, which would equate to possible competition for them. They probably figure that the less they interfere, the more time they have to progress. That's how I would look at it. I think we already have UFO's. Area 51 is very real, and there are probably more places like Area 51 that we are unaware of.

There may be alien races that are working with us and talking with us, but there are also alien races that feel very differently and don't want to be involved at all. They may say they're here to help us, but nothing is for free. There is always a price, no matter what. If alien races are here and they are helping us, I would find that very questionable. Maybe their intentions are true, but I doubt it.

Actually, I don't think there are many alien races here; they're very few and far between. Most people live their entire life without seeing a single UFO in the sky. That's the majority of people; although, not everybody's looking either. As for those people who make claims that they have seen one; most of what they've seen can be easily explained. There is a very small margin of things that are going on *out there*. The Goodyear blimp, meteorites, and helicopters in the distance that can't be heard are some of the things often mistaken for a UFO.

There are some accurate sightings though, and that is what we should be very careful to discern. You have to figure out what the truth is without assuming anything. Don't get caught up in the hysteria of other people's thoughts just because they seem convinced or sure of themselves. That's my take on this, and I certainly do believe there's an alien race here, but to what degree, I'm not sure. I think they're here observing; they're studying. If they're not studying the human race, they're studying the planet. They're studying the mineral content, the oceans, the air, the ozone, the magnetism, and the dimensional vortexes. There are so many things to study here on Earth.

What are your views on the government and the alien races? If alien races are partaking and observing us, do you think they are in contact with parts of our race? Do you think the government would have any role in that?

Let's get something straight, I think we have a great government. I think, like anything else, power breeds corruption. Yes, there are problems, but I think our government is probably much better than many other governments in the world. I have a great respect for our government.

Our government was created to serve the people; that's the first problem. What happens is that every man in office becomes greedy. They all have a desire for power. It's something that's primitive like with every species, animal or group, they are all constantly competing. If you look at most species, you will see competition for mating and for patriarchal position; the same thing goes on in politics. As much as they try to put the people's interest's first, it becomes a personal thing of who will get the power. You're not going to remove that. It's something that's just going to be there.

Having said that, I do feel the government is involved with aliens on some level. You may think it isn't right for them to keep this a secret, but I disagree. I think they have a right to keep it a secret because there are millions of people in the United States, and a portion of these people are ignorant. They're stupid, and they think UFOs or an alien is the devil coming down from space. Somebody once used a verse from the bible to say that the devil will come down from the skies. So, right away these ignorant people assume aliens are going to be taking over the government, and the government is run by aliens.

The government can't admit to having any information on aliens until society is ready and truly evolved. It would cause national hysteria. Just watch a movie depicting alien intervention and you will understand how society still views this. We sit here and say, "Well, there's no reason for that, we're ready." Yeah, maybe the people reading this book are ready, but what about the rest of society? What about your parents? What about your grandparents? What about all the people that you're not affiliated with? Just because you think the way you do, you haven't taken into consideration all the religious people who attend churches: the Mormons, Jehovah's Witnesses, Jews, Baptists, Protestants, Catholics, and everyone else who can't even begin to conceive the idea of aliens. They would go into a frenzy if that happened.

I think the government is probably correct in controlling the release of this information. It's unfortunate. The real question should be who is in charge of that kind of power and technology, and can they be trusted?

If America is the land of the people, run by the people, for the people, then I say we do have a right to know. It's a duality of what's right and wrong. It's very easy to corrupt people. It's very easy to allure, tempt, and convince them that you're doing the right thing.

A lot of officials or *"people in the know"* have come forward and said they believe in UFOs. However, many of them recant their statements because the government comes to them and says,"We know you're a congressman and don't doubt that you have seen what you claim. People are going to respect what you say, but this is national security. If you confirm it then there will be mass hysteria. There will be people freaking out and it will result in deaths. There will be riots and we're going to have to use guns and gasses to calm the people down. You've got to trust us on this; you can't go forward with your statements. You have to recant. You have to say it was all a mistake."

Usually, they're convinced but if not, then I'm sure the government will threaten them or destroy their career. What choice do they have? It's either recant and get on with your life, or pay the consequences. Obviously, the power that's against them is more than they can deal with. That's why I think the people who really know what's going on are convinced that they shouldn't say anything. If they do, they're threatened. I believe the government knows what's going on. I think we really should be more concerned about a government within the government. There are some people who believe in what is called a *Black Government*. It is what they're calling negative.

It's either:

a   A group of powerful people from all over the world, or

b   They're Americans who manage to filter large quantities of money back to themselves in order to build facilities, such as Area 51. They control or have the ability/technology to control Congressman, Senators, even the President. They basically tell the President, "You're here to run the country. We're here to take this technology, keep it under control, and keep it from being exposed to ensure world security. If you knew about this information, it would be a problem."

Maybe one of the presidents learned about this, agreed with it, and signed some documents saying that a president does not have enough clearance to go above this "other government." It's a separate acting organization inside of our own government, and it doesn't affect what our government does and visa versa. This is what I fear has happened; and all because one president signed the papers. It means the other presidents can't veto it without making a huge scene. This black government has become so financially and politically powerful by the people who are involved that no one dares to go against them because they would lose.

Taking this all into consideration, I believe in the people. I believe in the government, but that doesn't mean we should be oblivious to what is happening around us. We have to be cognizant of what's going on. We should question everything and not just trust the news and TV on blind faith because it's all about the media, and it's controlled. I don't believe in full capitalism; I just don't think it's the right way to go.

I don't think the government would expose any alien information either, but you always have to look for the "government within the government." You may think it's impossible to keep things under wrap when people report seeing a UFO; however, in Chicago, the entire city saw UFO's and it was never broadcast. There are several other instances where there have been major UFO sightings, but most of the time it is never broadcast; it's all controlled.

I don't believe that it's impossible to keep a secret in this day and age. It's not true anymore. Even if a story does get out, there is something called *spindoctors* who put out counter stories and make them sound very convincing. The spin-doctor does a profile on the person who saw the UFO, emphasizing their credentials and credibility. Then they start putting out stories to attack everything about the person: the quality and authenticity of whom they are, looking for any dirt they can find on the person, and elaborating to make it more sensational than what it is.

That's how they destroy somebody's credibility. So if something does get out, they blow it out the door anyway. And then the media doesn't have a leg to stand on to report it because they will look like idiots. That's how it's done.

Chapter 13

OTHER ORDINARY LIFE:

SUPER BEINGS & IMMORTALS

Let's discuss super beings and immortals. Do they exist? The answer to that is very simple; yes, they do. There are beings that are born human and are abnormal, super beings, which have capabilities that other human beings don't have or demonstrate.

Let me start by explaining the vampire phenomenon. Let's just say there are people walking the Earth who live forever. It's hard to believe, but let's look at one of the oldest texts we have – the gospel. The first Bible states there were people who lived for thousands of years. If you look at the age expectancy of some of the people in the first Bible, you're going to see ages from 500 to 1000 years old, which is very interesting.

For instance, let's examine the religious story of Cain. Cain was cursed by God to walk the Earth forever; that means he lives forever. There was also the Roman soldier, Longinus, who stuck the spear into the side of Jesus. He was cursed to walk the Earth forever until the End Times. If the story has any truth to it, and they were immortal, then it is very likely they're still walking the Earth today. They're still here in the same physical body.

So, taking that into consideration, let's take a closer look at the whole vampire lore. There are people out there who have a disease where they need blood. There is a platelet in blood they need to take into their body. A craving is your body telling you that you need a certain food because you need a certain nutrient that food contains. For instance, your body knows what nutrients apples contain because it is familiar with those nutrients. That's how it recognizes and craves it. Well, if it's blood you need and your platelets are low, your body will say, "You have to get this blood from a human being." How do you know? Because when you were a kid, maybe you sucked your own blood when you had a cut and realized this, or you sucked somebody else's blood by accident. Who knows? But somehow that identification is present.

Is it possible to become immortal?

Without saying yes or no, let's look at this theoretically. Humans categorize all disease as bad because they assume it destroys the body. But what if there's some kind of disease that prolongs or preserves the body? It doesn't know right from wrong. It's not a thinking virus that says, "To kill is what I'm out to do." Viruses don't think; they just do what they're programmed to do. What if there was a virus that is programmed to fight the aging process? It fights and eats up the chemical that ages you.

Your body stops producing a chemical that keeps you youthful at the age of 19 or 20 years old. If it can be produced for X amount of years, but why does it have to stop at all? Why does your body start deteriorating? There is a certain quantity of cells in your body, and when they are used up, that's it. What if they were replaced by something artificial that kept reproducing itself in your bloodstream? You would never age. I believe biologists already know what causes the aging process, and I believe they already have the capability of slowing or stopping it. It cannot be released yet because if it is, the population of the world would explode. Even to extend human life for another ten years is asking a lot. The ratio of expansion of the human race would be astronomical just for a simple ten year add-on. But I do think it's likely that there are immortal people out there.

What about people who have certain abilities, or people who can do certain things?

I will reiterate something that I mentioned earlier. Radiation is what determines your basic abilities. Your capabilities on this planet are determined by radiation. What if somebody was affected by a higher or lower form of radiation while in the womb? Wouldn't the circuitry of the brain develop differently from others? Maybe the body looks the same but the interior is definitely different.

Most people have never seen a 2-headed snake, but that doesn't mean it doesn't exist. I've seen one, they do exist. There's not a vast quantity of them; most of them will die in nature unless they're caught by someone who takes care of them.

There are children born with two heads. In the town of Chernobyl, Russia where the nuclear plant blew up, there are babies being born cyclops, meaning they have one eye in the middle of their head. They preserved those aborted babies so they could study the effects of nuclear radiation. What if those children had lived? What if they had one eye that was functional and useful? What would those children be capable of if they had lived?

What if one of the children had telepathic abilities because of the pressure placed on the brain from the eye? What if that child was capable of doing something totally different? What if it only needed a tenth of the oxygen to breathe because it had a different way of processing it?

The possibilities are endless. I believe there are people in remote places of the world, even here in the United States, that have undergone significant genetic changes. Most of them probably don't live, but a small percentage is able to adapt and survive. The child may walk, talk, and look like the rest of us, but it is different in imperceptible ways. I find that very interesting.

Other than being educated by somebody who has those special qualities, what is the advantage of being able to connect and relate to somebody like that?

Just think of the knowledge they could share with you. Think of what they've seen, what they've done, and what they've experienced. We live for an average of eighty years, but only forty of those are prime years. The rest are either rearing years or decaying years. Basically, you've got maybe forty years of good life. That's just a flash compared to someone who's lived for double that amount of time. Let alone for 10, or

100 times that length. We can only guess at what our ancestors did. We can only look at literature so much; it only goes back so far, and even literature has been misunderstood and misinterpreted over time.

In this case, you have someone who understands how and why certain historical events took place because they were there and saw how it really happened. The benefits of having that kind of information are astounding. A person who lives longer than the average life expectancy has also mastered a greater percentage of their brain. If you only use 12 -15% of your brain, what are the capabilities of someone who has lived for 300 years or more? They obviously would be pushing the limit of their brain. Sooner or later, they would start reflecting on it. So who's to say what there is to be learned? There is a great deal to be experienced and learned.

What about survival skills?

If you're intelligent enough to know that you're not going to die, you might live a hundred years just scraping by. Sooner or later, you're going to start collecting artifacts. You'd come to realize that 100 or 200 years down the road, you're going to sell them for thousands of dollars. You're going to become very wealthy. You're going to be so wealthy that you probably don't have to be bothered by people or civilization at all if you don't want to be.

I suspect that those people who are immortal, or have lived for any extent of time, are not going to be the average person. Even if they were average to begin with, over time, they're going to become very wise.

They're going to speak over 20 languages, without ever going to school, just from being in different parts of the world.

The only way you're going to run into people like that is if they have a reason to mingle with the population, such as somebody who would need blood platelets, like a vampire. Someone who's become immortal, well – it's very likely they're the type to refrain from the public's eye. It's also very likely they will stay in a stable, remote, or isolated part of the world, apart from the possibility of a war that would disrupt their life because they could be exposed.

The world is very similar to the human body: white cells, red cells, there are all forms of life. They contribute to the world, and all the life in your body contributes to the whole. It's very similar there: the macrocosm-microcosm; it's a very similar situation over, and over, and over again throughout the universe no matter how large or how small. There are cycles in your body, in nature, in the solar systems, and solar systems have cycles around universal systems. Everything follows the same pattern, only the scale changes.

The human body not only produces red cells as the main workers; it also produces white cells. Sometimes it also produces super antibodies to fight viruses. These super white cells are more prepared because of the data received from other white cells. A vaccine is often made from weakened or dead forms of the microbe, its toxins or one of its surface proteins. A vaccine is introduced to your body in order to educate the white cells to look at it and recognize it for what it is. The white cells can then look for the living ones that look identical. The difference is, one's dead and one's alive. It's education. You have the white cells that don't have a clue, and you have the newer ones that do. The body is constantly dealing with different things and adapting to suit those circumstances. This adaptation results in different beings with different capabilities born on the planet.

If there are gifted children born who are recognized and socially acceptable - that's the key: socially acceptable – they can do miraculous things. Take a close look at how Mozart could use his ability. His brain had to have been different than most human beings because human beings cannot mimic what he did. He was different. There was something about him that was different than most people. Some call it talent; I say it's genetic. I think it's in the brain because he was capable of hearing music and creating music in his head, just like you can hear a stereo blasting right now.

Some artists are more gifted than others, no matter how much schooling or talent they have. There is a certain function in their brain that makes it possible for them. Some people have the ability to physically balance their brain and adapt it to new situations.

I once heard of a blind person who learned to click with his mouth so he could use the echo as a mechanism to see. He was able to ride a bicycle around poles without harming himself. He's one hundred percent blind, yet he can hear the clicking sound bounce off objects. He uses that sound to see the structure of everything around him.

These are all examples of the abilities of the brain. You haven't reached the full capabilities of your brains yet because you haven't been put into a situation where you had to.

There will never be documentaries about these people; they will live and die because the general public cannot understand them. In fear, most people will say "It's the devil," or,"They are possessed," or they might even kill them.

I've been reading about Joan of Arc. She was put to death because she was very bold and outspoken. She had highly developed senses and a lot of common sense that people didn't want to accept.

The human race has a big social problem: if you don't conform or mimic everyone else, you are attacked. It's very common in all living organisms, whenever there is competition. In nature, it's survival of the fittest. In the animal kingdom, if you stand out from the herd, you are attacked and challenged for position.

Human beings do the same thing as any other living organism. If you stand out from the crowd, it is miscon-strued as leadership tactics. People fear what they don't understand. They attack and destroy it because human beings are still very primitive. This is demon-strated all the time with religion. Religion has de-stroyed some of the most creative people in the world because some talented or gifted people thought differently, were artistic, or musically inclined. The religious leaders thought it was 'music from the devil' or 'artistry from the devil' because it was superior to what they were able to conceive, so they destroyed it.

This is a flaw in nature; nature is not perfect. In-stead of having the ability to recognize this flaw, nature accepts it. Gradual evolution is acceptable to nature. Anything that's a product of advancement - was born ahead of the evolutionary process - is unacceptable and must be eliminated. It's as if, somehow, a gene, which wasn't supposed to kick in for another 20 human generations, is activated. Some of them accidentally kick in too fast and the rest of humanity attacks it; destroys it.

There are wolves in Canada that are known for attacking other wolves and for the longest time, no one could figure out why. The only thing biologists could determine was that the lone wolf being attacked had a mild genetic difference, and the other wolves sensed it. This genetic difference could have been a leadership pattern, or something that was demonstrated in its behavior. The other wolves were able to sense it, and they didn't like it. It was unfamiliar to them, and they had a natural instinct to attack and kill it.

Change is also very difficult for human beings to accept; they attack anything they can't comprehend.

When you break everything down and easily explain it, because there is a common pattern whether it's in our bodies, the world, or the universe; I think that humanity should be more evolved and could figure things out better than it does.

To paraphrase Albert Einstein, the world is filled with stupid people. Those of you who are intelligent will always be under scrutiny of *the many*, and *the many* are stupid. So, no matter how brilliant you are you will always be suppressed by all the stupid people because they are *the many*; they rule. That's the problem: *the many* are uneducated, *the many* are simple-minded. You are the few who are the perceivers, the imagintors, and the dreamers. But you will always be attacked because of it.

I remember reading a story about this guy who dreamed of travelling by train in Europe. He said "This is what I'm going to do," and he built this train of his dreams. Everybody said, "What are you doing? Why are you wasting our money? Are you crazy? Nobody can tolerate moving faster than 30 miles per hour. The human body can't withstand it and it'll rip apart."

People really thought that?

Yes. This just shows you the ignorance of man. They tried to prevent him from building the train because of their ignorance. There are hundreds and hundreds of stories just like this. In 1930 there was a scientist who said that all scientists should stop developing new things because everything in the world has already been created; there was nothing left to be invented.

There's a little bit of truth to that; everything has been created but that doesn't mean it can't go to the next level.

We haven't even begun to tap into what is out there yet. There are many things to put into the human equation. It's unfortunate, but that kind of thinking is seen on many different levels, whether it is religion or society. It's not what you see up front that I'm concerned about. It's the implications connected to it that you aren't seeing yet. If you submit to something idiotic from society, and agree with it, then you also infuse yourself with everything that's connected to it. That's where you have to be careful.

Society is really a collection of rules that are decided

by a group of like-minded people. If like-minded people from other cultures get together and come up with a new thought or a new concept, 'they' - whoever is *the many* - are the ones who are dominant. That is how the rules are set. For example, in this country you can only marry one person. That's it and that's the way it should be. In Saudi Arabia, men are allowed to have up to four wives, provided that they can support all the wives equally. This practice is reportedly in decline.

They still do that today?

Yes, there are countries in the world that instill that kind of belief. There are so many different things that we, in the western part of the world, find culturally shocking, but are considered acceptable in other countries because of *the many*. You were raised to believe and accept what you were told and not question it. You don't question half of your beliefs. As a nation, we think we are superior to the rest of the world and know it all, and there is no reason to question how we became that way in our society. We think right away, "Well, it's all good. I can't think of anything that's bad about it."

The point is, there are many things that are bad about it, and it is only half the problem. I'm not saying there is a perfect way; I'm saying the system is as good as any, and I can accept it for what it is, but I will not allow it to limit my thinking.

When you allow society to control your decisions then you also allow society to control your thinking. You become part of the group rather than an individual. You do it without even realizing it. That's what you have to be careful about. You have to stay very open-minded no matter what the subject is and no matter how controversial it is. The minute you narrow your thinking with even the most basic ideas, you close your mind to every other thought; all of it is connected. This is why immortals, or people with unusual abilities, will never publically surface. Anybody's who's ever been unique in that sense has been murdered.

Let's look at Rasputin. Rasputin was a Russian who had certain abilities. He made predictions that were highly accurate and highly detailed on a whole different level that could affect his country. He was also human and he had flaws. Just because you are talented does not mean you are flawless.

He seduced a lot of women in his lifetime. He took advantage of his sexuality because he was a man as much as he was spiritually gifted. His ability was genetic, everything else about him was very normal. He followed his human instincts like anybody else and that got him in trouble. Rasputin obtained a level of power where he could affect kings and queens. It's what I would call a *Judas Effect.*

Judas thought Jesus was very talented, but he also believed that he knew more than Jesus, that he had a greater wisdom. Judas couldn't convince Jesus to do what he wanted him to do, so he decided to take the situation into his own hands. He figured if he told the guards where Jesus was, they would come get him and all the people wouldn't want anything to happen to Jesus. But his plan was flawed and Jesus was crucified. Judas immediately regreted what he had done, but by then it was too late.

This kind of thinking is very dangerous; the same thing happened to Rasputin. Rasputin's predictions were very accurate and they should have been used in a more useful way. There were people who wanted power and wanted to maintain that power. They felt Rasputin was a threat to their career, not to society, but to their position of power. Therefore, they poisoned him and shot him in an effort to kill him. He lived through most of it, but eventually they did manage to kill him. Again, this is a demonstration that anybody who has any kind of ability should never come forward. History is repeated over, and over, and over again. Almost every prophet in the world has been murdered, and every great teacher has been attacked.

Question everything – that's my motto. I don't believe everything I hear. I'm always looking for that loop-hole. I refuse to be one of those blind people that are part of the masses. I would rather be the one who stands out in the crowd; that's the best way to go. It makes me angry when I think how society deals with people who are very intelligent and articulate, people who stand out, risk everything by removing themselves from *the machine*.

Chapter 14

ECHOES OF CONSCIOUSNESS

We live in very challenging and often difficult times and, because of that, some of my students have expressed a concern about White Cells who may turn to the Darkside. How would it affect your soul if you're in this dimension as an enlightened being but you turn to the Darkside? How is this possible?

Well, it all comes down to the choices you make. This dimension is about duality. You could be living life as a really good person but something horrible happens to you or someone you care about. For instance, a man has a family whom he loves. He's a very good, spiritual man. He does good things and joins organizations to help people. Then, one day, a man kicks the door in and rapes his wife and children in front of him. He kills the wife and children but the husband survives. As a result, the husband becomes absolutely bitter, extremely jaded, and hateful. All of a sudden, he's into revenge, hating people, and wanting to kill them.

For this spiritually advanced person, he doesn't remember who he really is while residing in the physical body. Let's say he turns to the Darkside. Now his enlightened consciousness is coming in from *who he really is* and, at the same time, he has all this darkness coming into him. There's going to be a duality there that's fighting for dominance. Either his positive, enlightened, self is going to consume the negative and he'll find forgiveness and compassion in his heart, or the Darkside is going to consume him as an advanced spiritual being and he'll turn to the Darkside and be a very, very dangerous foe.

It has happened. It comes down to choices; it's just very fast in that state of consciousness. There's going to be turmoil. It's similar to the Star Wars scenario when Darth Vader, while he's still Anakin, is starting to turn to the Darkside. He feeds into the power and the emotional crisis he goes through. In the end, when Luke is trying to get him to come back to the Force, Anakin surrenders that Darkside. He has all this crazy contemplation in his heart.

If you speed that up a thousand fold, that's what's happening momentarily while this person who is filled with hatred is receiving all the memory of who he really is. If he has attained a level of enlightenment, it's hard to shake that state of mind. He is going to realize the error of his ways. The positive will consume the negative and find a way of releasing that anger and that pain. In his next life, or lives, there will be a greater sense of purpose for this person to help humanity because he will have a deep sense that he did some-thing critically wrong somewhere.

I've talked about reincarnation in the past. I'd love to say that Hitler is going to burn in hell for what he did, but God does not think in the same terms we do. In one sense, Hitler is evil because he murdered all these people; so we've made him a villain. But if another person goes to war, drops napalm on thousands of people, kill hundreds of the enemy, he's honored for what he did.

At my level of consciousness, I've got some problems with that perspective. I have a lot of problems with the way human beings, at this stage of their evolution, perceive things. When somebody says to me, "He should burn in hell," and then another person defends someone who has wiped out millions of people in wars, I'm shocked at their level of arrogance in these matters. How do they decide who is bad and who is good? Everything seems very cut and dry. They sort their consciousness to fit their perspective, and they seem incapable of looking at it from a different standpoint. I can't say that's always the case because I think there are scholars out there who are really saying what I am.

On reincarnation, some people believe if you do something very bad, you're punished for that when you come back in your next life. Or you have to work off that bad history or those negative energies. That's just ludicrous to me. It's just absolutely ludicrous. It's not that the Universe has no method. How is it determined who gets into the higher levels and who doesn't?

By their frequencies?

That's right; when you look at the sum total of what you are when you leave an organic life, your highest level of purity or refinement of consciousness is your energy form. That form has a frequency and that frequency determines which level of dimension you can access. In dimensional terms, it's like every millisecond is a whole other universe. There are frequencies that you tune in to. It manifests and you transition from the one you were currently in. The level of frequency or dimension you go into is decided by the vibration you're carrying in your heart.

So this person who was enlightened and did all these negative things may have been able to move to higher states and be in the presence of God. That is where we sit and feel healed. We feel love. It's like living in Oregon where it's rained for two months; then, all of a sudden, there's a 72° day. You walk outside and you can smell the flowers and the grass and the sunshine is warming your body. There's a deep healing that comes from that. It's not that the rain did something wrong to you. You had just forgotten how much you really craved and loved the light. It's the same concept.

As an energy being, you want to be in the presence of this vibration. You want to get as close to it as you can because it just feels better. It feels *right*. It feels deeply *correct* within you like it's healing and nurturing you. But this being is not allowed to stay in the higher frequencies of God.

It's a buoyancy thing. He has this extra weight now that he has to iron out in his own conscious. He might be able to do it right away depending on his level of awareness, but what is the best way to get rid of that kind of vibration? What is the one thing that can remove the deeper, darker energies within your frequency?

Surrender.

True, deep, remorseful surrender is the only way. You cannot fake it. No matter whom you are or how righteous you are; no matter how strongly you feel about what you did or didn't do. You can't remove that in the eyes of the Universe. It's like saying that a scale can't pick up a single hair that falls on it. If it was a high-powered microscopic scale, it's going to detect the weight of that hair. The Universe is so attuned to frequency that it can detect the minutest level of change beyond the molecular. So It decides.

You're trying to get your perceptions, your feelings and your consciousness to match God's. You have a part of God in you, and that's what's calling you. That's the Navigator. There's a need to get back to it and the only way to get back to that Source is to mimic Its vibration so the vibration fits; it's a seamless fit. If you can see the seams, you haven't hit that perfect vibration yet, but it's wonderful that you're getting that close.

Human beings simplify things in a crude and very wrong way. The real question is – what's right? To the Universe, there really isn't a level of life and death. We relate to it because it's like a beginning and an end. But as an energy being, there's not a sense of a beginning or an end; there is just consistent transformation. So when it comes to life and death, your experiences are what matter. What transpired during your life? What did you amass in your consciousness from your experience? What transition did you go through? Death is not perceived like it is in this dimension. It's a beginning and an end, but it's really just like an entrance; it's a departure and an entrance.

So, when you think of murder, do you use this dimension's interpretation? Once you go into the other dimension, you look at it differently. It may not be as bad or as intense as you're thinking. But you're thinking from this perspective and that's the hardest thing to overcome. It's something for you to reflect on. Things are not exactly the way you think they are. Whenever you try to conceive of what these judgments should be of what's right or wrong, you always have to remember that you are conceiving it from the perspective of this world, this reality, this consciousness. There's always that duality. Do you want to look at it as a truly spiritual being, or do you want to look at it from your present reality?

Look at gambling. If you illegally ran a little casino operation from your house just for fun, you might get five years imprisonment. But if you did it from Las Vegas, there's no penalty at all; in fact, you're financially rewarded. People tell you what a wonderful thing you're doing, and what a great casino you've got.

The human perspective is your greatest enemy. When you say, "I really want to become more spiritual," you must delve into these deeper philosophical perspectives and see them for what they are and respect them. This is the environment you're in. By the same token, there is this other level where you see things for what they truly are. Don't let it blind you and hold you in a certain state of consciousness.

The same mindset that you're using to make your judgments now is based upon what you think is right or wrong. The same thing is determining your spiritual growth because you have expectations ideas and concepts without even thinking about them. That's why you constantly have to consider the best route to avoid that.

What's the best route? Non-thought: To think in a clear state of consciousness without thought. The judgmental thoughts from your consciousness are coming from the organic brain which is simply an echo or an absorber of this reality. It's echoing the laws, bylaws, and social structure. Your soul still remembers what it's like to be a dimensional being, even if it's a new one. This is why you get into conflicts and why you despair living in this dimension. You just don't know why you're depressed. It's passing judgment. That's really what it comes down to and these are things that you have to take into consideration. It's a very difficult thing to do when you exist in this environment.

What's ticking through an enlightened person's mind? How do you think? How do you see the world? How do you perceive things? I give these things a lot of thought. I try to teach everything from my perspective so that you can take it on and try to mimic it, and see what it does to you. That will begin to transform you. It is very beneficial, but you've got to *get it*. If you don't get it, then there's no point to it.

Here's a way for you to think of things: When you think about other dimensions, you think about other realities or other worlds. When you think like this, I would propose that you should go to another reality and change this whole reality. Then you would exist in another reality. You would see how people lived and existed and, if you were stuck there, you would start to think and act like them, take on their customs, and learn their language. You would understand how they communicate and interpret. You would know how different it is from what you do.

You would obviously grow from that experience because it's giving you a whole new concept of how you perceive things. If you went to another world and had to stay there, you would be able to sample completely different things from that reality; things that you possibly never would have imagined before in your life. The interesting thing is, when you go to this other dimension, everybody automatically perceives what it's going to look like, to a certain degree. Everybody usually thinks human body forms, different nationalities, and houses that are different colors. You see houses of some type, as well as the basic structure of what you perceive reality to be. Put a lemon twist to it by changing the colors, clothing, or simple things.

For most human beings, just to experience some other dimension will be absolutely mind bending. If you ever go to another country, you'll find that there's a part of you that resists the cultural change. Can you imagine going to a whole other dimension and having to exist there and adapt to it? Your brain is wired for this dimension with its specific content, smells, flavors, and textures. If you went to another dimension, you would feel extremely out of place but, as a spiritual being, this is what you have to do. You have to come here and adapt. At the same time, you are also awakening to a higher state of consciousness, remembering who you are.

Instead of thinking about traveling to other dimensions, tone it down a little bit. Why not start to see other realities within your own organism here in life? You create a certain reality and you perceive things a certain way.

What if this was a bubble dimension? Everything that you see out in the world you see from your spiritual perspective. Imagine being able to step out of your bubble and go into another bubble. Let's say you have the bubble of people who participate in medieval reenactment, or the bubble of Goth people, or the people who are into vampires, or Asian Americans who have their own little social world. What about the bubble of 'Valley Girl' people! It goes on, and on, and on. You never think about the way these groups see each other; it's a whole other dimension. I didn't say it was going to be anything like this dimension. A whole other dimension could be something you cannot even conceive, but yet you structuralize it.

That's what you do with other people in the world. You structuralize from your perspective. What if you were to visit one of these other realities and incorporate yourself into it as a bystander, visitor, or time traveler who has a much greater knowledge? You've absorbed yourself into this other world and you're mimicking yourself so you can experience it. How would that change your perception? Would that change how you see things? To see the world from somebody else's perspective, how would that reinvent you? How would it affect you? Would it change you? Would it change your personality? Would it change you emotionally?

An experience like that would change you far more than you could ever imagine. This is how I see the world. There may be different social classes or social structures, but if you can recognize them as globes of perspectives, you can reflect on it and reach a state of enlightenment. I reside in a certain state of consciousness, in a particular bubble but, when I move into higher states of consciousness, I step out of it. All I see are the bubble realities all around me. The only neutral ground is in between these bubbles. That's the only place of true clarity. Look at other people, see their patterns, and you will raise your own consciousness.

On a much larger scale, it's interesting to see the functionality of the planet as a living organism. In this living organism, like the human body, these organisms play many different roles. In many cases, they all live in the same place but they don't interact with one another. Rarely is there a shared communication.

When I see the world, I see all of these different roles. I see things happening just like an organism. Everything in your body is really working for one purpose, and that is to maintain your life, your existence. The planet is doing the same thing, working for a larger organism, for its progression. Once you can start to see the other organisms in life, once you perceive it, that's what will change your consciousness.

You're moving forward in consciousness because when you look at things differently, you can get a completely different experience. That changes you. Now take it to a whole new level and say that by looking at it, and seeing other people in whatever bubble they're in, you realize they really live in a whole different reality.

Think of it this way. Let's say you go to the movies and watch a film on bears; then you go camping. If you hear a rustling in the woods, your brain immediately says, "Oh, that's probably a wild animal." If you watch a movie that's about a killer, when you hear a rustle you are immediately alerted toward a sense of danger rather than, "Oh, it's just an animal." If you watch a UFO film, you perceive the noise to be aliens.

You set your mind into motion for interpreting things. You set standards on your expectation of reality. You do this and are set in a certain way of perception without even knowing you are in it. It's about realizing how you're interpreting, or how you're automating on a very complex level. By recognizing it and thinking about it, you can actually release yourself from that expectation. When a person is athletic, their perspective is all about sports. When they talk to other people they do not see the complexities of their particular interests; they see certain things, but they also begin to assess you. They formulate a perspective of whom and what you are. It's a filter and they're interpreting it from the perspective of an athletic reality from the athletic bubble. Whatever they immerse themselves into is how they interpret reality.

You can still work in there, but they don't see anything but those functions that they administer to you. Sometimes, you are able to bridge the two bubbles. The bubbles push into each other. You are getting somebody into spirituality and they're getting you into athletics. You find some kind of connection between the two and something interesting comes from it. The bubbles then depart from each other.

For the most part, you tend to see what happens in life from your perspective. You can create a perfectly happy, cozy world for yourself but somebody else might not recognize any of that. From their perspective, they just see you as someone who is lost. That is just one interpretation of reality blending into another and it's this blending and mixing that creates a total consciousness for the planet. It's what holds this vibration for this place that is reality. Collectively, it's what makes what we call the norm for reality, the norm of how we experience things.

Each of these bubbles can be looked at in two different ways. You can look at the bubbles as being safety zones. For example, let's look at Christians. The Christians have their bubble and then they have little bubbles inside that where they don't get along with the other Christians. For the most part, they perceive the world as problems that can be protected through prayers. They find comfort in the Bible. It's like recipes in a book that say, "This is the way it is. If you do it this way, this is what you get." This creates a sense of comfort. It gives them a sense of, "When I die, I have this place to go." These beliefs are what create their happiness or their despair. The Christian bubble molds your consciousness by accepting a certain way of looking at things. If that's what you exist for, that's how you see everything.

If you read a really good spy novel while you're flying on an airplane, there's a part of you that feels that you could be a spy. You start looking around and seeing things the way a spy would. You become more observant. You watch somebody move his lapel and there's a metal clip underneath it. You wonder what that lapel pin could really be. Could it be a small camera? Because you're now in this level of interpretation, you see what you want to see. You're now defining this lapel pin through the tinted glasses of a spy.

If you read Anne Rice's, *The Vampire Lestat*, there's a part of you that now sees human beings as cattle and when these beings come down to feed on them, there's a part of you that can believe that. When you are that into a book, there is a part of you that doesn't want it to end because you love the state of mind that it puts you in. That's why Goth bars were formed. Vampire people actually take it to the next level.

When you immerse yourself into that culture, it becomes the reality you exist in. It becomes your social structure, and before long, this is your reality and you can no longer fully relate to the other people outside the world you're living in. The athletic person sees everybody as athletic. Suzy Homemaker looks around thinking, "Somebody needs to fix the makeup on that girl." When you see Suzy worrying about things like that, you realize she doesn't have a clue. These people might as well be mindless. You begin to see it in a different perspective.

These bubbles can consume you. They can put you into a trance and put you to sleep. Then you're in another reality and it soothes you, it rocks you, and it comforts you. Now, all of a sudden, you're in this other bubble and you don't even know you've leapt from one bubble to another. You begin to forget and rewrite your consciousness in a sense – slowly, methodically – into some other new perspective.

Someone might inquire, "How do you know you're not in this bubble yourself and have this same ability? How do you know you're not seeing everything through your own perspective?" You probably are but the difference is that you're also acknowledging it and saying, "That's probably something outside of my bubble."

What is the next level? What's the next level for your spiritual teachings? Eventually, you need to expand outward. You need to take it to the next level and practice your perception of all of these social mechanisms, which are really conscious mechanisms within the Gaia mind. By separating yourself, you may be able to rewrite yourself into it differently, or have greater control of what's happening in the matrix.

By acknowledging something and seeing it consistently, you begin to separate yourself from the matrix. You're no longer looking at it from within your own world saying, "I feel spiritual," or, "I see how mundane or how plastic they are." It's a different perspective now. You're extracting yourself in a different kind of state of consciousness by pulling yourself out of what you know to be different states of mechanisms and consciousness groups. By doing so, there is a revelation that cannot be expressed. It must be experienced. This is what a very advanced spiritual person perceives and sees. They immerse themselves into it and then they step out. They immerse, and step out. This is what's going on.

That's something a spiritual person figures out and starts doing. Just by being aware of it now, you may begin to become conscious of it. That may be what catapults you into a state of enlightenment. True, it can be a lonely place, but it's also a beautiful place because it gives you that sense of inner peace. There's a certain peace that comes from it and you're really grateful, but there's another part that separates you from everything and makes you feel very isolated. When you start separating your organic body from your spiritual body, everything seems good or bad. You start to try to feed your spiritual body, or your dimensional body, with the things it requires. You're so used to starving it that it simply assumes that's the norm. It's conditioned itself to accept it and it doesn't think about it. So, now you start feeding it and it's going to want more. You're going to have this conundrum between the two. That is the spiritual person's burden in life to deal with. A lot of people deal with it already on the micro levels but it just intensifies.

What is the point of all of this? What does this mean? Practicing techniques allows you to experience certain things. Applying a certain way of doing something or perceiving something is an effort. Anything that's an effort is really the norm in this reality. It's a process. Whenever you want to push or change this reality, it requires effort. If you want to become more muscular, it can be painful. It takes effort and work to do that because you're changing the norm of whatever program you're in that's on auto pilot.

So, whenever you want to step out of the program, there seems to be some kind of effort involved that changes you. There's always this resistant energy. It's always trying to keep you in your bubble. So when you work with this material, you're going to pay a price. There needs to be some kind of effort from you to redesign yourself until you pop into one of these other levels where there are other advanced spiritual people. You're going to have to do your work to get there.

This is the duality of what I'm saying. If you want to get there faster, you're going to have to work at it. You're going to pay the price with effort. Here are the methods and the techniques to practice. You'll psychically build yourself and then it'll lead to a higher level of spirituality faster.

Simultaneously, you want to remove yourself from everything. Once you've accepted that, you should be able to perceive what I'm saying to you more clearly. You may be able to do that on your own, but it's not going to be enough. That's why people who have done this for 20 or 30 years realize they need something more. Listening and learning is a slow way to transform yourself. By coupling the two together, you're going to have even faster and better results.

Everything on the planet procreates. Trees pollinate and create new life. Cells divide. It goes on and on because everything has a method of procreation. The planet is a living organism. Everyday people who are working for the planet are Red Cells. They are linked to the consciousness grid designed to progress the planet that will eventually pollinate the Universe.

White Cells are actually spiritual beings who are more in tune with the Universe; although, some of them are in tune with the Earth. They each serve a different kind of role. Most of the White Cells are people who are still on the same frequency in their own way. My goal is to find those White Cells and try to help them awaken. They need to realize a birth within themselves in order to progress to the next level of awakening. They need not think about procreation as a man or a woman, or a hermaphrodite creature mating with itself and creating a third. The third is actually an acknowledgment by the Universe that, as a White Cell, you're doing what you're supposed to do. If you're not doing the will of nature, nature works against you.

By being a White Cell, you are actively doing what the Universe requires you to do in order for it to acknowledge you and to empower you. Most people have figured out the physical and the spiritual, but they haven't figured out or even realized that there's a next level to that physical/spiritual process. That is an enlightenment state of consciousness.

So, what is God's connection to all this? In a sense, you must see yourself differently. You must see yourself as an independent supercell in a body. There are red cells and there are white cells, but we also know through science that there are supercells that lay dormant within the body. They have super technology to fight ancient viruses that can wreak havoc on a body. So when the white cells are all getting beat up and wiped out by these old and powerful viruses, the body somehow awakens these ancient, powerful white cells to come forward to do battle. If there's enough time, they'll win the battle. If they're too late, the whole mechanism, the inner universe collapses, meaning the physical body, and the person is going to die.

You must get the Universe to acknowledge you. You must get the Universe to acknowledge what you believe that you are, an advanced Super White Cell. You must learn to see yourself and experience yourself as being a White Cell in that sense so that you can reflect this need. You must also learn to do whatever it needs to do. What does the Universe want you to do? As organisms, what is the way that you would procreate what you are? It's very simple. What am I doing right now? I'm creating a third by teaching. I'm mating the physical organic with the spiritual. I'm pollinating you with this spiritual knowledge. It's DNA. Every word I give you and every experience you're feeling is a kind of DNA; it's just a matter of you thinking outside the box. By teaching you and by giving it to you, the Universe is saying, "Oh, this being is doing his role, by procreating *his* species."

Species doesn't simply mean flesh and blood. Species is what moves the whole Universe to exist. There's a dynamic force behind it that's invincible that tells all life to progress and not to kill itself or die off. It wants you to live. It's the same Force that's saying, "Okay, the Red Cells are doing their job. The birds and bees are doing their job, but are the White Cells doing theirs? Are they at the point where they've matured their spiritual knowledge?"

It's no different than the aging cycle. You begin as a baby; then you grow into a toddler and into your youthful years. You work your way through until you get to adulthood. Are you now going to procreate what you are? Will the Universe acknowledge that you're doing what you're supposed to do? You need to teach. You need to show the Universe that you are giving this knowledge and that you're seeding other beings that are designed to receive it. Nature is looking for certain aspects, and if you only perceive yourself as being a man or a woman, then you've already created the bubble of your reality and the limits by which your mind can consciously conceive and move into.

Not only are you organic, but you're also of a spiritual vibration. You have a biological need inside of you to procreate, too. You might say, "I don't feel the need to have children." That's fine, but I guarantee you at some point you're going to feel the need to teach. That's going to be a way for you to pollinate and procreate. The Universe sees you as a living organism. It sees you as a White Cell, a spiritual being. The Universe is saying, "I'm willing to assist you but what are you willing to do in return? Why should I empower you or make you more powerful if I don't see you reciprocating what I'm giving you?"

The Universe will make you more powerful if you simply reciprocate the need for it because you're doing what you need to do. Name one great teacher who has never taught anyone. The greatest spiritual teachers, throughout history, the ones who have created the greatest miracles, have taught hundreds of people, if not thousands. To get the Universe to respond to your needs, you must tell it, "I want to awaken to the powerful being that I AM."

You have not come here to only do one specific job. Is your job just to mate? Isn't there also a level of interaction required? What about co-creating life? We need to have experiences because it programs the DNA within us to have greater data for survival as an organism. Spiritually, you're not just designed to save the world. Part of saving the world also contributes to the future of the world by sharing that data, information, and DNA. It's the same pattern, regardless of the frequency. It's just a matter of how complex it gets.

Enlightened people worked on finding their enlightenment but, at some point, they also decided to start teaching. Forget about whatever religious beliefs you have adopted now. They're all flawed. It is in the blemishes that you are now sifting to find the secrets that were lost. You're going to find that enlightened people were already teaching in the process of their own awakening. That's what's been lost. The Universe will recognize you when you get to a state of consciousness where you're communicating what it is that you're trying to share. The fact that you're trying to share it is what makes you tune into this other Source.

Some of my students also teach. They often speak about a state of mind they get into that is incredibly gratifying. They feel an ecstasy, an orgasm, in the process. It's the Universe gratifying you for your efforts. If you teach and you do a good job, you'll get into that zone and you'll understand.

To move to the next level of your development, you have to decide that you're ready to teach. You have to say to the Universe, "I'm not a waste of your time. I'm not an incomplete being that is just going to eat from your table but is not willing to give back." The Universe wants to assist you, but there is a protocol of life in this dimension. For it to work with you, you have to work with it. You need to reciprocate that relationship. You do that by raising more White Cells and contributing to the purpose of White Cells.

Where do White Cells come from if nobody teaches? In this living organism of a planet, there is a dynamic purpose. There is an absolute need as much as there is a need in your body for white cells. What if white cells suddenly stop proliferating? What if they didn't carry that data over to the next white cell? You never have the same cold twice. Why is that? After the white cells fight and they win, somehow the information about the way they beat the virus is immortalized. Then they can keep fighting it.

What are you doing to hand out what you've got? What's going to make you stronger? What's going to make the Universe recognize you as being an absolute pearl amongst White Cells to empower you even more? The same thing it did for Krishna, for Buddha, and for Milarepa. There comes a time when you step outside of the bubble you're in and acknowledge that you're ready to teach, that you're willing to take on that role.

You live to serve in the same way you go into another dimension and see purple houses and human beings with arms, a head, and eyeballs. You set the conditions, but that's not true servitude. You can't say in your heart that you're willing to serve, because the Universe wants you to teach and that's not in there. You really want glorification as if you're going to save the world through some lightning bolt from your hand or some echo coming from your body that suddenly purges everybody in the world of evil.

By teaching, you free yourself and allow your consciousness to move into higher places, but there is a point when you say, "I need more." You don't even need to say that you need more. Your students are eventually going to ask for an experience, and you're going to have this thought in your mind of not being able to provide it. You will be put under pressure, but you're going to perform. There will also be a part of you that thinks, "If I fail they won't really hate me, so

I'll just have to work it out." And there is another part of you that says, "Let's do it. It should work."

The Universe is not going to let you down. It's going to back you up. It's going to make the rain fall from the sky. It's going to help you to heal somebody that's sick. It's going to allow you to do what you've not yet believed you can. Remember the power of belief. The reason most people do not achieve psychic or spiritual things is because they don't believe in their heart they can change reality. They have self doubt, and it's a blind doubt that they are not able to see within themselves. It's fear of error. It's fear of not being able to find that place inside to manifest it. That is the bubble you're in.

If you can get outside of the bubble you created, if you can acknowledge that you need to procreate, if you can get the Universe to see that you *are* procreating, the Universe will reciprocate with the energy you need. It sees you doing what needs to be done. It sees you working as part of the ecosystem of the Universe. You've accepted your true higher role, so it will allow you to manifest and change reality. If you do not decide to teach, you're only going to reach a certain level, like 90% of the other White Cells out there. Even most of the White Cells out there are still in a deeper kind of bubble.

It sounds negative to compare yourself to others, but you have to, even though you're told you shouldn't. It's another one of these programs. In this dimension, you have to acknowledge where you're at with things so you can gauge where you need to go.

There's going to be a time when you want to help reproduce God's vibration at the highest level. This is why I push for Higher Balance Institute. It's why I want people to start teaching. I've said for years, "You need to teach," but very few students do. There's plenty of material out there and there's plenty of learning going on. It's only a matter of whether you choose to apply it.

Do you choose to just sit and bask in it, or are you going to apply it and be truly dedicated? And what will you do if you reach enlightenment? Your job is to merge the physical world into the higher dimensions. Prepare it and encourage it. Help it get there and guide it. Without that, God is doomed. You are not just in this world. You are throughout the entire Universe in multiple dimensions. If you fail to do what needs to be done, you fail God. But you need to maintain that continued existence.

It is imperative that you understand that you are not just part of a collective organism. *At times, you have to see yourself independently as a super cell.* You must acknowledge to the Universe that you're ready to carry out its desire, but also acknowledge that you're worthy. You need to show the Universe that you truly aren't trying to tell It what It should or shouldn't be doing. God doesn't think in words. God doesn't think in the way we do.

When you do something, a feeling is created somewhere in that action. It's that other dimensional communication within you that isn't expressed with words, but you can feel it. It's that same feeling of gratification you experience when you start to teach. You reach higher places and suddenly your student ties their success to you, and they say, "Wow, I feel it! I get it!" *It's that moment!* What do you call that moment of gratification? It's not unlike bliss. Yet, it's even more than that.

You need to reach those levels. You need to let the Universe know that you're willing to do whatever It wants you to do without trying. You need to teach. You need to give. You need to reciprocate this knowledge. You need to let the Universe know that you are not just a dead end that's going to sit on this knowledge and never procreate.

What is the purpose of getting this far? Is it so you can do some big miracle? So you can help the planet on a certain date at a certain time? The Universe understands the concept of natural selection. It understands that weaker species get beat out by the more dominant species, and if the other one can create a better defense, it will continue to exist because it can hold off the aggressor.

The Universe knows that many of you are going to fail. It knows many of you are lazy. It already knows that you're just eating at the table but you're not willing to contribute. So, it tries to procreate in numbers. It creates more in hopes that maybe two puppies in a litter of ten will survive in the end. There are universal laws in nature that are true in the Universe. God is no fool. Whether or not you can see these truths depends on the flexibility of your mind. So, you need to show the Universe that you're willing for it to empower you to the levels of an enlightened being; that you're willing to do the other chores that come along with that responsibility. Do you think God would choose to make one person enlightened and assume that this one person is going to be able to save the world? Or would God find as many people as possible to attain enlightenment to ensure that the job gets done?

You must present yourself to the best of your ability if you really want to achieve enlightenment. That doesn't mean that you have to do it in the next two years, five years, or ten years. It doesn't mean that you have to see yourself as the utmost important enlightened being of all time. Maybe you will choose to get there in your next lifetime. That's perfectly acceptable.

It's very important for you have this knowledge so that when you decide the time is right to teach, you will understand why. Most people that go on their spiritual path do so for selfish reasons. They're looking for inner peace and inner bliss. They don't reflect on serving God. They simply reflect on experiencing God. They just want to bathe in the sunlight, but they don't want to help It. They don't want to help other things enjoy the same sunlight. Ironically, the sunlight has intelligence. It has a purpose. It has a desire and it expects something from you in exchange for what It's giving you. Nothing in this universe is free. God's love is unconditional, but if you want to get something higher to stimulate your consciousness, there has to be reciprocation.

You must acknowledge in your heart what you are. You're a Super Cell. Do not allow ego to get in the way. Do not allow judging yourself to get in the way. You will only judge yourself based upon your perception from your own box. Most of you may never be able to judge yourself outside of the box. So don't get caught up in trivialities. Freeing yourself from those trivialities will free you from the box.

The laws of the Universe are designed to nurture and help you. God doesn't want you to fail. You just have to trust God that it's going to unfold for you correctly, but you also need to have some desire for momentum. How will you know when you're ready? How does a tree know when it's ready to give fruit? Does it give fruit as a seedling? Does it give fruit in its first year? How about in five years? How does it decide when it's ready? Is it because of climate change? Is it because of the rotation of the planet? Is it seasonal? What in nature is communicating to it? You'll know when that time arrives. If you have to ask, it's not the right time, but you can prepare yourself by practicing it. You know it exists. You're not oblivious to it.

Effort is important. It's just like someone who's very athletic. The athletic person doesn't think about what they have to do. They just do it because that's their passion. It's the world they exist in. It just makes sense to them. When you are starting from an organic body, attaining enlightenment always takes work. How bad do you want it? Do you have a good teacher? Someone who works out a lot needs a good personal trainer. In the same way, you need a good teacher. A good personal trainer motivates his client to exercise just as a good spiritual teacher will help you if you need it.

Can you explain the difference between the `I`s and the bubbles?

The `I`s refer to the consciousness within your brain. The `I`s are like little micro bubbles and your own reality is like a living organism, or living thing, like Gaia. Now, look at the macro and see the bubbles of Gaia's mind. Where's your role?

If you want to go and meditate up in a mountain like a Tibetan monk, that's good. But there are plenty of Buddhist monks doing that already. It's time to take a different course. If you want to do it that way, that is your role as you've chosen to serve the organism of the Universe. It's a lesser role than actually working directly with someone. The results will be different.

Globally, there is a balance for the Gaia mind as the Buddhist monks emanate a peaceful energy, which is like rain, and it helps all of us. We all benefit, just like a whole forest benefits from the rain. Buddhist monks are a different kind of White Cell. They are fulfilling their role and holding the planet in a certain balance versus the Darkside. There's constantly a conflict between the Darkside and the Force.

There's a balance that comes out of that constant conflict. There's a weight and a counterweight, and it's what keeps it steady. There may be a rock here and there due to outside effects but, for the most part, it holds steady. All these Buddhist monks hand down this information from one to another, but as the planet becomes more complex, it needs to proliferate itself, too. As the planet progresses, there are fewer advanced monks being able to broadcast that frequency. It's an old technology. The Universe is now replacing it with a newer technology, and Navigators are it. That's a very bold statement, but our approach is a notch above the rest. It is better to teach someone so that they can reach enlightenment instead of only teaching them to meditate and broadcast. Teaching them an array of other skills in addition to meditation makes them much more useful to the Universe.

Spiritual masters on this planet have performed miracles that are outside the laws of physics. On a remote planet where the laws of physics may be much looser, can others do similar things?

Absolutely, they can. No matter where you go in this Universe, there seems to be a practical sense of physics.

Now, it might mean gravitation is a little stronger, a little weaker, or that there are different levels of gaseous forms or less dense waters. For the most part, there's consistency throughout the Universe. Consistency is a major factor for the intelligent life of any living organism in the Universe and the way it trickles down into other life forms. So, you'll see a level of similarities. There are advantages in some places while there are certainly disadvantages in others. It's the roll of the dice.

Let's say you were going to another galaxy. Do you think you would find something completely different from our galaxy? No. You would find a consistency throughout the Universe at certain levels. They're not all identical. Certainly new things can be brought in from those perspectives. That's the whole point of incarnating and moving throughout the Universe. However, there is also a level of consistency and similarity.

Can I access the Akashic Records and the greater grids of data beyond that?

Sure, but you're still looking at it from a human perspective. In order to access the Akashic Records, you must be able to think about and create things in your mind that you've never even been introduced to in any way. You must be able to interpret information in a way that is very foreign to the human brain. If you follow the logical process of building a solid foundation of consciousness and get through to the Akashic Records, you will gain an understanding of the flow of knowledge. It will just happen.

Why must you always fixate on whatever is next? Why not allow the Force to continue to grow throughout your journey rather than become perplexed about what is next? Allow this beauty to grow and flourish. Allow that to continue.

In order for God to give you what you want or what you need, you must perfect yourself in the eyes of God. Just because you want more knowledge right now does not mean you are ready to handle it. You may think of yourself as indestructible in spiritual terms, but do you have the tools to deal with it mentally or emotionally?

Anybody can have a nervous breakdown. And that's purely a crash of the mind. You may not crash physically or feel physical trauma, but you can crash mentally. You can grab onto something that is more than the structure of your mind is designed to handle. Your mind is built to deal with the complexities of this reality. If you don't have the mechanism to handle that information from other realities, it's going to burn out all your wiring.

It's similar to a high voltage charge. You think, "Well, electricity powers my computer and provides a certain speed to compress data. What happens if I take 550 volts and plug it into a 110 volt outlet? It's not designed to handle it, so it would destroy the whole thing! Just because you know that the 550 volts is there, does it mean you should use it?

Wouldn't it be better to continuously work with the mysteries and the revelations that the 110 volts is giving you? That is still profound considering that you started off years ago with a 9 volt battery. You can't expect to understand the knowledge you're going to receive at more advanced levels if you don't have the faculties to comprehend it.

If you don't have a solid foundation, there's nothing to support you when you reach the higher levels. God will deny no one, but God isn't going to hand over something that you're not at all prepared to understand.

You must allow yourself to evolve. A caterpillar doesn't just pluck wings out of its body. It goes into a cocoon. For a caterpillar, that's like its meditation, its process – its dance with nature. In the meantime, it survived to the cocoon stage without getting eaten or killed. It ate and it chose wisely. There was a metamorphosis that took time; it didn't happen in an instant.

How would you advise your students to teach?

As a White Cell at a certain level, you want to be exposed to this information because it builds you up multi-dimensionally. It nourishes your soul. This information helps filter out everything that's preventing you from growing. It liberates you from other beliefs that are holding you back and in so doing, you are able to awaken.

When you begin to awaken and you begin to build your foundation, your consciousness moves a certain way. There's going to come a time when you want to do something with it. The key thing to remember is that you are still growing and evolving. There's no reason why you can't start reaching out to other people in reciprocating this teaching. *Should you listen to all of the material before you start teaching? No,* if you listen to one thing and you work on it and you get to a level that you know it well, then you're ready to teach that one thing. You can continue working on yourself, but share as you go along. Pay it forward. You will find that the more people you work with, the quicker you're going to move to even higher and higher levels.

You were talking about the bubbles through which we perceive things. How can I perceive things differently?

You need to teach and it won't be easy. You have to know you're going to have both successes and failures. You may try a hundred times before you find that "sweet spot," but you have to teach. The sooner you can accept that in your heart and not care about ridicule, the sooner you will achieve your goal. It's that simple.

Once you reach your goal, it doesn't mean that you're going to stay there either. It still takes effort, but it's a lot easier. It takes mindfulness. You can't *unknow* what you know. That's the beauty of it. You need to put yourself in a situation where you don't have any other choice but to teach.

Don't think about what you're going to do; just sit yourself in front of your student and teach – don't even think about it. Begin by teaching meditation. Make the effort to find a room, schedule a time, and put a flier together. Make a commitment to teach that meditation. And when that day and time arrives and only one person shows up, you will teach that one person because you won't really have another choice.

You will teach and you will start to feel a lack of self-confidence. But because they've never heard any of this before, they're going to think you're very interesting. The student will ask you questions and you will have the answers. All of a sudden, you will start getting into the groove of teaching. And that's how it begins.

Is there a technique to assimilate a group of people outside of your normal perception of reality?

For starters, you can put on your husband's or your wife's clothing to get the *feels-like*. There's a certain vibration and feeling that comes from that. It's very intense because it's very physically oriented. You can also put yourself into environments that you would normally not put yourself into, but don't analyze it from your perspective. Try to get yourself in the zone so you can understand it as the person next to you is receiving it. And try to get into the mode of appreciating what you're hearing. Forget what you know; just for an hour, *unknow what you know*. Try and feel what it is to be Suzie Homemaker making cupcakes. Or what it is like to be a mom or a dad. Or what it is to be a rock star. You need to try different things. Try on some different clothes than what you would normally wear and try to discover who you are creatively.

The reality TV show "Wife Swap" is a perfect example of people experiencing realities different from their own. In one episode, a rigid "All American" mom swapped places with a mom from a Goth family. Initially, things got off to a rocky start as both families had to adjust to the change.

The more traditional mother was far stricter about chores and didn't allow the teenage daughter to wear makeup or jewelry while the Goth mother was far more relaxed about maintaining the household. She encouraged the children to unwind and have fun. They started to get a different perspective. After a few days, the rigid mother allowed the girls in the Goth family to give her a makeover. They dressed her up in some *punk clothes*, and did her hair and makeup in their style. Once she saw the results, she was feeling it! She said, "Wow, this is kind of liberating. This is kind of fun!" She had never allowed herself to experience something like that before.

She got on the drums and she did some karaoke. She laughed but, remember; initially she was horrified when she went to that household because she had a certain perception of what this other bubble had to offer. Until she went and experienced that bubble, she wasn't able to see the other complexities and the good in them. When she got into that mode, she realized these people weren't so different from her. Afterwards, she said it was a good experience for her. It also helped build a better relationship with her daughter who was being a little bit rebellious. It brought her a different perspective of her consciousness.

The Universe has been doing this since the beginning of time. It's like reincarnation; it's just done on a larger scale. It's like time itself. If you want to do it on a micro scale, you can accelerate it in your own way. There are things to be learned, even when you think there's nothing to gain from it. It's the same thing. So, by looking a little deeper at this situation, all of the family members actually gained something from the swap. Sometimes, it is beneficial for you to experience certain things. Not horrible things. Not things that are going to put your body or health at risk. Everybody knows right from wrong. But you can recognize these different realities and visit them.

You could visit another reality as an outsider: a time traveler, a space traveler, or a traveler of some other kind. You could dress up and fit in with these other crowds. Go to church someday. Dress up for church. Go to some book reading at a book store that you never would have otherwise attended. Be open-minded and you will find there is beauty in most anything. And the secret is not so much that there's beauty. The secret is in developing the skill to discover that there's beauty in everything. That's part of enlightenment.

**At the start of this conversation, you spoke
of removing yourself from the machinery of it all.
Do you perform the scanning technique from
the space in between the bubbles?**

Of course, that's where I'm operating from. I'm removing myself from these emotional perspective places, because I couldn't teach if I was in one of those. If I was in one of those bubbles, my teaching would be as mundane as most other spiritual teachers. The reason people get at the edge of their seat when I teach is because I'm teaching things that nobody else talks about. I've removed myself from even that bubble. I have to remove myself from typical spiritual systems and that is why I have a resistance to learning Hinduism in depth. I don't want to get encapsulated in one of those bubbles. That's how I interpret everything. This is why I've always admired my self-stylized progress. I've always embraced a certain level of absolute truth to students.

If you reflect on this, you'll see the truth of it and you will be grateful that I was honest with you instead of wasting ten years of your life telling you something you found more acceptable to your current perception. I don't want to pamper anybody. I want to tell you the truth. If you get upset about it, that's fine; I know you'll get over it. How do I know you'll get over it? I've already been down that road before. And you'll be grateful.

These are my suggestions and my warnings. These are the things that I'm putting out. If I candy-coat it, the only reason would be to get you to a higher tonal. It's not my job to make people like me; rather, it's important that I'm true to my heart. That means telling you the absolute truth the best way that I can. I'm not saying that I don't candy-coat things sometimes because I certainly do; but it's more of being blatant. It's more of a hesitation to say certain things. There is certain material that's not appropriate for someone just starting out because they aren't ready to understand it. It would just discourage them. But, if the student follows their progress, this will make absolutely perfect sense to them, and they are going to embrace it wholeheartedly. They will go, "If only I had heard of this six months ago, I would have thrown this whole other program out the door."

Is watching TV a good way to study different bubbles?

It's a horrible way to study bubbles. TV offers you a regurgitated concept of these bubbles. It only gives you the surface of it. It's just Lego blocks made out of plastic and they're all white. Lego blocks now in wood form. Lego blocks made out of cement. Lego blocks made out of multi-colors with magnets in the back of them.

You really need to experience something in the third dimension rather than the first or second dimensions. You might see it, but you can't really taste, smell, or touch it. You need all five senses involved and, hopefully, a sixth sense, to really get it.

You might also get a surface judgment from watching it, but then you're watching it from your couch in your bubble having a perception of that bubble. It's only when you throw yourself into it that you're consumed by it. Either the bubble will consume you and you will become it, or you will be able to function in that bubble and have enough strength to pop back out of it.

It's like diving underwater. You can hold your breath; you can see the fish; you can see the bottom; you can swim around and you can experience what it is to float. But, eventually you're forced back up to the top for air, unless you drown and then you're part of the lake. You can't get the full sensation of swimming under water from watching TV.

When I first became a student, I assimilated different environments and experienced different things. As I developed more of my sixth sense, I realized that I had to physically experience that environment to get the most out of it.

People do it naturally; it's an aspect of life. As far as the organism goes, you get married. You get into religion. You get out of religion. You get into your idea of what a marriage is and you find out it's not right for you or you find out it's wonderful for you. There are plenty of people who start off in one career and then switch to a different career. They find their inner peace and their inner bliss, but it took them time to figure how to get there. More advanced people, like the kind I'm teaching, take a more direct and active role in controlling those decisions, so maybe that speeds the process up.

When I was a teenager, I would actively seek out churches where they were doing healings through prayer. I would let them put their hands on my head. I also loved going to the carnival and letting myself sink into that feeling. Sometimes it's nice to go to other environments and visit them. They're really micro worlds; that's why I call them globes. I like to just go into this world where everything is like a child's concept of a magical circus. Then I revel in the idea of no more problems, pressures, wants, money, or bills and I enjoy visiting that world. But, you eventually have to pop out of that world; you can't stay there or you will forget who you are. It's fun for a little while.

There are those little pieces of something that you walk away with. If I was patient enough to look, I always left with something useful from every place I've ever visited in these globes or worlds. I walked away with something that gave me a deeper understanding of life, reality, and the Gaia consciousness. I realized that each one of these globes was reminiscent of the other.

In seeing those simple truths, it gave me certain realizations about the goodness of humanity. It removed a lot of bitterness from my perception of humanity. I now have a choice of how I see the world: I can choose to see the ugliness or I can choose to see the beauty. Fortunately, I chose to find the beauty in all of my journeys. Which one will you choose?

Good Journeys,
Eric Pepin

CONTINUE YOUR JOURNEY

Thank you for joining me on this journey. My hope is that you take what you have learned, apply it, and watch your life transform as your spirituality flourishes. The light of knowledge is vital on your journey, but you must apply it. That is why I am giving you additional tools, you can download for free, to assist you in putting the methods you have discovered here into practice.

Before you do that, there is one thing I would ask of you: leave a short, honest review at Amazon.com or wherever you found this book.

Higher Balance is a dedicated, grass-roots organization. We rely on the power of people to help spread this knowledge. Assist others out there searching, like you, find this book.

ADD TO YOUR EXPERIENCE
READERS ONLY FREE MATERIAL

As a reader you receive special reader-only bonus material you can download for free. You will get new tools and knowledge to enhance all the practices found in the book.

Receive:

Guided Mind Projection: Eric Pepin guides you on an audio Mind Projection session. You'll go step-by-step through the entire process you can use for practice and to better experience your initial projections.

Feels-Like Video: While you learn the language of Feels-Like in the book, the *emotional* element is difficult to capture in print. Watch this video of Eric showing you how to use Feels-Like and what it is.

Shadow People: Advanced Knowledge: An entire advanced course on the energy beings commonly called Shadow People. The discussion begins in the book in the chapter on Energy Beings. However, there is so much information and dis-information on the internet Eric sat for a video explaining in greater detail what Shadow People really are. Then he followed up with a 90 minute lecture giving the most in-depth knowledge to-date on the topic.

Go to *www.guildofpsi.com/readers-only*

Appendix · Glossary of Terms – Book 5

Akashic Records

The *Akashic Records* is a term for the dimensional data of the Gaia Mind (see *Gaia*). It is an energy vibration that contains a record of any and all planetary events, actions, thoughts, and feelings that have ever occurred or will ever occur in the future. These records can extend beyond the planet into all universal experience since the beginning of time, and are stored permanently in an energy substance named "Akasha."

Assimilation

Assimilation is a mental skill that allows you to experience the world around you. Through assimilation, you experience things as they experience themselves. For example, have you ever experienced life and viewed the world as your dog or cat? Have you ever thought like your cat or dog? Assimilation is a skill that allows you to do this. Assimilation is the starting point for countless other psychic abilities. Even if you already have some skill in other abilities, practicing assimilation will quickly improve your other skills.

Astral Planes

Astral planes are really dimensions. Culturally, there were times when people didn't know how to explain these other realities. Sometimes they were so surreal compared to how they perceived reality that they deemed it the 'astral plane' or the 'ethereal plane.' (See *Dimensions*).

Astral Projection
An "out-of-body experience" often occurring during sleep or a meditative state during which the ethereal or astral energy field of the body separates from the physical body and travels over great distances to other locations. It is a process that sends conscious energy out from the physical body to collect information to bring back for experience.

Awakening
The phrase used to describe the transformation or process of becoming conscious from a prior state of unconsciousness, or unawareness. A dynamic of discovery during spiritual development. To wake from sleep. (see: *Enlightenment*.)

Auras
An aura is a field of subtle, luminous radiation surrounding a person or an object. Higher Balance has a video on how to see an aura. You can access it on their site: *http://youtu.be/aYlb_XtNP7c*

Babbler, The
A term to define repetitious, involuntary thoughts pervading through the mind. Uncontrolled babbling will naturally occur as a result of never learning how to manage the rational thinking process while growing into adulthood. It is also referred to as "Mind-Chatter."

Biochemistry
A term that summarizes the "chemical" functions of any "biological" organism. For
example, this term would include human brain chemicals such as Serotonin, Dopamine, Acetylcholine, Phenylethylamine and others that directly relate to states of awareness.

Calibration
A word to explain the conscious or unconscious adjustments or optimizations that take place in one's energy, mind, or physicality. These different energy calibrations are often very subtle and not noticed; they occur all the time as a person adjusts to experiences in life. They are most often felt during meditation or clear states of consciousness.

Chakra
A name for the intersection areas of energy meridians (or electrical pathways) in the body. There are seven primary chakras along the spine. They extend from the tip of the tailbone to the crown of head. These seven are located (from the bottom up) in the rectal area, near the genitals, behind the navel or solar plexus, at the heart, at the neck, between the eyebrows, and on the crown of the head. Each chakra corresponds to certain states of consciousness, emotions, body organs, nerve networks, colors, and energies. There are over 2000 of these energy centers or intersections of this energy in the human body.

Collective Consciousness
Humans serve as the planet's central nervous system; the collective consciousness is a term for the planet's mind state. It is the planetary energy field of humanity's entire evolutionary experiences and expressions. This mind-field or collective consciousness is enriched as humanity develops, whether the development is in language, art, music, technologies, cities, spiritual awakening, or any other area of endeavor. As this consciousness evolves, each succeeding generation of conscious individuals will inherit and be influenced by this collective consciousness and add their own experiences to it.

Crystallize
Although this term is also used in its basic form, crystallizing is when one's modes of thinking are set into somewhat permanent patterns. The calcification of the pineal gland is a major contributor to this event causing spiritual inflexibility. Although the age of this biological and psychological event varies for each person, the average age is said to be twenty eight. During late stages of life, one commonly experiences a relaxing of these modes around the age of the late fifties.

Darkside, The
A term commonly used in the movie trilogy "Star Wars" to describe a destructive energy in the universe that destroys any manifestation or potential of creation.

Deep Resonating Aums
A meditation music CD featuring layers of recorded Aums by Eric Pepin while he was in a meditative state. Working with *Deep Resonating Aums* will raise your vibratory tonal exponentially. The Aums will quite

literally resonate and permeate all objects around you, effectively re-writing all undesirable environmental energy programming.

Desiderata
A 1927 poem by American writer Max Ehrmann.

Dimension
One of the countless realms of reality or space. Alternate dimensions of reality can be experienced in degrees, from subtle to total immersion. There are countless dimensions of reality. These concepts are now being used in modern physics to develop theories of reality, such as String Theory. The term referenced by Eric is usually one of parallel dimensions where entities exist.

Doe (or Do)
'Doe' is the first and lowest tone of the diatonic scale. This term is used to define the primary vibratory state of the planet's consciousness. Spiritual states of existence are much higher in tonal. The "Doe" signifies a vibratory state that is limited to the immediate physical dimension which does not recognize higher energy frequencies. Within the 'Doe' state, immediate desires of the body outweigh the subtle urge for spiritual awakening. It is sometimes termed 'Doe.'

Dreamscape
A therapeutic tool for revealing and handling issues that are troubling your mind. It provides a means to explore various possible higher states of consciousness. It will guide you into a vivid dream-like reality, opening doors that are normally only available to you

in a dream state. In contrast to typical dreams that occur while asleep, Dreamscape "dreams" may be much easier to interact in, shape, and remember afterward.

Elongation
When entering deep states of meditation, an individual may feel as if their physical body is expanding upwards or outwards. It is actually an initial spontaneous movement of subtle energies of the body and often leads to "projections" of many types. The most common, Astral Elongation, is a result of specific energy frequencies being stimulated, through practicing non-thought, that link the physical body to its subtle energy bodies.

Empathy
The ability where one can tune into another person's feelings or emotions and then experience them as if they were one's own. This is experienced primarily through the heart chakra, although the understanding of the feeling would be enhanced by bringing the mind chakra into play. Empathy without understanding would be of limited value.

Energy
A term that refers to the simplest essence, condition, or state in all things. A dynamic and flexible word that can be used to express the relativity, vitality, and intensity of anything that exists.

Enlightenment
A higher state of consciousness in which a person transcends beyond his or her ego, and becomes aware

of his or her divinity; a state where a person is one, or whose consciousness is existing near or at the frequency of the Multidimensional Universe or God.

Entity
A term that defines any living thing in existence. It is also used to describe a spirit normally assumed (often wrongly) to be that of a dead person. Sometimes in reference to a spirit or a being from another dimension.

E.S.P.
An acronym for Extra Sensory Perception. Not only does it define the state in which all five body senses deliver a greater amount of information for the brain, it also encompasses 'paranormal' or psychic abilities such as: telepathy, precognition, psychometry, photometry, telekinesis, psychokinesis, projections, clairaudience and clairvoyance.

Expansion Modules
In-depth audio courses which offer specialized techniques and advanced information on specific areas of interest not covered in The Foundation Set from Eric Pepin's book "Meditation Within Eternity." If the Foundation Set creates the core of development, Expansion Modules just add onto or expand that core. These can be accessed at:
http://www.higherbalance.com/products/

Feels-Like
A "tag" or "feels-like" is what something feels like in your chest intelligence. Everything has a feels-like - a computer screen, a table, chair, pen, paper, etc. Without

touching an object, you can imagine the texture, temperature, density, and clarity of it. You know how the object feels – its frequency.

Force, The
A term and concept for the positive life enriching conscious energy of the Universe. It is commonly used in the "Star Wars" movies to describe the life energy of the universe which binds any manifestation of matter together.

Frequency
A term used for the property or condition of an occurrence taking place at frequent intervals. Any form of existence has a range of frequency in order for it to exist. Frequency is a form of energy.

Gaia
(Greek - Goddess of the Earth) The Gaia Hypothesis, formulated by James Lovelock, states that all living matter on the Earth contributes to a single living macrocosmic organism. Retrospectively in the system of a living earth, the collective consciousness of humanity would be considered the central nervous system.

Governor
An unconscious pattern and function of the brain that binds a person's awareness to the physical world. It is a specific vibratory state which subsequently contributes to the rejection of all things that are not normal or that have yet to be discovered. (see: *Doe*)

Grid, The
An invisible planetary energy web that interconnects all living things. If one can plug into this grid, they will have

access to planetary collective experiences existing in higher dimensional vibrations. (see: *Akashik Records*)

I's, The
The alternate personalities, roles, or egos within a person. A product of unconscious functioning, these I's unconsciously assist a person in coping with the environment.

In-Between, The
To be consciously shifted. There is a place between matter and energy where one can exist and be aware of both simultaneously. Not simply to be aware of yourself but to be in a special state of consciousness.

Innerverse
The inner universe of the human body. Like the world of intelligent life that we experience, there are also intelligent life forms within our bodies; experiencing within their own universe.

Intent
Something that is intended consciously or unconsciously; an aim or purpose. Intent precedes any choice or course of action.

Kirlian Photography
A photographic process using a high voltage, low amperage field of 50,000 volts or more. This process was invented by Semyon and Valentina Kirlian. It captures the radiation around objects and humans which is not visible to the naked eye. It is often used to photograph the energy field (Aura) that surrounds the human body and the energy transmissions when different forms of organic life cross each other.

Kundalini
The elemental energy of the human body which, like a serpent, rests coiled at the base of the spine. Everyone uses Kundalini energy or power to maintain conscious-ness, but it very seldom rises up the central spinal channel beyond the first chakra center (the groin chakra). The Foundation meditation practice can be used to ascend to and activate the higher chakra centers.

Lotus, Full
This traditional body position provides a solid base for the practice of meditation and
Prana breathing exercises. The spine is erect; the legs are crossed over one another; and the flow of blood to the legs is constricted and redirected to the internal organs.

Traditionally the posture is a reminder to emulate the lotus plant, with its roots in the earth and its face reaching towards the sunlight. It is also the basis of many other yogic postures.

Lotus, Half
This seated meditation posture is almost identical to the Full Lotus position stated above. However, with the half-lotus, one foot rests on top of the opposite thigh with the sole pointing upwards, while the other foot rests on the floor, as in the common Indian position. (see: *the meditation map provided with the Foundation Set in "Meditation Within Eternity."*)

Lucid Dreaming
Dreaming while knowing that one is dreaming. Lucidi-ty usually begins when the dreamer realizes that the experience is not occurring in physical reality, but is a dream.

Magnetic Pill
A revolutionary supplement designed to "supercharge your neural network." It is a scientifically proven brain supplement designed to give you deeper meditations, expanded consciousness, and all the benefits of a body that is fine-tuned to greater levels of development. Its main ingredient, magnetite, develops psychic ability and enhances this sensory.

Matrix
The Matrix is a term or allegory that dramatically conveys the view that ordinary appearances do not depict true reality and that gaining the truth transforms one's life. The Matrix is the sensational world that traps one into believing that nothing outside the five senses even exists. The matrix is also a term for the apparent fabric of the reality in this dimension.

MDC
Multi-Dimensional Consciousness. (see: *Consciousness*)

Metronome
A device used to mark time by using regularly recurring ticking sounds or flashes at adjustable intervals. An effective tool for inducing states of deep trance or hypnosis.

Micro-Macro
A term to reference zooming from micro (the very small) to macro (the very large).

Micro-verse
A micro version of the universe. A universe of the very small (micro).

Middle Pillar
A term in reference to the deepest core of one's consciousness that is completely interconnected with the universe and all manifestations of life: It is the ultimate Self without a notion of ego separation.

Mindfulness
Discipline in which the mind reflects on a single point of reference. The state of attention or reflection of the mind's activities. The trait of staying aware. Using desired thought.

Navigator
The subtle urge everyone has in them that drives them to evolve and seek out the experiences of life to the fullest extent. It is an intuitive mechanism of the causal spirit used to perpetuate and direct the will of the Force.

Non-Thought
When masters suggested having non-thought, they meant to not have verbal words in one's head. It's thinking at a higher level without using the words. When you understand and internalize this concept, you can transcend the boundaries of everyday life.

OBE
An acronym for Out-of-Body Experience. An experience (similar to Astral Projection) which occurs when the astral body or etheric body leaves the physical body while the individual is in meditation, at rest, asleep, near death, or temporarily dead.

One-on-One (or 1-on-1), sometimes called "personal reading"
A private one hour session with Eric Pepin on a variety of subjects including but not limited to spirituality and personal refinement. Usually the person having the session will ask Eric questions that pertain to their spiritual life and Eric will give personalized advice and answers.

Paranormal
Beyond normal. Beyond the range of normal experience or scientific explanation. Beyond or above normal human ability or senses. (see *E.S.P.*)

Parapsychology
The study of E.S.P. and any other sort of psychic phenomena. Dates back to the foundation of the English Society of Physical Research in 1882 and continued through laboratory research at Duke University Parapsychology Laboratory, Stanford Research Institute and elsewhere.

Pineal Gland
A small endocrine gland in the brain situated beneath the back part of the corpus callosum; secretes melatonin; realized by many to be 'the seat of the soul.'

Planes of Light
A blissful vibratory state usually attained after maintaining deep prolonged focus during meditation and consistent Prana circulation. Perceived as an all-encompassing brilliant illumination that internally and externally surrounds the meditator.

Prana
This is originally a yogic term for cosmic energy or the evolving life force of the Universe. Prana is thought to flow through the body, enriching and aligning health and vitality. It is considered the vital link between spiritual dimensions and material dimensions. Harnessing this energy through meditation enables people to accelerate the development of psychic states and the ability to perform miracles.

Psychokinesis
The power of mind over matter without the use of physical or sensory means. Together with ESP, psychokinesis (PK) includes telekinesis (the paranormal movement of objects); levitation and materialization; mysterious events associated with given people or houses, hauntings, and psychic healing. Since the 1930s, PK has been a major research interest among parapsychologists, especially in the United States and Russia.

Psychometry
The ability to gather information or impressions that are hidden to ordinary sensory perception from a physical object. The vibratory information and impressions could be the history of the object and its history of people and events associated to it. The term was coined in the mid-nineteenth century by an American physiologist named Joseph R. Buchanan.

Red Cell
A person who lives according to the natural purpose of Gaia and the vibration of the 'Doe' and is unconscious of the urge to pursue their full spiritual potential.

Remote Viewing
The practice of using the sixth sense to describe details about a target that is inaccessible to normal senses. A remote viewer might be asked to describe a target (person, place or event) on the other side of the world or perhaps describe a person or an activity, without being told anything about the target.

Samadhi
Samadhi means being in the state of undifferentiated being. It is a state of consciousness whereby one realizes the oneness of self while other I's are put aside. Eric's reference of Samadhi is one of an ecstatic state of bliss.

Scan
A technique of psychically receiving information from, but not limited to, a person, place, or thing.

Siddhartha
Siddhartha Gautama, known as the Buddha, was born in the sixth century B.C. as a son of a chief in what is now modern Nepal. Siddhartha left a life of wealth and submitted himself to rigorous ascetic practices. Not fully satisfied, he discovered a path of balance rather than extremism. He called this The Middle Way. Buddha attained enlightenment, thus earning the title Buddha, or "Enlightened One." Buddha preached the Dharma in an effort to help others reach enlightenment.

Sixth Sense
The Sixth Sense is the ordinary term for the faculties of Extra Sensory Perception. (see *E.S.P.*) The Sixth Sense is

the ability to receive or send information beyond the realm of the five senses of sight, sound, taste, touch, or smell. The term was coined by German researcher Dr. Rudolf Tischner whose book "Telepathy and Clairvoyance" was written in German in 1920 and published in English in 1925. The first serious paranormal research was done by Dr. J.B. Rhine, Professor of Parapsychology at Duke University, North Carolina.

Shangri-La
A mythical country allegedly located in the mountains of Tibet, created by James Hilton in his novel "Lost Horizon," in which he describes the perpetual
youth and vigor of its residents.

Sleeper
Someone who lies dormant. One who has yet to awaken their Sixth Sense but can feel the impulses of their Navigator.

Soul
A term for the life energy of an individual; an energy body of the non-physical self. That part of the individual which survives death and lives on into the hereafter, before being reincarnated.

Star Reach Program
Prior to the Journey program, Higher Balance offered specialized personal training with a Star Reach instructor. The personal instructor worked directly with the participants to determine their goals. The instructor then coached them to overcome weaknesses, enhance their strengths, and helped them through the rough spots.

Super Being
A White Cell who has fully awakened and become a Super White Cell. (see: *White Cell*.)

Telekinesis
The ability to move physical objects by force of will or mental energy alone. (see: *Psychokinesis*)

Third Eye
The Mind Chakra. The area approximately between the eyebrows, thought to utilize intuitive sense. Also believed to be the center of psychic vision.

Tones, The; sometimes called 'Bars' or 'Pitches'
The "Voice of God." A high pitched frequency usually heard on one side of the head – either the right or the left. Comes from within your consciousness. Focusing on it allows it to become louder and louder.

Tonal
This term refers to the vibratory degree of frequency that the energy of a person, place or thing exists at. (see: *Frequency; Vibration*)

Vibration
A particular frequency or resonation of a thing or event in existence. Not necessarily specific to that person or entity. (see: *Frequency; Tonal*)

White Cell
One who lives their life according to the divine will and direction of the Force or Universe.

GET FIRST HAND EXPERIENCE

Higher Balance is dedicated to giving you all the tools and knowledge you need to empower yourself and transform your life. The purpose and mission of Higher Balance is to awaken the world one mind at a time. Toward fulfilling that goal, we know that the greatest results come when you can experience something for yourself, rather than just reading about it.

Visit *www.higherbalance.com/experience*
for retreats and programs.

Higher Balance Institute
515 NW Saltzman Road #726
Portland, OR 97229
+1-503-646-4000

www.higherbalance.com/experience

Sit vis vobiscum.

CPSIA information can be obtained at www.ICGtesting.com
Printed in the USA
LVOW11s0418130315

430412LV00002B/3/P